Maritime Terrorism and Piracy in the Indian Ocean Region

Unregulated or lesser regulated maritime spaces are ideal theatres of operation and mediums of transportation for terrorists, insurgents and pirates. For more than a decade, the Indian Ocean waters adjoining Somalia have been a particular locus of such activities, with pirates hijacking vessels, and Al Qaeda and Al Shabab elements travelling between the Horn of Africa and the Arabian Peninsula, operating lucrative businesses and even staging deadly operations at sea. However, these operations and threats remain, by and large, understudied. Responses to the two threats have varied, highlighting the lack of cohesive regional and global institutions with the mandate and the capacity to address them. Those scholarly deliberations on Indian Ocean maritime security focus on piracy and armed robbery at sea, while their terrorist/insurgent counterparts have eluded sustained scrutiny. This volume helps in closing that gap by looking at both from the field in Somalia and Yemen, within broader frameworks of regional maritime security and port-state control, and international maritime law and the ongoing search for maritime resources. The European, African and Middle Eastern case studies add salience to the regional and international complexity surrounding maritime security off the Horn of Africa. This book was originally published as a special issue of the *Journal of the Indian Ocean Region.*

Awet T. Weldemichael is Queen's National Scholar in African History at Queen's University, Canada. He is currently researching contemporary Somalia and its adjoining waters.

Patricia Schneider is a Senior Researcher at the Institute for Peace Research and Security Policy at the University of Hamburg, Germany (www.ifsh.de) and teaches in the Peace and Security Studies program. She is an expert on maritime security and terrorism and co-edits the quarterly journal *Sicherheit und Frieden – Security and Peace.*

Andrew C. Winner is a Professor of Strategic Studies in the Strategic Research Department at the US Naval War College, Rhode Island, USA. He is the co-chair of the Indian Ocean Regional Studies Group.

Maritime Terrorism and Piracy in the Indian Ocean Region

Edited by
Awet T. Weldemichael, Patricia Schneider
and Andrew C. Winner

LONDON AND NEW YORK

First published 2015
by Routledge
2 Park Square, Milton Park, Abingdon, Oxon, OX14 4RN, UK

and by Routledge
711 Third Avenue, New York, NY 10017, USA

Routledge is an imprint of the Taylor & Francis Group, an informa business

© 2015 Indian Ocean Research Group

All rights reserved. No part of this book may be reprinted or reproduced
or utilised in any form or by any electronic, mechanical, or other means,
now known or hereafter invented, including photocopying and recording,
or in any information storage or retrieval system, without permission in
writing from the publishers.

Trademark notice: Product or corporate names may be trademarks or
registered trademarks, and are used only for identification and
explanation without intent to infringe.

British Library Cataloguing in Publication Data
A catalogue record for this book is available from the British Library

ISBN 13: 978-1-138-85064-4

Typeset in Times New Roman
by RefineCatch Limited, Bungay, Suffolk

Publisher's Note
The publisher accepts responsibility for any inconsistencies that may have
arisen during the conversion of this book from journal articles to book chapters,
namely the possible inclusion of journal terminology.

Disclaimer
Every effort has been made to contact copyright holders for their permission to
reprint material in this book. The publishers would be grateful to hear from any
copyright holder who is not here acknowledged and will undertake to rectify
any errors or omissions in future editions of this book.

Contents

Citation Information	vii
Notes on Contributors	ix
Acknowledgement	xi

1. Introduction: Maritime terrorism and piracy in the Indian Ocean Region   1
   Andrew C. Winner, Patricia Schneider and Awet T. Weldemichael

2. Maritime corporate terrorism and its consequences in the western Indian Ocean: illegal fishing, waste dumping and piracy in twenty-first-century Somalia   4
   Awet T. Weldemichael

3. Spanish maritime security governance in the Indian Ocean Region   21
   Annina Cristina Bürgin

4. German maritime security governance: a perspective on the Indian Ocean Region   36
   Patricia Schneider

5. Yemeni security-political dynamics and maritime security in the Indian Ocean Region   59
   Stig Jarle Hansen

6. The abundant sea: prospects for maritime non-state violence in the Indian Ocean   67
   Martin N. Murphy

7. Maritime security and port state control in the Indian Ocean Region   82
   Sam Bateman

8. International law and counter-piracy in the Indian Ocean   96
   Douglas Guilfoyle

Index	119

Citation Information

The chapters in this book were originally published in the *Journal of the Indian Ocean Region*, volume 8, issue 2 (December 2012). When citing this material, please use the original page numbering for each article, as follows:

Chapter 1

Editorial: Maritime terrorism and piracy in the Indian Ocean Region
Andrew C. Winner, Patricia Schneider and Awet T. Weldemichael
Journal of the Indian Ocean Region, volume 8, issue 2 (December 2012) pp. 107–109

Chapter 2

Maritime corporate terrorism and its consequences in the western Indian Ocean: illegal fishing, waste dumping and piracy in twenty-first-century Somalia
Awet T. Weldemichael
Journal of the Indian Ocean Region, volume 8, issue 2 (December 2012) pp. 110–126

Chapter 3

Spanish maritime security governance in the Indian Ocean Region
Annina Cristina Bürgin
Journal of the Indian Ocean Region, volume 8, issue 2 (December 2012) pp. 127–141

Chapter 4

German maritime security governance: a perspective on the Indian Ocean Region
Patricia Schneider
Journal of the Indian Ocean Region, volume 8, issue 2 (December 2012) pp. 142–164

Chapter 5

Yemeni security-political dynamics and maritime security in the Indian Ocean Region
Stig Jarle Hansen
Journal of the Indian Ocean Region, volume 8, issue 2 (December 2012) pp. 165–172

Chapter 6

The abundant sea: prospects for maritime non-state violence in the Indian Ocean
Martin N. Murphy
Journal of the Indian Ocean Region, volume 8, issue 2 (December 2012) pp. 173–187

CITATION INFORMATION

Chapter 7

Maritime security and port state control in the Indian Ocean Region
Sam Bateman
Journal of the Indian Ocean Region, volume 8, issue 2 (December 2012) pp. 188–201

Chapter 8

International law and counter-piracy in the Indian Ocean
Douglas Guilfoyle
Journal of the Indian Ocean Region, volume 8, issue 2 (December 2012) pp. 202–218

Please direct any queries you may have about the citations to
clsuk.permissions@cengage.com

Notes on Contributors

Sam Bateman is a Professorial Fellow at the Australian National Centre for Ocean Resources and Safety, University of Wollongong, Australia.

Annina Cristina Bürgin is based at the Institute of European Studies, University of Coruña, Spain.

Douglas Guilfoyle is Reader in Law in the Faculty of Laws, at University College London, UK.

Stig Jarle Hansen is an Associate Professor at the University of Life Sciences, Ås, Norway.

Martin N. Murphy is a Senior Fellow at the Atlantic Council of the United States, a Research Fellow at the Centre for Foreign Policy Studies, Dalhousie University, Halifax, Canada, and has taught in the Security Studies programme at Georgetown University, Washington DC, USA.

Patricia Schneider is a Senior Researcher at the Institute for Peace Research and Security Policy at the University of Hamburg, Germany (www.ifsh.de) and teaches in the Peace and Security Studies program. She is an expert on maritime security and terrorism and co-edits the quarterly journal *Sicherheit und Frieden – Security and Peace*.

Awet T. Weldemichael is Queen's National Scholar in African History at Queen's University, Canada. He is currently researching contemporary Somalia and its adjoining waters.

Andrew C. Winner is a Professor of Strategic Studies in the Strategic Research Department at the US Naval War College, Rhode Island, USA. He is the co-chair of the Indian Ocean Regional Studies Group.

Acknowledgement

We would like to acknowledge the funding of the Australian Research Council Discovery Project DP120101166: 'Building an Indian Ocean Region' for their generous assistance in the conduct and completion of this book.

INTRODUCTION

Maritime terrorism and piracy in the Indian Ocean Region

Terrorist attacks have been carried out at sea and using the sea by nationalist-separatist groups, leftist extremists and Islamist fundamentalists. Prominent cases in the Indian Ocean region include al-Qaeda's attack on the USS Cole in 2000 and on the French tanker Limburg in 2002, as well as Lashkar-e-Taiba's use of a maritime approach in its terrorist attack on Mumbai in 2008. Other terrorist groups that have been active in the maritime realm in the Indian Ocean include LTTE (Sri Lanka) and Al Shabaab (Somalia). Despite the gravity of these attacks and the potential for terrorist groups to continue using the relatively less-regulated maritime realm, the phenomenon remains relatively understudied. Indeed, over the past decade, much of the scholarly discussion on maritime security in the Indian Ocean has focused on piracy and armed robbery at sea. National and international responses to the two maritime security issues in the Indian Ocean have varied widely as well, highlighting not only the difficulty of addressing the issues per se but also the lack of a shared framework or institution in the region with both the mandate and the capacity for addressing both phenomena.

The international community has so far responded to maritime terrorism and piracy in the Indian Ocean with a mix of legal and regulatory frameworks and cooperation agreements such as SUA, ISPS and C-TPAT, as well as joint and independent naval responses (coalition task forces under the aegis of Operation Enduring Freedom, EU NAVFOR Atalanta) and United Nations Security Council resolutions on piracy. The effectiveness of these measures is difficult to assess, particularly in regard to the less-frequent phenomenon of terrorists' use of the maritime realm. What can be done is to look at some cases as well as a range of responses to identify the breadth and diversity of the challenges, as well as the span of tools available for national and international policy-makers to use when combating maritime terrorism and/or piracy in the Indian Ocean.

This special issue has its origins in a panel on maritime security that took place at the April 2012 International Studies Association (ISA) Annual Convention in San Diego, California. The panel aimed to draw attention to the concept and phenomenon of maritime terrorism (with a focus on the Indian Ocean) and review the international countermeasures and preparedness to overcome it. What was discovered during both the writing of the papers and the discussions at the panel was that the issues of, and responses to, maritime terrorism and piracy in the Indian Ocean are sometimes intertwined. To complement the papers that were presented at the panel, we sought additional contributions from established scholars of relevant geographical and thematic fields: Douglas Guilfoyle, Stig Hansen and Martin Murphy.

MARITIME TERRORISM AND PIRACY IN THE INDIAN OCEAN REGION

The articles in this special issue can broadly be placed into three categories: four case studies of specific maritime security challenges and national responses to them; one examination of the overarching issue of non-state actors and maritime security; and two that discuss international legal and regulatory responses to maritime security issues in the Indian Ocean. In the first category, Awet T. Weldemichael's piece on Somalia frames illegal fishing and toxic waste dumping as corporate terrorism at sea and reconstructs the evolution and typology of piracy off the coast of Somalia from a Somali perspective. He concludes that sustaining the gains against piracy requires reining in international corporate crimes, and joining hands with the Somalis, who, carrying the heaviest brunt of piracy, have been fighting it from within.

Annina C. Bürgin and Patricia Schneider analyse Spanish and German regimes of maritime security governance, respectively, as they play themselves out in the Indian Ocean. Whereas both countries take an active part in multilateral counter-piracy operations in the Indian Ocean – mainly EU NAVFOR Operation Atalanta – Spain facilitates the deployment of private security companies onboard Spanish-flagged vessels operating in high-risk areas. Although Germany, as a leading maritime nation with a large container shipping industry, is heavily affected by Indian Ocean piracy and its ship-owners have repeatedly asked for state or private vessel protection, it has until recently avoided facilitating private security companies. Both authors offer convincing explanations for why two EU members have different approaches. Bürgin emphasises, among other factors, the significance of the fisheries sector to the Spanish economy and the overall influence in Spanish politics of groups and companies active in the maritime industry. For her part, Schneider shows the near-paralysing conflict of interest among the very diverse German stakeholders and the complex German federal system that bestows responsibility for maritime security on various authorities, both from the federal states and Berlin.

Stig Hansen analyses maritime security concerns as they relate to, and are affected by, Yemen against the backdrop of state weakness and its ongoing conflicts. He concludes that Yemen's geostrategic location along two maritime highways and in the midst of regional rivalries is of importance not only to that country but also to maritime security in its adjacent waters.

Martin Murphy's piece perhaps offers a bridge between the case studies and the deeper examination of legal and regulatory responses to maritime terrorism and piracy. He touches on the diverse and multifaceted actors (states and non-states alike) across the wide Indian Ocean region. By focusing on non-state actors within a context of overlapping rivalries among states for resources and geostrategic positioning, he argues that the Indian Ocean will continue to offer opportunities for the use of violence to promote one's interests, terrorist or otherwise.

This potential of using the maritime realm for violence or other illegal activities will continue to affect shipping in the Indian Ocean for reasons that Sam Bateman expounds in his article. Bateman shows how, although flag states are in principle responsible for safety and security standards on vessels, in practice it is the regimes of Port State Control, and adherence to and implementation of those regimes by the port states, that makes the real difference. Weak to non-existent Port State Control mechanisms in the western and north-western Indian Ocean have, however, enabled non-seaworthy vessels to operate in those waters, endangering themselves and their crews to maritime predation and the environment to accidental pollution or slicking.

Finally, Douglas Guilfoyle brings the discussion back to international rule of law through an analysis of how piracy off Somalia has been treated in legal parlance. Studying the various international conventions, Guilfoyle shows that pirates are neither combatants to a conflict nor do their actions fit the extant legal framework against terrorism. As a result, he demonstrates that international responses to piracy have so far been in the realm of law enforcement legal paradigm, despite the prominent use of naval forces to patrol areas of the Indian Ocean and notwithstanding the often overlapping methods of piracy and maritime terrorism.

Andrew C. Winner
Professor of Strategic Studies, Strategic Research Department,
Director, Indian Ocean Studies Group,
US Naval War College

Patricia Schneider
Senior Researcher, Institute for Peace Research and
Security Policy at the University of
Hamburg (IFSH), Germany

Awet T. Weldemichael
Department of History, University of Kentucky, and
Unité de Recherche 'Migrations et Société' (URMIS)
Université Paris Diderot – Paris 7, France

Maritime corporate terrorism and its consequences in the western Indian Ocean: illegal fishing, waste dumping and piracy in twenty-first-century Somalia

Awet T. Weldemichael[a,b]

[a]*Department of History, University of Kentucky, Lexington, KY, USA;* [b]*Unité de Recherche 'Migrations et Société' (URMIS), Université Paris Diderot, Paris, France*

This paper identifies the root causes and general typology of the widespread phenomena of piracy off the coast of Somalia. It shows that piracy in this region started as a direct response to illegal fishing, with widespread claims of hazardous waste dumping offering added moral justification. It argues that the two international crimes that are the root causes of Somali piracy constitute corporate terrorism at sea. The alacrity of the earliest illegal trawlers that were captured by the fishermen to pay ransom unleashed the scourge of criminal/ransom piracy that has overshadowed – in figures and discourse – 'defensive' piracy. Restoring the state and combating poverty can help minimise the favourable conditions that latter-day pirates exploited to launch their trade, but will not eradicate piracy without successfully containing the corporate terrorism that triggered it in the first place. Moreover, combating poverty among fishing coastal communities require the eradication of illegal fishing.

1. Introduction

Piracy is an age-old crime. In the words of Martin Murphy (2010, p. 1), 'when the maritime Abel slipped his boat into the water for the first time Cain was close behind'. In Somalia, however, it is a relatively new phenomenon. In a recent overview of Indian Ocean piracy, pioneer of Indian Ocean world studies Edward Alpers (2011) rules out the historicity of Somali piracy. The fact that *buraad badeed*, the Somali phrase for piracy (meaning bandits of the sea), entered the lexicons of daily Somali life no more than two decades ago is also indicative of piracy's recent advent into the country's conflict-ridden political economy. This does not mean that attacks against ships did not occur in Somali waters before. It only means that they did not occur sufficiently to enter public discourse. But when they did, there emerged a dilemma in explaining why they have been steadily rising since 2001 and exploded as of 2005.

Many analysts agree that the nexus between hazardous waste dumping and illegal, unreported and unregulated (IUU) fishing prompted Somali piracy (Menkhaus 2009; Tharoor 2009; Waldo 2009). In 1997, a United Nations consultant, Mahdi Gedi Qayad (1997), sent an early warning that 'the absence of a national government and the availability of huge natural marine resources in Somali waters attracted the international poachers and also motivated the illegal fishing and the damaging of the previously unpolluted ecological system'. Ten years later, a United Nations body concurred with Qayad's findings and noted its consequences.

In 2008, the United Nations Somalia Monitoring Group (2008) reported that 'the ecology and economy of these areas have been adversely affected by years of illicit overfishing by foreign vessels and the dumping of toxic waste into Somali territorial waters'. The group went on to say that '[g]enuine economic hardship, whether directly related to these factors or not, and a sense of grievance against foreign exploitation of Somalia's maritime resources, not only inspire many pirates, but also serve to legitimize their activities in the eyes of their communities'. Similarly, Mohamed Abshir Waldo (2009) writes that, since the collapse of the central government,

> poaching vessels encroached on the local fishermen's grounds, competing for the abundant rock-lobster and high value pelagic fish in the warm, up-swelling 60 kms deep shelf along the tip of the Horn of Africa. The piracy war between local fishermen and IUUs started here.

Based on an analysis of documented cases of piracy off the Somali coast, Stig Jarle Hansen (2009, p. 10) contradicts these claims. Accordingly, 'Somali pirates have always targeted non-fishing vessels'. But the unpredictable ebb and flow of pirate attacks before 2005 made piracy an unexplained puzzle, leading him to the conclusion that there 'is some truth to all' the views that hold 1991, 1994–1995, 2003 and 2005 as start dates for Somali piracy (Hansen 2009, p. 19). Although Hansen accurately captures the conflicting views as to when piracy started, hence the puzzle, the widespread tendency to lump together criminal gang attacks in par with attacks by the rebel Somali National Movement (SNM) and aggrieved fishermen is the source of the confusion.

That confusion is also partially a reflection of the international community's double-standards in dealing with the multitude of challenges that Somalia presents. In the words of Scott Coffen-Smout (1999), the 'international community encourages local Somali administrative entities to take responsibility for governance of the region, but when authority is exerted over coastal waters the individuals are labelled pirates'. Speaking of Somali piracy as a phenomenon that started in 1989 may be factually accurate but it is analytically unhelpful in understanding why piracy exploded in the new millennium. Doing so also inadvertently hides rampant corporate terrorism at sea and its concomitants – local complicity and international duplicity – which are at the heart of the epic explosion of Somali piracy in the third millennium.

Martin Murphy (2011, pp. 11–15) offers a useful preliminary typology that can help us overcome the puzzle. After analysing Somali predation at sea since its earliest days in the late 1980s, as Hansen did, Murphy goes on to distinguish between 'predatory' and 'defensive' attacks. Where Murphy deferred further analysis to a future date when improved security environment granted researchers better access, Abdi Samatar *et al.* (2010, pp. 1384–1386) further elucidate that typology. Accordingly, 'political, resources, defensive and ransom' piracies are distinct but interrelated categories, some of which followed the other while others coincided. SNM attacks constituted political piracy, illegal fishers are the resources pirates, self-declared defence vigilante and fishermen defensive pirates, and finally criminal gangs who are after the ransom money.

SNM attacks constituted the struggle of a political organisation seeking to assert its authority and, upon the establishment of Somaliland in 1991, came to an abrupt end. Until the early 2000s, piracy by criminal gangs in the rest of Somalia remained so few that even Hansen (2009, p. 20) writes '[i]n 1992 there were simply no recorded piracy attacks in Somalia. In 1993, there were fewer recorded incidents of piracy in Somalia than in Italy'. While relevant in the broader sense and no less criminal, the pirate attacks of the last decade of the twentieth century are too few and far between to make Somalia synonymous with piracy any more than the Italian attacks made Italy a pirate hub.

Building on extant secondary material and drawing from recent fieldwork in Puntland (the autonomous north-eastern region of Somalia), this paper identifies the timeframe and root causes of defensive piracy of the fishermen, which was a precursor to the widespread phenomena of ransom piracy. It shows that Somali piracy started in reaction to the latent and manifest violence that resource pirates wreaked on the coastal communities, with widespread claims of waste dumping offering added moral justification. Once it started, the inflow of ransom money burst open Pandora's box and it took a life of its own. Poverty and the gaping absence of order-enforcing apparatus after 1991 did not of themselves cause piracy,[1] they offered a fertile ground for those genuinely trying to push back against encroaching resource pirates or those claiming to be doing so. I argue that the crimes of IUU fishing and waste dumping are classic cases of corporate maritime terrorism that ought to be of global concern. Ecological, moral, political and security imperatives demand that they are urgently contained. Restoring the state can help end the scourge of piracy but only if it succeeds in containing the corporate maritime terrorism that triggered it in the first place. Or as Waldo (2009) puts it, 'the notorious shipping piracy is unlikely to be resolved without simultaneously attending to the fraudulent IUU piracy'.

2. Structural violence and corporate terrorism in a Somali setting

Because the interaction between and consequences of corporate terrorism and violence are crucial for our understanding of the Somali predicament, it is important that both violence and terrorism are nuanced. In spite of near universal repugnance at terrorism, there is no consensus about its definition. In this paper, terrorism is understood as a violent act – or the threat thereof – against innocent civilians and/or their property in order to achieve one's objective(s) directly or indirectly by intimidating and instilling fear among an audience other than those enduring the violence or the threat (Primoratz 2004, pp. 3–29). Moreover, the defining feature of terrorism as a self-evident phenomenon is the act (as opposed to the actor), and that it is committed – and resorted to as a method – by states and non-state actors alike (Arndt 1953, pp. 303–327; Primoratz 2004; Blakeley 2009).[2] This then begs the questions of what violence is.

Since the Norwegian sociologist Johan Galtung's (1969, pp. 167–191) typology of violence, the world has by and large come to grips with its varied forms. As a system of imbalances built into recognised structures of a given society (or among societies) that cause otherwise avoidable harm to individuals and communities, the concept of structural violence has particularly gained traction. We now speak of structural violence '[w]henever persons are harmed, maimed, or killed by poverty and unjust social, political and economic institutions, systems, or structures' (Köhler and Alcock 1976, p. 343). Building on Amartya Sen's argument that underdevelopment is caused when people are denied agency in their development, Kathleen Ho (2007) convincingly equates the structural violence that makes such a denial possible with human rights violation. If violence is not always physical, therefore, and structural violence is in fact a necessary precursor to manifest violence or the threat thereof, it follows that latent violence can also be classified as terroristic.[3]

Whereas terrorism of the weak 'targets the few in a way that claims the attention of the many' (Crenshaw 2007, p. 4), terrorism by the powerful *ipso facto* gains the attention of the many who are indiscriminately targeted. With profit maximisation its sole driving force and consumers and profit-seeking investors its audience, corporate terrorism is similar in a sense, in that it targets anyone who stands in its way. In the process, the environment is destroyed, livelihoods ruined, human lives lost, people injured and so on. All of these or their combinations take place in an environment of corporate terrorism, with the ultimate effect of either instituting a structurally violent system or reinforcing the pre-existing one that made corporate terrorism possible in the first place, hence a vicious cycle. The latent and manifest violence that attended – and in many ways continue to do so – IUU fishing and waste dumping in Somalia are thus considered classic cases of corporate terrorism.

3. The waste dumping – illegal fishing nexus

International conventions and codes of conduct admonish states and non-states alike to adhere to sustainable fishing and responsible disposal of toxic waste.[4] Nonetheless, toxic waste dumping and illegal, unreported and unregulated (IUU) fishing remain daunting global challenges, differently affecting countries depending on their governance capacities.[5] In 2006, a high-level international High Seas Task Force (High Seas Task Force 2006) estimated that US$4–9 billion was lost annually to illegal fishing. Sub-Saharan Africa lost an estimated US$1 billion a year, which was equal to a quarter of its annual fisheries export. A few years later, a rare worldwide analysis of illegal fishing by a group of international experts indicated that, beyond its environmental effects, the monetary value of the practice ran between US$10 and $23 billion (Agnew *et al.* 2009). The global challenge of toxic waste emanates from jarring human incapacity to sustainably manage the byproducts of highly industrialised – or fast industrialising – and excessively wasteful societies. In 2010, for example, EU countries produced 8.6 million tones of electronic waste, only 36% of which was properly handled. INTERPOL reported that the remaining 5.5 million tones disappeared into 'complementary streams' (United Nations 2011a, p. 13). In the past two decades, Somalia has been a particular locus of these two international crimes, perpetrated by corporate greed.

Waste dumping

The tale of waste dumping in Somalia is still shrouded in secrecy. But it is now established that as early as 1992, possibly even earlier, toxic waste was being disposed of in Somali territorial waters (and undisclosed locations inland). Initially these dumping were reportedly carried out in return for weapons to the powers that be in Mogadishu, but are believed to have continued after any semblance of local government to partner with disappeared (MacKenzie 1992; Greenpeace-Italy 2010, pp. 20–29). It is important to briefly review the little that is known and that has been said and done – or not – in order to show its significance to piracy.

According to the Italian chapter of the international environmentalist group Greenpeace-Italy (2010, pp. 20–29), there is documentary evidence dating as far back as December 1991 that shows Italian waste-trading companies (some possibly fictitious) and known Swiss financiers making deals to export solid waste to and build waste storage facilities in Somalia. Upon learning about the deal, the then outgoing Executive Director of the United Nations Environmental Programme (UNEP), Mostafa Tolba, blew the whistle in September 1992 and shared some of the signed documents with the media. Whereas UNEP convened an inconclusive meeting with the Italian and Swiss governments that 'aimed at stopping millions of tonnes of European toxic waste being dumped in strife-torn Somalia' (MacKenzie 1992), only in 1997 did the UN dispatch a consultant on an assessment mission.[6]

Documenting the scattered waste canisters along the Somali coastline, the assessment mission reported how 'some Somali fishermen underlined that *they sleep and wake with fear, sorrow and unpromising future* due to the presence of such unclassified tank in their fishing area' (emphasis added). Moreover, 'tankers routinely discharge oily waste' in Somali waters, with detrimental effects on Somalia's marine resources (Qayad 1997). As the Qayad report failed to generate any attention, the discharge of such waste by passerby vessels was worsening due to two inter-related factors peculiar to the north-western and western Indian Ocean regions.

According to the Australian expert in maritime safety and security Sam Bateman (2012), these factors are the poor quality of many of the ships that sail in those waters, and the lack of waste management facilities in the region's ports. Significantly stricter regimes of Port State Control (PSC) in the developed world relegated a higher concentration of old, deficient and wasteful ships to waters off the less developed coastal states with weak or altogether non-existent PSC mechanisms. Not only do these unseaworthy vessels pose significant risk to sailors, ports and the environment, but they also face higher risks of being victims of maritime predation.

To make matters worse, countries along the northern and western coasts of the Indian Ocean were unequipped to handle the waste of the vessels that called at their ports until 2004, when the Omani port of Fujairah opened the only facility in the region to recycle ship-generated waste.[7] What that meant was that the 20,000 or so ships that traversed those waters had nowhere to dispose most of the sludge and solid waste that they generated on a daily basis, other than in the water. Whereas the weakness of the countries in the region and the collective ineffectiveness of their PSC regimes may have encouraged the ships to irresponsibly handle their waste, the virtual absence of maritime authorities – hence any risk of being caught – in Somalia removed any deterrent function that even weak states serve. As a result, UNEP estimated as early as 1992 ship discharge of such waste in Somali waters at 33,000 tonnes a year (Qayad 1997). In spite of the fact that ocean currents transport maritime pollution beyond the borders of individual countries, neither the discharging of heaps of ship-generated refuse nor the deliberate dumping of more hazardous waste in Somali waters drew sustained attention of the international community.

Not until the December 2004 tsunami washed more of the waste canisters up the beaches was toxic waste dumping in Somalia thrust back into public discourse, albeit fleetingly. In the immediate aftermath of the tsunami, UNEP dispatched a fact-finding mission to Somalia and found out that the tsunami had

> stirred up hazardous waste deposits on beaches around North Hobyo and Warsheik, south of Benadir. Contamination from these waste deposits has thus caused health and environmental problems to the surrounding local fishing communities. Many people in Somalia's impacted areas are complaining of unusual health problems including acute respiratory infections, mouth bleeds and skin conditions. (UNEP 2005, p. 11)

Shortly afterwards, in May 2005, another fact-finding mission composed of multiple UN agencies spent four days in Puntland, i.e. north and north-east of the locations that UNEP reported on. Four months later the Nairobi-based highest UN official for Somalia reported back with their findings (*Reliefweb* 2005): 'the mission had found no traces of toxic waste from the samples taken in the three coastal locations and tested in Nairobi'. The Resident/Humanitarian Coordinator followed that up with what became an unbreakable routine: there remained an urgent need 'for a more comprehensive assessment of the natural environment of Somalia, which would include further investigations of alleged toxic waste sites on land, and dumping of toxic waste at sea'.

In mid-2008, UN special envoy for Somalia Ahmedou Ould Abdallah blew the whistle yet again on illegal fishing and toxic waste dumping off Somalia. Convinced that 'there is dumping of solid waste, chemicals and probably nuclear' waste and that it was 'a disaster [for] the Somali environment [and] Somali population', the Mauritanian diplomat claims to have asked international NGOs to investigate, to no avail (*AFP* 2008).

Only in 2011 did the UN Security Council (United Nations 2011b) take public notice of this matter. On 11 April 2011, the Security Council demanded an investigation into why 'allegations of illegal fishing and dumping of toxic waste in Somali waters have been used by pirates in an attempt to justify their criminal activities'. Seven months later, the 'Report of the Secretary-General on the Protection of Somali Natural Resources and' (United Nations 2011a) reviewed the allegations against the backdrop of existing conventions and prohibitions. The report concluded that 'prevailing security and resource constraints have limited a thorough examination of the evidence' and that 'more robust investigations need[ed] to be carried out' in order to ascertain the allegations.

Such farcical recycling of reports, hesitant claims, assertive counter-claims and repeated calls for further study by the United Nations is revealing of international duplicity regarding this globally-consequential crime. As a result, no one has to this day ascertained many aspects of the export of waste to Somalia: the exact source(s) and levels of toxicity of the hazardous material; how much of it was dumped where in Somali territory and territorial waters; and if dumping has at all stopped. Nevertheless, impressive Somali capacity – as an oral society – to spread news and retain information has made the claims of toxic waste dumping in Somalia household stories across the country. These stories evoke strong feelings among Somalis. They also offer legitimate grounds for anyone to rise up against the reported violations or serve as moral justification for those who claim to be doing so.

Meanwhile, repeated and categorical United Nations condemnations of Somali piracy vis-à-vis its insufficient attention to IUU fishing and blatant disinterest of hazardous waste dumping only help fortify the righteous indignation shared by many Somalis.

Illegal, unreported and unregulated fishing

Unlike waste dumping, Somali encounter with illegal, unreported and unregulated (IUU) fishing is direct and across the long coastline,[8] and their reaction was generally more robust, as international attention to the latter was swifter. In the immediate aftermath of the 1991 collapse of Somalia's government in Mogadishu, foreign industrial fishers aggressively entered Somali waters (what would generally be considered EEZ and territorial waters; Menkhaus 2009, p. 22). To fully appreciate the implications of their doing so, it is important to briefly see a parallel internal Somali process that was destined to clash with illegal fishing interests.

Since the late 1970s, small-scale fishing cooperatives had been selling their catch to the government and in 1981 the state co-owned Somali High Seas Fishing Company (Shifco Co.) started operating an Italian-built fishing fleet. Around 1988, small-scale Somali fishermen aggregated their operations to launch a sizeable private fishing sector, especially active in the export of demersal fish (Jo'ar, interview, 2012). During the chaos of state collapse and worsening civil war, many north-eastern Somalis flocked back to their home regions and found economic sustenance and alternative livelihoods in the under-exploited fishing sector.[9] It offered the most entrepreneurial of the townspeople with lucrative business opportunities, gainful employment to others and subsistence to many. Several private companies emerged and by 1993 there were at least 20 of such individual and joint ventures between Garacad and Hafun in the autonomous Somali regional state of Puntland (East African Fishing Company, Al-Shaab33 Fishing Company, and AGfish Company, interviews, 2012).[10] The population of traditional fishing villages exploded in parallel. According to the current District Commissioner of Eyl District, between 1991 and 2005 the population of the historic fishing village of Eyl grew by nearly tenfold and reached close to 10,000, most of the population of which lived directly or indirectly off the fishing sector (Mayor Yusuf, interview, 2012).

The 1990s thus saw an unprecedented boom of the locally-owned, export-oriented fishing sector in Somalia, which also went a long way to meeting localised subsistence needs. Young men and boys who joined in the rush early on started to emerge as a new 'class' in their own right. Identified by their long, expensive *me'awis* (traditional sarong-type outfits worn from the waist down) and crowding together during non-fishing seasons, these fishermen came to be envied by their peers, looked up to as role models by the young and aspired after by the ladies. Whereas school-age boys dropped out of school and ran off to coastal fishing villages,[11] young ladies sang *quusoa ma tahay, aan kula qoslee?* ('Are you a diver, so I can be dear to you?')[12] Throughout the 1990s, therefore, Somali subsistence and commercial fishing did well by most accounts, in spite of the tough competition against industrial fishers and deteriorating marine environments.[13]

The rudimentary model of commercial fishing that generated much profit in the 1990s constituted of entrepreneurs or company owners at the top tier. These entrepreneurs invested capital to procure equipment – from nets and traps to fishing boats, trucks and freezers – for their own fishing companies and to give on credit to smaller-scale fishers. The entrepreneurs also gave out unsecured, competitive loans to other fishermen, who would pay their debt back with their catch, turning the transaction into a form of localised, small-scale resource backed loans. Besides the limited number of permanent employees, these companies also hired hundreds – and in some cases thousands – of seasonal employees (both expert divers and labourers). With established routes and networks of exporting the fish in bulk, the bigger companies partnered with independent smaller-scale fishermen and fisherwomen who owned their own boat(s) and equipment, hired their own limited number of seasonal employees or used family labour and sold their catch to the bigger companies (see Figure 1).

Meanwhile, illegal trawlers aggressively encroached into the inshore waters that had been the traditional preserve of Somali artisanal fishers, subsistence and commercial. The number of such trawlers lighted the coastline so much that Somali officials and international personnel of UN agencies and other organisations consistently likened the sea to Paris or New York. But Somali fishermen experienced these mobile cities of light quite differently. Coming as close as five miles in some areas and two in others, the illegal trawlers destroyed the gear of the artisanal fishermen. Eyl fisherwoman and latterly anti-piracy activist Asha Abdulkarim Hersi (interview, 2012) says that the wasting of so much time, fuel and energy in search of the missing nets and traps – only to conclude that they had been 'taken away' by the trawlers – worsened their losses of fishing gear. On average, replacing lost gear cost close to US$1000, which was too expensive for the artisanal fishermen to afford (Mayor Yusuf, interview, 2012).

Whereas generalised claims that illegal trawlers fished the Somali waters empty have to be scrutinised against the backdrop of fast shrinking fish stocks and catch across the Indian Ocean (Rumley *et al.* 2009, pp. 1–17), the methods of the trawlers are beyond recourse. Fishermen consulted from Bandar Bayla to Eyl and Garacad are consistent in their description of the factory ships' fishing methods, including dynamiting underwater crevices and coral reefs in order to more easily catch the

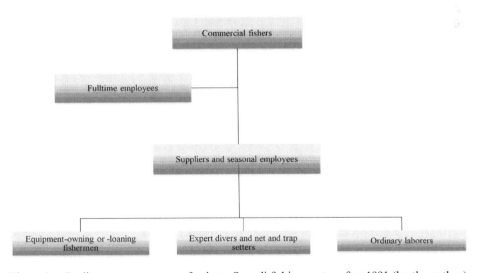

Figure 1. Rudimentary structure of private Somali fishing sector after 1991 (by the author).

crustaceans and demersal fish. The environmentally-conscious fishermen were furious about the implications of the humming, vibrations and frequent explosions that kept them awake at night. 'It is one thing to steal the resource', said a fisherman from Garacad, 'nature has its ways of replenishing itself. But to destroy the environment! These people were also endangering the future of the following generations' (Abdulkadir, interview, 2012). Meanwhile, some artisanal fishermen have been run over by the gigantic fishing fleet or their crafts destroyed in the waves of the passing trawlers.

The losses that the Somali fishing companies continued to suffer made it impossible for them to continue investing in upgrading their equipments, procuring new ones or giving out loans. Their increasingly-outdated gear and that of their smaller-scale partners – especially in the face of fierce competition from industrial fishers – in turn diminished their catch as well as their capacity to retain their employees. This cascade of troubles was compounded by a natural disaster that pushed the short-lived lucrative sector on a fast downward spiral. The devastating tsunami of December 2004 consumed huge capital costs of the local fishing companies and further reduced the catch of those who persisted in fishing. Lacking safety nets to fall back on – in the form of either a state government or insurance arrangements – the local Somali fishing companies never recovered from their losses. Many went bankrupt and closed shop while the remaining few continued to operate on massive deficit. Based on statistics from a representative company with a complete data set, Table 1 best demonstrates the above phenomenon.

4. The legitimate local response that went awry

Artisanal subsistence fishermen, the local fishing companies and their smaller-scale suppliers immediately protested the illegal trawlers' repeated violations. As a young community activist, the current Director General of the Ministry of Fisheries Abdiwahid Mohamed Hersi (aka Jo'ar) and like-minded activists mobilised the communities and appealed to SSDF leader Abdullahi Yusuf (Hassan and Jo'ar, interviews, 2012). In response, former coastguards joined the local fishermen in defending against illegal trawlers with immediate effect, capturing more than six of them in the first half of the 1990s – all within five miles of the coast (Jo'ar, interview, 2012).

After the establishment of the autonomous Puntland State of Somalia the responsibility of issuing fishing licenses and protecting Somali waters from illegal trawlers fell on two private security companies: Hart Group (1999–2002) and Somali-Canadian Coast Guard (SomCan; 2002–2005, and 2007–2009). Although the full story of these security companies is still murky, from the extant secondary literature and interviews with informed personalities in Puntland, not only have they failed to contain illegal fishing but they also exacerbated piracy. In the words of

Table 1. Tones of lobster exports by a private Somali fishing company (by the author).

	1994/ 1995	1998/ 1999	2003/ 2004	2004/ 2005	2005/ 2006	2010/ 2011
Al-Shaab33 Fishing Co.	103	127	148	100	80	20

retired General Ali Badey, Hart Group 'took the licensing idea but did not take the patrolling' component of their contract (General Badey, interview, 2012). Similarly, on SomCan, Canadian journalist Jay Bahadur (2011, p. 65) quotes Jo'ar as saying: 'SomCan was keeping the security of their own licensed ships instead of keeping the security of the sea'.

Under the protection of Hart and SomCan coastguards, foreign trawlers continued fishing deep in inshore waters, except this time they were protected under the authority of the state. In the process, they destroyed local fishermen's gear and in many cases their heavily armed guards fought with community defence vigilantes. Whatever the merits of these security solutions, the local fishing communities did not see them any differently than the armed foreign trawlers that stole their fish at gun point, almost literally. In the words of General Badey (interview, 2012), 'the hungry [Somali] people could see that their own government was involved in illegal fishing, piracy', in a sense the government protected illegal fishers. Thus, left to their own devices, the local fishermen took matters into their own hands and, in due course, criminal gangs took advantage of it.

With his company's headquarters in Kulub (12 km north of Garacad), Mohamed Abdulkadir 'John' (interview, 2012) planned to confront the trawlers from the mid-1990s through to the early 2000s. He first bought his fishermen weapons and allowed them to use his speedboats to capture the trawlers with the intention of sinking them or burning them with gasoline, which he also provided.[14] By his own account, in the early 2000s, John even tried – but failed – to procure sea mines to plant in Somali territorial waters in order to prevent the trawlers from coming into their fishing grounds and blow them up if they did. 'The idea', he said, 'was to send a strong message and prevent others from coming to our waters.' Similarly in Eyl, when the first illegal trawler was captured and brought to the harbour in 2000, many, including the current Mayor of the district, wanted to pull the vessel out of the water and let it 'die' on the beach. It was expected to become a visible reminder to the other illegal trawlers of the fate that awaited them should they continue to pirate Somali resources (Mayor Yusuf, interview, 2012).

The owners of the local Somali fishing companies claim not to have been interested in money. They only wanted the foreign industrial fishers to get out of their waters. Neither moved by such pleas nor prepared to give up their fishing crafts, the owners of captured trawlers proved eager to pay 'fines' in order to secure the expedited release of their vessels and go on with their business without the embarrassment or potential lawsuit. And the ordinary fishermen – the divers and labourers – who did the hijackings and remained in charge of the captured vessels wanted money (out of greed and/or for their subsistence needs). So when the first trawlers were captured in 2000,[15] the frontline hijackers and the owners of the trawlers outmanoeuvered the Somali commercial fishermen by striking deals in which the hijackers released the trawlers upon receiving undisclosed sums from their foreign owners. Thus started ransom payments, which lured increasing numbers of pirates into attacking fishing vessels.[16]

Meanwhile, the industrial fishers increasingly armed themselves and/or secured the protection of either local warlords or the privately-organised Somali coastguards. It only took a few encounters for the artisanal fishermen to realise that they had been outgunned and overpowered. 'Our boys lost hope when they realized that the trawlers' licensees supplied them with armed militias to overpower opponents', said a fisherman in late 2000 (Khalif 2005). Whereas some fishermen who genuinely took the gun to defend their waters thus gave up, many others took to attacking every vulnerable vessel they encountered at sea. The tipping point for this emerging epidemic of ransom piracy took place between 2003 and 2004, when a few men introduced an attractive business model of harnessing the enormous potential they saw in hijacking ships for ransom (Hansen 2009, p. 23ff). Their trade quickly took on a life of its own.

The evolution of defensive piracy to predatory business was helped by many factors, principally by the 2004 tsunami that dealt the withering fishing sector an irreversible blow. The incapacity of the marine environment to replenish itself at the same pace that it was being plundered and the inability of local fishing companies to recuperate pushed many more subsistence and employed fishermen out of their legitimate line of work and into the warm embrace of ransom piracy. In the absence of strong law enforcement, this reservoir of experienced seamen living in abject poverty offered an ideal ground for the few business-minded organisers to recruit and train men for hijacking ships on the high seas, leading to the epic phenomenon of modern-day piracy. The escalation of ransom piracy thus eroded the fishing sector even more and the two have since developed an inversely proportional relationship, the reversal of which promises to offer a sustainable Somali solution to the scourge of piracy.

5. Current dynamics and trajectory of illegal fishing piracy off the coast of Somalia

Suggestions that piracy and a large-scale international maritime presence in Somali waters may have scared illegal fishers away remain hard to ascertain, because the illicit nature of the business makes it impossible to establish its extent before the outbreak of piracy and after. What is certain is that illegal, unreported and unregulated fishing in those waters continues unabated. At the height of piracy and the presence of international naval flotilla in April 2009, the Somali Deputy Prime Minister and Minister of Fisheries and Marine Resources at the time, Abdirahman Ibbi, stated that hundreds of European and other foreign vessels remained active in illegal fishing off Somalia (*EUobserver.com* 2009). The Director General of Punt-land's Ministry of Fisheries is specific on the hundreds of vessels (Yemeni, Iranian, Spanish and other Asian and European boats and ships) that continue to illegally fish in Somali waters (Jo'ar, interview, 2012). Somali fishermen consulted from Bandar Bayla in the north to Garacad in the south claim that it still goes on. Residents of Bandar Bayla mobilised to wage peaceful resistance against illegal fishers by sailing in small boats with banners and loud speakers, announcing to the big ships that they were fishing in Somali waters and that they had to leave. As recent as January 2012, their attempts have been responded to with a hail of bullets from the fishing vessels. Unarmed, the protesting artisanal fishermen fled back to the coast on each of those occasions (Mayor Ali, interview, 2012).

Meanwhile, moving from actively supporting the men who captured fishing vessels, Somali coastal communities started asking and challenging as early as 2008 why commercial vessels were being attacked and brought to their waters. The repertoire of pirate leveraging over these communities ranged from invoking clan and family ties, hence protection, to corrupting local elders and threatening to resort to violence. As residents of these coastal communities would never fail to point out to visiting researchers and journalists, the pirates were armed to the teeth while the local communities were either unarmed or their arms did not match those of the pirates. Several inter-related developments took place between 2008 and 2009 that fully awakened coastal communities to the peril of piracy taking place in their midst, while at the same time helping accelerate piracy.

First, the inter-clan-based and commercialised organisation of pirates broke down when the three principal leaders fell out with each other,[17] leading to the emergence of clan- and sub-clan-based pirate groups (Hassan, interview, 2012). Explaining the secret of the business successes of his countrymen, a Somali businessman related to BBC journalist Mary Harper (2012, p. 116) that trust lied at the heart of it all: 'People will come to you, they will give you their money without signing any document, they will say, "Here is my money, help me", and five or six people will come together entirely due to trust'. Just as in legitimate business ventures, so too in piracy trust emanating from primordial ties played some role. One pirate (confidential interview, 2012), for example, related how on his return to Garowe after a successful pirate operation in late 2008, 'there was this rush by investors who offered money for future missions'. Although Harper's conclusion that the 'clan system guards against deception in business dealings' (Harper 2012, p. 119) does not fully apply to the piracy business because there continue to be intra-clan, -sub-clan and -family rivalries and double-crossings, the increased homogeneity of pirate groups assured previously reluctant investors, who then rushed to offer capital to groups from their own clans or sub-clans.

Second, after several months of going without pay, many soldiers of the autonomous Puntland State of Somalia abandoned the defence force and started searching for alternative means of supporting themselves and their families. Many of these well-trained and disciplined men were recruited into pirate groups. With the increasing number of soldiers-turned-pirates and disintegration of inter-clan pirate groups, the existing 'code' among pirates disappeared. Pirates started to double-cross each other across and within clan groupings. The consequent tension and violence within and among pirate groups led to increased insecurity of local communities wherever the pirates landed.

Third, Abdullahi Yusuf's loss of the Presidency of the Transitional Federal (TFG) Government in Mogadishu and the simultaneous collapse of the private coastguard ventures between 2008 and 2009 added – in diversity and numbers – to the pool of soldiers-turned-pirates in Puntland. In late 2004, Abdullahi was elected to preside over the internationally-backed TFG, whereupon he took with him the Ethiopian-trained and battle-hardened SSDF fighters who had constituted the bulk of Puntland's forces, to the detriment of the autonomous region's security sector. In 2008, however, he lost that position and the TFG under President Sheikh Sherif Sheikh Ahmed and Puntland lacked the political will and/or financial and institutional capacities to absorb into their fledgling forces Abdullahi's well-armed and seasoned fighters. The latter returned to their home region between late 2008 and early 2009, with nothing to show for their time or support their families with. Around the same time, the last private coastguard company lost its licence, leaving the trained and armed sailors without a fallback option. It is widely rumoured in Puntland that men coming from these two forces have a strong presence in the organisation, leadership and financing of many of the successful piracy activities off the coast of Somalia.

Finally, investors' and pirate groups' rush to outdo rivals by attracting the better skilled and bigger number of recruits led to previously unheard of extravagance. Before 2008, pirates went into 'hibernation' after every successful hijacking. They spent their loot in relative hiding, and did not come out until they exhausted their money and needed to prepare for another mission. After 2008, however, investors started to pour money (on credit) – in cash and in kind – to lure the non-pirate youth into piracy and retain the committed pirates.

The consequences proved devastating to the local communities and eroded what little support pirates had enjoyed among their hosts. Over-consumption of alcohol, khat/qat and other drugs by gun wielding young men, including children, led to commotion and disturbances among communities that had previously lived in relative peace. In several cases there were violent fights within and among pirate groups as well as against the coastal communities. Security deteriorated. In the words of a young resident of Eyl who represented the non-pirate youth in their campaign against pirates, insecurity increased to such a point 'that our wives started to miscarry'. The explosion of open prostitution undermined the morals of devout, conservative Muslims and offended the sensibilities of the more open tolerant ones. Young men and boys without previous driving experience started owning and driving brand new automatic (as opposed to stick shift, which are the more difficult to drive) sports cars, causing numerous accidents that the locals had neither experienced nor seen before. Accompanied by many dependents called *shahat*,[18] the pirates borrowed massively from local businesses under hefty interest rates but in many cases disappeared upon receiving their share of the ransom money.

The combined effect of pirates undermining social and religious values of their willing or unwilling hosts, disturbing their security, setting bad examples to their children and defaulting on their debts cost the pirates the sympathy of and business relations with the local communities. Many coastal communities started organised campaigns as early as 2008, which are still ongoing. Awareness campaigns by religious leaders, titled traditional elders, elected office holders and an array of activist groups persuaded many pirates to abandon piracy, dissuaded many young men from joining pirate groups, encouraged parents to refuse to marry their daughters to pirates and warned young women of the real risks of marrying pirates. While all these moves helped ostracise many pirates, perhaps most effectively, local businesses – and especially women food vendors – refused to do business with pirates. These anti-piracy efforts have so far evicted pirates from Bandar Bayla in the north to Garacad in the south.

6. Conclusion

Maritime dangers know no boundaries and maritime corporate terrorism has not only caused piracy off the coast of Somalia but it also continues to pose grave dangers to the world. Legalistic hairsplitting to suggest that one cannot speak of Somali territorial waters or EEZ, hence also of illegality of economic or other operations there, is a lame and morally bankrupt justification of robbing people of their meagre livelihoods; a justification not different from that used to justify imperialism and colonialism. Moreover, international obsession with piracy and repeated declarations that they can be crushed militarily are nonsensical,[19] for pirates are not an armed force seeking or waiting for battle; instead they are loosely organised groups that can easily dissolve into their respective communities under pressure and reassemble at an opportune future date.[20]

Piracy has wreaked incalculable damage to the Somalis themselves and it would make more sense – from moral, political, economic and security points of view – to join them in their own fight against the scourge they are confronting from within. While a relapse cannot be ruled out, the coastal communities have made important gains in that regard with limited help from the state and none from the outside world. Those gains must be capitalised on to fortify local communities' anti-piracy resolve by putting an end to the repeated violation of their waters (at least the inshore waters), helping them restore the fishing sector and find additional alternative means of supporting themselves. A sober appreciation and resolution of the root causes of piracy parallel identifying its moral, social, economic and security consequences on the Somali people, and capitalising on their resolve to fight it would only bring about a semblance of normalcy as a thin veil over the ominous structural violence, a phenomenon Galtung (1969) calls bad peace.

Acknowledgements

I am thankful to Hamburg University for exploratory funding and the Gerda Henkel Foundation for the research grant that made the fieldwork for this paper possible. I also thank Patricia Schneider, Sam Bateman, Andrew Winner and the anonymous reviewers for their valuable feedback.

Notes

1. Menkhaus (2009) correctly notes that many scholars, commentators and policy makers have 'seized on [this piracy story] to plead for a durable political solution to the 19-year crisis of the state collapse in Somalia'. But not only does this view exaggerate state capacity in Somalia before 1991 (or generally of the African state for that matter), it also ignores the fact that poverty in Somalia is not something that has come with the civil war.
2. For a contrasting view, see Laqueur (1987, p. 146).
3. The widely held view that 'political end' is a defining feature of terrorism is unhelpful because it disregards the similar physical and psychological significance of terrorism that are more tangible than the final goal that may or may not transpire. It is my view that the most recent shooting spree of a lone terrorist in Toulouse or the Oklahoma City bombing by a lone criminal is not any less terroristic than the East African embassy bombings or that of the World Trade Centre.
4. Until the early 1970s, toxic waste was dumped in the seas with limited restrictions. See Sjoblom and Linsley (1994)
5. This paper adopts the definition of IUU fishing as stipulated by the Food and Agriculture Organization (FAO) of the United Nations in Paragraph 3 of the 2001 *International Plan of Action to Prevent, Deter and Eliminate Illegal, Unreported and Unregulated Fishing*.
6. The closest anyone had gotten to discovering the truth about toxic waste dumping (in exchange for arms) was Ilaria Alpi, the young Italian journalist who was murdered in broad daylight in Mogadishu in 1994.
7. The former chair of IMO's Marine Environment Protection Committee (MEPC) believes that oil slicks in the north-western Indian Ocean is also likely to have ameliorated due to improved technology in ship design that, according to Sam Bateman (conversations in April 2012, San Diego, and correspondences in July 2012), 'reduces the need for tankers to clean cargo tanks (by what they call 'loading on top'), and [the construction of] double hulls and segregated ballast tanks that reduce the need for tankers to load ballast water into cargo tankers, which then leads to a requirement to discharge dirty ballast water before loading their next cargo'. Also see Bateman (2009, pp. 109–117).

8. The convenience of blanket application of IUU to all fishing operations in Somali waters since the collapse of the state hides as yet untouched legal minefields. While it is important to bear in mind that the legality of some fishing operations or the illegality of others cannot be put in black-and-white terms as a result, there were and still are many fishing trawlers that have not even bothered to seek the green light of any of the competing power centres nor the local communities in whose waters they fished/fish. Moreover, fishing vessels can just as easily be considered in violation of whatever law they may be operating under – or become altogether illegal – when they operate outside the prescribed zone, use prohibited methods or arm themselves to the teeth (as they often did) under the guise of defending themselves. Many of these are textbook cases of IUU in waters off the Somali coast.

9. At least since independence, many nomadic and settled Somalis left their home villages and small towns and flocked to the capital, Mogadishu, in pursuit of a better life: education, careers, salaried jobs etc. When the state imploded, these townspeople found safety in their respective home regions, impoverished as they may have been due to the decades-long loss of their human resources to the capital that has suddenly ceased to be *the* political centre.

10. All three companies emerged in the early 1990s and still maintain a reduced presence, while most of the others went bankrupt under the heavy weight of illegal fishing, tsunami, piracy and now aggressive counter-piracy operations that have made their fishing ground a no-go zone.

11. My driver during my travels between Garowe, Bosaso, Eyl and Galkacyo was one of those teenage boys who quit school to become a fisherman.

12. I am grateful to members of my research team, Abdinasser and Sakaria, for the lessons about such very revealing songs, anecdotes and tales that a foreigner would be hard pressed to come across.

13. Interviews with scores of fishermen and fish exporters show that the income of a Somali commercial fisherman reached as high as US$20,000 per season and that of an average diver reached US$5000. There is a good chance that these figures may be a little exaggerated but they give an indication of the overall wellbeing of the trade and popular optimism it generated.

14. Had 'John' succeeded in this scheme, this would not have been the first time that a vessel was set on fire in Somali waters: in 1991, the MV Naviluck was reportedly set on fire by pirates aboard three attack boats. See Murphy (2011, p. 12).

15. According to 'John', between late January and early February 2000, a Taiwanese fishing vessel was the first to be captured by the fishermen near his company headquarters in Kulub.

16. I spoke with five commercial fishermen, numerous artisanal fishers, five regional/district administrators, two retired generals, three colonels, three legal experts including the current Attorney General and even pirates who blame these early ransom payments as the source of the current problem of piracy.

17. These are Mohamed Abdi Hassan 'Afweyne' (belonging to the Hawiye clan from the Hobyo-Haradere area), Abshir Boyah (Darod clan from Eyl), and Garad Mohamed (of mixed Hawiye-Darod parentage, operating between the two piracy sectors).

18. Literally meaning beggar in Arabic, *shahat* in this Somali context is considered more dignified than a simple beggar.

19. 'We could very easily crush the Somali pirates', said one panelist at a recent shipping industry conference in Stamford, CT, who went on to blame lack of political will to do so (Lee 2012).

20. From a security point of view, they constitute what Peter Chalk characterised as 'gray area phenomena', whereby the foe is not easily definable and the conflict non-linear (Chalk 2010). See Guilfoyle (2012) for a legal analysis of how the laws of war do not apply to Somali pirate attacks and counter-piracy measures.

References

AFP (2008), 'UN envoy decries illegal fishing, waste dumping off Somalia', 25 July. Available at http://afp.google.com/article/ALeqM5gVV_gQDsp1m8v7nPcumVc5McYV-Q, accessed 20 August 2008.

Agnew, D.J., Pearce, J., Pramod, G., Peatman, T., Watson, R., Beddington, J.R., and Pitcher, T.J. (2009), 'Estimating the worldwide extent of illegal fishing', *PLoS ONE*, Vol. 4, no. 2, pp. e4570. Available at http://www.plosone.org/article/info:doi/10.1371/journal.pone.0004570, accessed 14 September 2011.

Alpers, E.A. (2011), 'Piracy and Indian Ocean Africa', *Journal of African Development*, Vol. 13, no. 1, pp. 15–38.

Arndt, H. (1953), 'Ideology and terror: a novel form of government', *The Review of Politics*, Vol. 15, no. 3, pp. 303–327.

Bateman, S. (2009), 'Maritime security implication of the international shipping recession', *The Australian Journal of Maritime and Ocean Affairs*, Vol. 1, no. 4, pp. 109–117.

Bateman, S. (2012), 'Maritime security and port state control in the Indian Ocean Region', *Journal of Indian Ocean Region*, Vol. 8, no. 2, pp. 188–202.

Blakeley, R. (2009), *State Terrorism and Neoliberalism: The North in the South*. New York: Routledge.

Chalk, P. (2010), 'Piracy off the Horn of Africa: scope, dimensions, causes and responses', *Brown Journal of World Affairs*, Vol. 16, no. 2, pp. 89–108.

Coffen-Smout, S. (1999), 'Pirates, warlords and rogue fishing vessels in Somalia's unruly seas'. Available at http://www.chebucto.ns.ca/~ar120/somalia.html, accessed 19 April 2011.

Crenshaw, M. (2007), 'Thoughts on relating terrorism to historical contexts', in M. Crenshaw, ed., *Terrorism in Context*. University Park: The Pennsylvania State University Press, pp. 3–24.

EUobserver.com (2009), 'Commission ready to investigate European illegal fishing off Somalia', 22 April. Available at http://www.illegal-fishing.info/item_single.php?item = news&item_id = 3804&approach_id = 17, accessed 10 June 2009.

FAO (2001), *International Plan of Action to Prevent, Deter and Eliminate Illegal, Unreported and Unregulated Fishing*. Available at http://www.fao.org/docrep/003/y1224e/y1224e00.htm, accessed 15 January 2012.

Galtung, J. (1969), 'Violence, peace, and peace research', *Journal of Peace Research*, Vol. 6, no. 3, pp. 167–191.

Greenpeace-Italy (2010), The toxic ships: the Italian hub, the Mediterranean area and Africa. Available at http://www.arte.tv/download/permanent/u1/somalie/Report-the-toxic-ship.pdf, accessed 14 July 2011.

Guilfoyle, D. (2012), 'International law and counter-piracy in the Indian Ocean', *Journal of Indian Ocean Region*, Vol. 8, no. 2, pp. 203–219.

Hansen, S.J. (2009), 'Piracy in the greater Gulf of Aden: myths, misconceptions and remedies', *NIBR Report #29*, Norwegian Institute for Urban and Regional Research.

Harper, M. (2012), *Getting Somalia Wrong? Faith, War and Hope in a Shattered State*. London and New York: Zed Books.

High Seas Task Force (2006), 'Closing the net: stopping illegal fishing on the high seas. Final report of the ministerially-led task force on IUU fishing on the high seas'. Available at http://www.illegal-fishing.info/uploads/HSTFFINALweb.pdf, accessed 20 April 2011.

Ho, K. (2007), 'Structural violence as a human rights violation', *Essex Human Rights Review*, Vol. 4, no. 2, pp. 1–17. Available at http://projects.essex.ac.uk/ehrr/V4N2/ho.pdf, accessed 15 December 2011.

Khalif, A. (2005) 'How illegal fishing feeds Somali piracy', *The East African*, 15 November.

Köhler, G. and Alcock, N. (1976), 'An empirical table of structural violence', *Journal of Peace Research*, Vol. 13, no. 4, pp. 343–356.

Laqueur, W. (1987), *The Age of Terrorism*. Boston: Little, Brown & Co.

Lee, R. (2012), 'Maritime panelists frustrated over Somali pirate inaction', *stamfordadvocate.com*, 19 March. Available at http://www.stamfordadvocate.com/news/article/Maritime-panelists-frustrated-over-Somali-pirate-3419172.php#ixzz1qGLlByTY

MacKenzie, D. (1992), 'Toxic waste adds to Somalia's woes', *New Scientist*, 19 September.

Menkhaus, K. (2009), 'Dangerous waters', *Survival*, Vol. 51, no. 1, pp. 21–25.

Murphy, M.N. (2010), *Small Boats, Weak States, Dirty Money. Piracy and Maritime Terrorism in the Modern World*. London: Hurst & Company.

Murphy, M.N. (2011), *Somalia: The New Barbary? Piracy and Islam in the Horn of Africa*. New York: Columbia University Press.

Primoratz, I. ed., (2004), *Terrorism. The Philosophical Issues*. New York: Palgrave Macmillan.

Qayad, M.G. (1997), 'Assessment mission to Somalia in connection with alleged dumping of hazardous substances'.

Reliefweb (2005), 'Somalia: UN mission to Puntland on toxic waste in the coastal areas of Somalia', 7 October. Available at http://reliefweb.int/node/186918, accessed 20 April 2011.

Rumley, D. (2009), 'Fisheries exploitation in the Indian Ocean Region', in D. Rumley, S. Chaturvedi and V. Sakhuja, eds., *Fisheries Exploitation in the Indian Ocean: Threats and Opportunities*. Singapore: ISEAS Publishing, pp. 1–17.

United Nations (2010), *UN Somalia Monitoring Group Report*, S/2010/91, 10 March.

United Nations (2011a), *Report of the Secretary-General on the Protection of Somali Natural Resources and Waters*, S/2011/611, 25 October.

United Nations (2011b), *UN Security Council Resolution 1976*, S/RES/1976, 11 April.

Samatar, A.I., Lindberg, M. and Mahayni, B. (2010), 'The dialectics of piracy in Somalia: the rich versus the poor', *Third World Quarterly*, Vol. 31, no. 8, pp. 1377–1394.

Sjoblom, K.L. and Linsley, G. (1994), 'Sea disposal of radioactive wastes: the London convention 1972', *IAEA Bulletin*, Vol. 2, pp. 12–16. Available at http://www.iaea.org/Publications/Magazines/Bulletin/Bull362/36205981216.pdf, accessed 15 April 2011.

Tharoor, I. (2009), 'How Somalia's fishermen became pirates', *Time*, 18 April. Available at http://www.time.com/time/world/article/0,8599,1892376,00.html, accessed 9 June 2009.

UNEP (2005), 'After the tsunami: rapid environmental assessment'. Available at http://www.unep.org/tsunami/reports/TSUNAMI_report_complete.pdf, accessed 10 June 2009.

Waldo, M.A. (2009), 'The two piracies in Somalia: why the world ignores the other?', *Wardheernews.com*, 8 January. Available at http://wardheernews.com/Articles_09/Jan/Waldo/08_The_two_piracies_in_Somalia.html, accessed 10 June 2009.

Interviews

Abdiwahid Mohamed Hersi (aka Jo'ar) (14 and 15 February 2012, Bosaso).

General Ali Badey (26 February 2012, Galkacyo).

Abdirizak Ismail Hassan (26 February 2012, Galkacyo).

Asha Abdulkarim Hersi (24 February 2012, Eyl).

Mayor of Bandar Bayla Saed Adan Ali (11 February 2012, Garowe).

Mayor of Eyl Musa Osman Yusuf (24 February 2012, Eyl).

Mohamed Abdulkadir (aka John) (27 February 2012, Galkacyo).

Owner of East African Fishing Company (5 February 2012, Garowe).

Three owners and executives of Al-Shaab33 Fishing Company (19 February 2012, Bosaso).

Spanish maritime security governance in the Indian Ocean Region

Annina Cristina Bürgin

Instituto Universitario de Estudios Europeos, Universidade da Coruña,
A Coruña, Spain

International maritime security issues are high on the agenda of many states and international organisations. Assaults in international waters on vessels flying the Spanish flag raised the awareness of piracy and other illicit acts at sea. Spain applies a twofold strategy in order to fight against piracy off the Somali coast and in the Indian Ocean: it takes part in the first maritime operation of the European Union (EU), *EU NAVFOR Atalanta*, and facilitates the deployment of private security companies (PSCs) on board civilian vessels sailing in international waters. Based on the security governance concept, this paper examines and compares the strategies regarding actors, the decision-making processes, legal issues and effectiveness. The article argues that the main reason for the change in security policy is that the actors involved assume a security governance approach to be more effective in solving a specific security problem.

1. Introduction

On 2 October 2009 the tuna fishing boat *Alakrana* was hijacked 120 nautical miles off the Somali coast (EU NAVOR Somalia 2009). The perpetrators demanded a US$10 million ransom and the return of their two comrades who had been captured by a Spanish warship. The ship was released after the payment of ransom, but it remains unclear which actors were involved. Merchant and fishing vessels flying the Spanish flag had been victims of maritime violence before, but the *Alakrana* case provoked an extensive debate on how *international* maritime security could be guaranteed and prompted the transformation of Spain's maritime security policy.

This article first provides an overview of the security governance concept and introduces criteria for analysis. Second, it describes two different security strategies. Third, it analyses the main causes for a change from security policy towards security governance and, fourth, discusses particularities of the security governance model. The article closes with concluding remarks.

2. Security governance: framework for analysis

The concept of security governance lacks a coherent theoretical background but serves as a useful analytical framework to analyse arrangements which address security issues (Kirchner 2006, p. 950). Security governance consists of two terms which have undergone substantial change: since the 1980s, the notion of security broadened and deepened with respect to issues, involved actors and addressees. The traditional state-centric notion of security has changed in that research now increasingly focuses on societies and individuals. Moreover, since the end of the Cold War, threat perceptions have changed significantly, since interstate conflicts are not considered to be main risks any longer and security conceptualisations turned towards non-military issues, thus including economical, political or ecological factors (Krahmann 2003, pp. 9–10; Kirchner 2006, p. 949). Furthermore, the concept 'governance' gained multiple applications. Nevertheless, all concepts describe how social interactions are managed and analyse the decision-making processes and the involved actors (Mayntz 2004, p. 66).

Applied in politics, governance focuses on a specific approach towards public policy administration. It describes a governing-mode which is less hierarchical and less centralised. Moreover, state authorities do not possess exclusive decision-making competence anymore. The term also implies the involvement of diverse actors and highlights the participation of non-state actors in policy-making and thus contrasts with the term Government. Governance emphasises processes and policies based on shared goals where compliance does not depend on the powers of an authority. Rosenau stresses that for governance, inter-subjective meaning is as important as formal rules, since this form of coordination only works if it is accepted by the involved actors (Rosenau 1992, pp. 4–5). The acceptance of an integrated approach towards solutions is not only based on shared norms, but also on the assumption that the cooperation might address a security problem more effectively than other strategies (Ehrhart, Petretto and Schneider 2010, p. 13).

The governance concept applied to maritime security describes and analyses involved actors and decision-making processes within this specific policy area. While the golden age for pirates ended in the eighteenth century, violence at sea has never ceased to exist (Sobrino Heredia 2008, pp. 89–97). In some regions attacks have increased and challenge both the Westphalian state and the international state system, which is why maritime violence is considered to be a transnational security threat and gives rise to new forms of governance. Therefore, the analysis of Spain's strategies in the fight against piracy in the Indian Ocean Region is based on the following criteria:

(1) involved actors;
(2) national legal issues and decision-making processes;
(3) driving force(s); and
(4) effectiveness.

3. Spain's maritime security governance model

The first *Spanish Security Strategy* of 2011 specifically mentions threats originating at sea and declares that 'maritime protection is of primary significance', as 90% of all imports and 65% of exports pass through Spanish ports (Gobierno de España 2011, p. 42). The Spanish Armed Forces further identified major maritime threats: proliferation of weapons of mass destruction, illegal trafficking of weapons and drugs, organised smuggling, illegal immigration, environmental damages, maritime terrorism and piracy (Fontán Aldereguía 2010, p. 285; Nieves 2010). This spectrum illustrates that maritime security is a broad concept, which requires actions by multiple diverse actors.

Spain's policy combating maritime violence in the Indian Ocean mainly consists of two complementary strategies: first, it participates in the European Union (EU) maritime operation *EU NAVFOR Atalanta*; and second, Spain facilitates the deployment of private security companies (PSCs) on civilian vessels in international waters.

3.1. Spain's contribution to Atalanta

In 2008, Spain advocated for a closer collaboration with European partners to fight piracy after several Spanish vessels had been attacked (Ruesta Botella 2009, p. 82). Based on the United Nations Security Council (UNSC) Resolution 1814, which evaluated the situation in Somalia as a threat to international peace and security, Spain co-sponsored Resolution 1816, which encourages cooperation among states, allowed them to enter Somali territorial waters and permitted them to make use of all necessary means to repress piracy (Bacas Fernández 2009, p. 168). Concurrently, Spain took a joint decision with France in June 2008 and both countries reached an understanding regarding combating piracy (La Moncloa 2008). Despite the coordinated action within the EU framework, Spain independently started the mission *Operación Centinela Índico* in September 2008, deploying a maritime surveillance aircraft using the French military base in Djibouti (Ejército del aire 2012). In November 2008, the EU Council passed the Joint Action 2008/851, which constitutes the legal basis for EU NAVFOR Atalanta.

Actors involved

There are two groups of main actors on the national level. Politically, the Parliament and the Council of Ministers exercise joint control of the armed forces; however, the Parliament has to authorise an international military mission. The Council has to inform the Parliament regularly and has to ask the representatives for another authorisation to prolong an operation. The Ministry of Defence is responsible for the implementation of the policies and serves as an interlocutor with international partners. Operationally, and with respect to Atalanta, units of the *Armada Española* (Navy) and the *Ejército del Aire* (Air force) participate in the maritime operations (MDE 2012, p. 15). Spain remained particularly committed to Atalanta from the beginning through substantial contributions. Moreover, the first commander of the coordination unit at EU NAVCO was a Spanish Navy captain, and until the end of 2012 it will have appointed most Force Commanders of the mission. Currently, Spain deploys a frigate and a patrol boat and operates a maritime patrol aircraft (CN-235 VIGMA). With 370 soldiers, Spain is the second largest troop provider (MDE 2012).

Operation Atalanta was launched within the *EU Common Security and Defence Policy* (CSDP). The Joint Action 2008/851 was adopted under the Treaty of Nice, but the basic legal provisions and the formal 'power structures' have not changed with the 2009 Lisbon Treaty and the intergovernmental character of the CSDP is still valid. Decisions on defence issues continue to be taken unanimously and without the involvement of the European Parliament (EP), which means that any EU Member State has a veto right. Moreover, the 'constructive abstention' clause allows Member

States to abstain from taking part in an operation, but requires them not to take any action which could impede the mission. Thus, participating in Atalanta does not automatically mean that Member States contribute operationally: currently, only seven EU Member States deploy naval vessels and/or warplanes, Spain included.

National legal issues and decision-making processes

International military missions are often criticised for their lack of democratic approval, since international 'general assemblies' do not participate in the decision-making processes and, often, Parliaments do not hold authority over the armed forces (Venice Commission 2008). Therefore, it is important to outline the situation in Spain and to explain recent developments.

Although Spain started to participate in peacekeeping missions as early as 1989 (Marrero Rocha 2007, pp. 172–173, 182), the law that regulates the deployment of troops abroad was not adopted until 2005 (*Ley Orgánica de la Defensa Nacional 5/2005*). The Constitution does not foresee an international military engagement and limits military duties to guaranteeing the sovereignty and independence of Spain. Even though the Parliament had limited rights in defence, affairs before these were not applicable to international peace or stability missions (Calafell Ferrá 2009, p. 381). The decisive factor for adopting a new legal framework was the intense debate following the Spanish military involvement in the US-led Iraq intervention in 2003–2004. A vast majority of the population and all parties except the governing *Partido Popular* (PP) were against the troop deployment in a non-UN authorised mission with a disputable legal basis (Aixalà i Blanch 2005, pp. 97–99; Marrero Rocha 2007, p. 192, 201; Herranz Surrallés 2008, p. 2). The terrorist attacks on 11 March 2004 in Madrid and the subsequent change of Government to the *Partido Socialista Obrero Español* (PSOE) facilitated the approval of the new law in 2005.

Accordingly, the Chamber of Representatives (*Congreso de Diputados*) must approve every troop deployment abroad a priori or a posteriori if the decision was taken in case of emergency. The Parliamentarians need to be informed regularly about the mission (Marrero Rocha 2007, p. 219; Puertas Cristóbal and Fernández Alles 2010, p. 46). Although this regulation is generally considered to be a milestone for parliamentary authority, critics emphasise that the law does not determine *how* the Parliament decides, i.e. in what composition, meaning, whether it needs to be done in a plenary session of the Chamber of Representatives or by the national Defense Committee (Marrero Rocha 2007, pp. 220–221). The Atalanta mission was approved in compliance with the strictest participation provisions: the Parliamentarians voted in a plenary session of the Chamber of Representatives.

The Parliament is a key actor in the decision-making process due to its right to authorise any foreign mission of the Armed Forces. Yet, the Council of Ministers also plays a decisive role for three reasons. First, any deployment is sketched and planned by this body. Second, the law does not clarify the decision-making process if the Government wants to extend a mission or how the procedures would be in the case of Parliament wanting to terminate a mission. In most cases, the particular mandate foresees a timeframe and specifies the decision-making procedures. However, the law is not specific here. Third, the law does not give explicit 'call-back rights' to the Representatives as provided, for example, in the German 'Parliamentary Participation Act'.

Driving force(s)

There are three main reasons why Spain participates in Atalanta. Firstly, piracy endangers Spanish national interests. The former defence minister highlighted that Spain defended the *mare liberum* in terms of free passage of persons and goods and the freedom to fish on the high sea. Admittedly, Atalanta was of vital importance for defending Spanish geostrategic and economic interests (Congreso 2009, pp. 3–5, 8). The left-wing party *Izquierda Unida* questioned the existence of Spanish geostrategic interests in the Indian Ocean Region, but accepted economic interests in the fishing sector (Congreso 2009, p. 9). On the military side, the Spanish Navy highlights that piracy is not only a threat to international security but endangers a specific national interest, the Spanish 'fishing activities' (Armada Española 2012). The Spanish Security Strategy is even more specific about African regions that are affected by piracy and emphasises geostrategic and economic interests in these areas (Gobierno de España 2011, p. 23, 35).

Secondly, there is a broad consensus that a unilateral military response to piracy is financially and logistically not feasible due to the vast expanse of the area: an estimated 1200 square nautical sea miles. To control the entire zone is not possible and it would be even less effective to act individually. Lastly, the contribution is strongly consistent with Spain's foreign policy. Since 1975, the guiding principle of Spain's foreign policy has been Europeanism (*europeísmo*; Jiménez Redondo 2006, pp. 30–31, 40, 121; Beneyto 2011, p. 44). Since becoming a member of the European Community (1986) and NATO (1982), the main goal was to integrate into the 'Western community', to normalise its international relations and to seek acceptance and recognition in order to overcome international isolation (Torreblanca 2005, p. 5). Therefore, Spain supported the development of a CSDP, joined the *Western European Union* in 1990 and contributed considerably to all subsequent missions (Barbé 2011, pp. 98–100). Concerning Atalanta, the Government underlined Spain's European orientation, i.e. acting within the EU framework to fight piracy, and clarified that it is in Spain's political interest to contribute substantially in order to improve its position within the European framework and better defend its national interests (Congreso 2009, p. 7).

Effectiveness

Atalanta's main objective is to secure *World Food Programme* (WFP) vessels, delivering food and equipment for Somalia (and the African Union Mission, AMISOM). The protection of other vulnerable vessels and the fight against pirates off the coast should only be pursued in the second place. Apart from despatching naval forces, the EU established the *Maritime Security Centre – Horn of Africa* (MSC-HOA), which provides 24-hour monitoring of vessels that transit through the Gulf of Aden and gives anti-piracy guidance. The Centre introduced the heavily protected *Internationally Recommended Transit Group Corridor* (IRTC), through which vessels were advised to pass the high risk area in convoys. Evaluating the mission against the backdrop of the mandate, the engagements might be considered to be successful. No WFP vessels were attacked once the EU (and NATO) started their missions. The same holds true with regard to the protection of vessels which are passing the Gulf of Aden using the IRTC, as the numbers of assaults there dropped from 117 in 2009 to 37 in 2011 (Kupferschmidt 2010, p. 76; CRS 2011, p. 10; IMB 2012 p. 5). However, in 2011 the total number of pirate attacks off the coast of Somalia again increased compared to 2010 (IMB 2011, p. 5).[1] The *International Maritime Bureau* (IMB) report for the first half of 2011 shows that the number of pirate attacks off the coast of Somalia was the highest. The situation became even more complicated as pirates expanded their range of operations to the Somali and Madagascar basin and to the Arabian Seas, as well as to the western and southern part of the Indian Ocean (Kupferschmidt 2010, pp. 76–78; Arteaga 2011, p. 2; Ehrhardt and Pretto 2012, pp. 33–34). Despite Atalanta's regular expansion of its operational area, the available military capabilities are not sufficient, since the contributing States have not increased their resources accordingly. Due to the European economic crisis, the deployment of troops has become evermore difficult and an increase of the capabilities is not likely.

The piracy activities in the Indian Ocean Region and the expansion of the area of attacks has affected the Spanish fishing fleet. The assaults on fishing vessels went on after the launch of Atalanta in 2008. In early 2009, and after the hijacking of the *Alakrana*, ship owners called on the Spanish Government for more protection. They insisted on a bigger deployment within Atalanta (EFE 2008; ABC online 2009; Europa Press 2010). When the Government refused to oblige, the business organisations requested the deployment of Spanish marines onboard commercial vessels (La Voz de Galicia 2009). The Government also rejected this demand, leading to discussions of new security measures.

3.2. Spanish maritime security policy and private security companies (PSCs)

Actors involved

Concerning official entities, four ministries are involved in authorisation processes, the training of employees and granting subsidies to designated ship owners. A key actor is the Ministry of Interior (MoI) and the two public security forces, the *National Police* and the *Guardia Civil*, as every PSC requires their authorisation. The National Police department (*Dirección General de la Policía*) issues the licence. Within the Police, the special unit dealing with private security companies (*Unidad Central de Seguridad Privada*; UCSP) processes requests and monitors the PSC's activities. The Guardia Civil carries out specific controls on armaments and reports to the UCSP (Dirección General de la Policía 2012). The second ministry involved is the Defense Ministry (MDE), assuming various duties. Firstly, the armed forces' facility *Instituto Tecnológico 'La Marañosa'* is placed at the disposal of the PSC personnel in order to train the handling of weapons and ammunition which had been approved by the Police. Secondly, the MDE organises requested transports of the PSC's armament. Only if the armament has to be shipped apart does the PSC bear the costs; in all other cases the MDE assumes the expenses (*Orden DEF/467/2011, de 2 de marzo: Séptima*). Additionally, the MDE is responsible for a favourable political environment. In September 2011 an agreement with the Seychelles was formulated, in which the Spanish tuna fishing fleet is allowed to carry on board large calibre weapons (La Moncloa 2011). Even though the vessels mainly fish in international waters, they are based in Victoria and sail in the territorial waters of the Seychelles, where the carrying of weapons is not only subject to Spanish law, but also to the legal provisions of the Seychelles (König and Salomon 2011, pp. 11–17). Closely related to the transportation of armament is the required authorisation to export the weapons used by the PSC (Law on Foreign Trade of Defense Materials and Dual Use Goods, *Ley 53/2007, 28 de diciembre*). This license has to be obtained from the Ministry of Industry, Energy and Tourism, which is the third authority involved. Finally, the Ministry of Agriculture (MARM) grants subsidies to the selected ship owners of tuna fishing vessels.

Non-state actors can be divided into two groups. First, the fishing industry dominates the discourse about maritime security in the Indian Ocean. The two main business organisations related to the tuna fishing industry, *Anabac* and *Opagac*, called on the Spanish Government to provide marines to protect their vessels because they considered this to be the most effective and economical solution (La Voz de Galicia 2009). However, the Government rejected this idea, stating that the deployment of armed forces on civil vessels is legally not possible.[2] The latter interpretation is convenient, as the Government had always shown high interest in a private security solution, declaring that the deployment of PSCs was more effective (La Moncloa 2010). A special category constitutes ship owners whose tuna fishing vessels receive subsidies from the MARM. The 17 tuna fishing boats belonged to six Basque and Galician ship owners and received subsidies because they contracted PSCs.

Second, there are private security companies offering maritime services. Several Spanish PSCs are working in this field, e.g. EULEN and Segur Ibérica. Even though it is hard to get correct information, it is public knowledge that these Spanish companies have provided or are still providing maritime security to the fishing fleet (Ibáñez 2009). Additionally, newspaper articles and Segur Ibérica confirm that security services are provided to tuna fishing boats in the Indian Ocean (Teleprensa 2009; Cerrada 2010).

National legal issues and decision-making processes

For the last 15 years, private security companies have flourished, triggered by the military interventions in Afghanistan and Iraq. The industry has fallen into disrepute because of the unlawful behaviour of several companies and mainly non-state actors called for more regulations. There has been some progress since international initiatives were launched and several countries have adopted new laws.[3] However, regulation issues remain a challenge (Bürgin 2011, pp. 59–66) and critics still advocate not cooperating with PSCs.

The Spanish Constitution states in Article 104.1 that it is the responsibility of the official Government security forces to guarantee security. Nevertheless, the provision of security services on civilian vessels by private security companies is legal. In 1992, Spain approved an act that regulates private security services provided by private natural or legal persons (*Ley 23/1992, de 30 de julio, de Seguridad Privada*) and states that private security services are complementary to public security and that PSCs are subordinated to public security forces. Moreover, the act determines the authorisation process and clarifies sanctions in case of infringements. Both the company and the employee need an authorisation issued by the Ministry of Interior and the PSC is recorded in a register. Breaches result in the withdrawal of the licence and, in severe cases, the payment of a fine. Furthermore, the provisions regulate the use of weapons and define the geographical scope of their activities (*Real Decreto 137/1993, de 29 de enero & Reglamento de Armas* and *Real Decreto 2364/1994, de 9 de diciembre*). Services provided abroad are not prohibited explicitly, but the decree delimits PSCs' activities on the *territory* of Spain, resulting in registered PSC operation in Spain only (Abrisketa 2009, p. 495; Iglesias 2010, p. 123).

In 2009, the Government modified the provisions. Then, vessels flying the Spanish flag which are not sailing in territorial waters and who find themselves in difficult circumstances, may contract private security using 'adequate armament' (*Real Decreto 1628/2009, de 30 de octubre*). The corresponding ministerial order specifies that adequate armament means the use of weapons of war (*armas de guerra*) and declares that only PSCs which are registered in Spain are allowed to provide these services (*Orden PRE/2901/2009, de 30 de octubre*). Moreover, in 2010 the Cabinet approved a decree regulating the subsidisation of contracting private security personnel to *tuna fishing vessels* operating in the Indian Ocean (*Real Decreto 1257/2010, de 8 de octubre*). It listed 17 tuna fishing vessels which extensively benefited from the financial assistance. Furthermore, it stated the financial contribution and the period of the assistance: the total contribution for all vessels amounted to €1,921,375 from the period of November 2009 to January 2011. Moreover, the Government bore maximally 25% of the costs, limited the contribution to €114,000 for the main fishing vessel and restricted the assistance for up to 12 months. In addition, it mentioned ship owners' obligations, e.g. that they had to bear at least 50% of the costs. The decree was extended in 2011 and the beneficiaries remained the same (*Real Decreto 803/2011, de 10 de junio*). However, this meant that Spanish fishing vessels and ship owners not included in the original list were not subsidised, even if they decided to contract private security personnel. Finally, the ministerial order of March 2011 allows PSCs to train in Armed Forces facilities and enables the latter to transport the armament used by the company (*Orden DEF/467/2011, de 2 de marzo*). Thus, contracting private security companies for international maritime navigation is legal but conditioned: a Spanish private security company must provide armed services on board a vessel flying the Spanish flag that sails in high risk waters. Furthermore, subsidies were only granted to the Spanish tuna fleet that operated in the Indian Ocean. The financial contributions have not been renewed in 2012 due to the economic crisis. However, the Basque Country still upholds financial contributions to the tuna fishing ship owners of €1.4 million for 2012 (EFE 2012).

The act of 1992 as well as the 2007 and 2009 amendments constitutes the legal framework that had to be adopted by the Parliament. In contrast, the norms regarding private security services provided specifically on board commercial vessels, adopted from 2009 on, are executive decrees or ministerial orders that do not require parliamentary approval. Even though the basic provisions were approved by the Parliament in 1992, all decisions taken with respect to the maritime situation – from allowing heavy guns to approving the support given by the armed forces to maritime PSC – have been taken without Parliament authorisation.

Main driving force

The key Government argument for supporting the collaboration between ship owners and maritime PSCs is the significance of the fishing sector – tuna fishing in particular – for the Spanish economy and Spanish fishing fleets' operations in waters with higher risks of maritime predation, justifying 'exceptional means' (*Real Decreto 1257/2010, de 8 de octubre*): the agriculture and fishing sector comprises 3% of the total Spanish GDP, 41,000 persons are employed in the fishery sector (MARM 2011) and every job at sea creates a further five to seven on land (Ramos 2012). It is clear that the fishing industry is a major economic factor for Spain: the country is the largest producer of fishery products in the EU, representing almost 25% of the whole EU production, and is number one regarding the total tonnage of the fishing fleet (Eurostat 2011a, 2011b).

Effectiveness

The predominantly positive attitude towards PSC protection of fishing vessels is due to the fact that no Spanish tuna fishing vessel operating in the Indian Ocean has been hijacked since armed private security personnel have been deployed on board.[4] Due to the limited information on PSC countermeasures, it is not possible to have a complete picture of their activities. According to articles and videos, the armed personnel takes preventive measures, e.g. using megaphones advising the attackers or firing off warning shots. However, it seems that PSC staff have also fired on pirates in the case of attack. Nevertheless, since the strategy is successful, it received great support and no opposition could be identified. When the new decrees were adopted in autumn 2009, some commentators critically assessed the existence of PSCs in general and in particular regarding maritime activities.[5] Ever since, the existence of PSC personnel onboard commercial vessels has mostly been reported, but rarely been criticised. The language use in the communications is informative: the use of PSC was considered to be right, as they 'defend' and 'protect' tuna fishing vessels. There is no sign that the PSC deployment is regarded as disproportionate or illegitimate nor is PSCs' supply of maritime services considered to be that of mercenaries. Rather, they are perceived as necessary because piracy attacks did not decline for years – 2012 being an exception.

4. Reasons for the change to apply a maritime security governance model

Several factors explain why Spain changed its approach in the fight against piracy and opted for a security governance model. Firstly, the hijacking of the *Alakrana* created significant public awareness and the crisis management provoked a public and political debate. As the pirate demands not only involved money, but also the release of Somalis previously captured by the Spanish naval vessel, the Government was involved from the beginning of the hijacking. The Government was heavily pressured and accused of poor crisis management, because of acting haphazardly and unprofessionally.[6] Even though the decree and the ministerial order were issued before the release of the *Alakrana*, the public reaction significantly influenced the Government decision to 'do something' to improve the protection of maritime trade, the fishing industry and their employees. The main business organisations of the tuna fishing industry called for more robust involvement in Atalanta. The Spanish armed forces, however, could not effectively protect the fishing fleet sailing under the Spanish flag in the Indian Ocean for the following reasons. As aforementioned, the affected space is too vast to be controlled extensively. The navies participating in

Atalanta are bound to the 'Northern Indian Ocean': in accordance with their mandate, the armed forces contribute to guarantee the functioning of the IRTC in order to escort vessels through the Gulf of Aden. Consequently, the Spanish navy is not present in the Mozambique Channel and around the Seychelles, where the Spanish tuna fishing fleet is operating. Finally, the Spanish armed forces do not have the capacity to deploy a naval force capable of fulfilling its obligations with Atalanta and the protection of the fishing fleet. Thus, a major role for the Armed Forces was not an option and the Government came under heavy pressure to find alternatives.

Secondly, the legal situation facilitated the decision to allow private security personnel to be deployed on commercial vessels. Spain applies the 'flag state principle' and therefore considers the vessel flying the Spanish flag to be Spanish territory. Hence, Spain applies the provisions laid down in the Law of 1992, which is why the authorisation process of a maritime PSC is handled as if it was an application by a PSC providing its services domestically and onshore. Thus, the decision to allow private security on board civilian vessels was uncomplicated; no laws had to be changed and everything could be handled by issuing decrees and ministerial orders. The only effort that had to be done was to conclude agreements with (coastal or harbour) states in this region to avoid difficulties for Spanish vessels with armed private security guards entering their territorial waters (König and Salomon 2011, pp. 11–18). The ease to allow PSC employment also holds true for the subventions granted to the 17 tuna fishing vessels. The subsidies were justified with 'public and social interests' that were at stake (*Real Decreto 1257/2010, de 8 de octubre: Artículo 4. 1*), corresponding with a law (*Ley 38/2003, de 17 de noviembre*) that regulates public subsidies and allows financial contributions in case of public, social, economic or humanitarian interest.

4.1. Some deliberations on the security governance models

The applied strategies in the Indian Ocean Region confirm the basic assumption of the security governance concept, i.e. that the involved actors cooperate in order to solve a problem effectively. In order to fight piracy, Spain opted for participating in Atalanta. However, one year after the launch of Atalanta, the numbers of attacks had increased and the hijacking of the trawler *Alakrana* and the subsequent public pressure impelled the Spanish Government to take more action. Since deploying more troops was not an option, the Government looked for alternative strategies. In order to protect vulnerable vessels, it not only encouraged closer 'private-private' cooperation, but actively supported this collaboration by issuing additional decrees and ministerial orders and facilitated financial contributions to the costs of contracting maritime PSCs. As no Spanish fishing vessel has been hijacked since the deployment of PSC personnel on these trawlers, affected ship owners, maritime security companies and the Government seemed to be satisfied with this twofold strategy: while the armed forces participate in a large-scale operation fighting piracy, private security companies defend vulnerable vessels in specific situations.

According to the Swiss foundation DCAF, the term 'democratic control of armed forces' is generally understood as 'the armed forces are subordinated to democratically-elected authorities and subject to the oversight of the judiciary as well as the media and civil society organisations' (DCAF 2008, p. 1). The majority of analyses focus on 'state' armies; however, DCAF stresses that the term 'armed forces' comprises all armed groups, also so-called 'non-statutory' ones. The outcome of the above analysis reveals an ambiguous role for the Spanish Parliament regarding this maritime case. With respect to Atalanta, the Parliament has comprehensive control rights as it approves all missions abroad. Thus, the democratic control of the *statutory* armed forces is high (Venice Commission 2008). Concerning the PSC policy, the Parliament was involved in the approval of the Law of 1992 on Private Security, yet the modifications of the legal acts since 2009 were adopted without parliamentary participation, but were issued as decrees or executive orders. One could argue that firstly, the adaptations were done by a Government with a majority in Parliament, which was the reason that the policy was not be dropped by the representatives; secondly, the adaptations were minor; and thirdly, neither the licensing nor the control procedures were changed. Nevertheless, one major order is especially important: the use of weapons of war on civilian vessels. Thus, the 'democratic control of the armed forces' in an international context is ambiguous: while the official army is controlled by the Parliament, it was the Government, acting alone, that initiated and approved the regulations on PSCs. Discussions about private security providers often turn on regulatory and legal issues. The Law of 1992 regulates PSCs comprehensively and includes an authorisation and monitoring process for companies as well as employees. However, it is questionable if the legal basis is adequate. The law is designed for *domestical* and *onshore* private security services. However, the circumstances for a PSC on a vessel sailing in the Indian Ocean and probably facing a piracy attack are considerably different from protecting a shopping mall: employees are deployed in a conflict situation, should meet higher requirements and should have received special training. Therefore, a new law is needed, approved by the Parliament, which takes into consideration the specific circumstances in which maritime private security companies are working. The elaboration of a new law would trigger a more profound discussion among parliamentarians and the public about the deployment of private security personnel abroad.

5. Conclusion

Since the hijacking of Spanish tuna fishing trawlers in 2008 and 2009, Spain pursues maritime security governance which encompasses two strategies: firstly, Spain plays a key role in the EU mission Atalanta; secondly, legal modifications made the deployment of armed private security personnel on civil vessels possible. The change to a security governance model was mainly due to the fact that the traditional approach alone did not solve a security problem effectively and national interests could not be protected sufficiently. The number of piracy attacks declined in Atalanta's activity area; however, in other parts of the Indian Ocean Region, vessels – from the Spanish perspective, mainly fishing vessels – are still victims of piracy. Apart from protecting maritime trade, the fishing industry is an important sector of the Spanish economy and is considered to be of national interest. The hijacking of the trawler *Alakrana* and the difficult process of freeing it demonstrated the inability of the Government to protect Spanish interests and Spanish citizens. Because extending contributions to Atalanta was not an option and the government rejected the deployment of marines on board civilian vessels, Spain promoted the private-private solution, i.e. the hiring of maritime private security companies.

MARITIME TERRORISM AND PIRACY IN THE INDIAN OCEAN REGION

This case study has shown that the responsibility for a Government to defend national interests effectively can lead to the adoption of new policy strategies and to establish new cooperation with diverse actors.

Acknowledgements

I wish to acknowledge the support of Prof. José Manuel Sobrino in the undertaking of this research project. My special thanks go to Dr Patricia Schneider, Dr Awet Weldemichael and the three anonymous reviewers for their constructive criticism and helpful comments.

Notes

1. The International Maritime Bureau IMB subsumes the following areas by the term 'Somalia': waters off Somalia, Oman, Yemen, Arabian Sea, Indian Ocean, Kenya, Tanzania, Mozambique, Madagascar, Seychelles, west India and west Maldives (IMB 2011, p. 6).
2. See for example *Cadena Ser* (16 September 2009), 'Chacón responde a los atuneros que no es posible embarcar militares en los pesqueros'. Available at http://www.cadenaser.com/espana/articulo/chacon-responde-atuneros-posible-embarcar-militares-pesqueros/csrcsrpor/20090916csrcsrnac_8/Tes
3. See for example the *International Code of conduct for Private Security Service Providers* (ICoC) or the so-called '*The Montreux Document*'.
4. See for example *RTVE* (18 October 2011), 'El atunero "Alakrana" consigue repeler un ataque de piratas en el Índico'; *La Opinion Coruña* (4 September 2011), 'La flota atunera refuerza la seguridad ante el previsible repunte de la piratería'; *Europa Press* (17 May 2011), 'Personal del buque Alakrantxu dispara al aire para repeler un ataque'; *RTVE* (9 November 2010), 'La seguridad privada del atunero Erroxape evita un ataque pirata en el Índico'; *RTVE* (2 October 2010), 'Se cumple un año desde la liberación del Alakrana'; *El País* (6 March 2010), 'Alerta máxima por la oleada de ataques en el Índico'; *RTVE* (5 March 2010), 'Detienen a 22 piratas después del ataque a tres barcos españoles en el océano Índico'; *Información Alicante* (18 January 2010), 'Los vigilantes de los atuneros tienen orden de disparar a matar a 600 metros'; *Diario Información* (10 January 2010), 'Vigilantes de los atuneros denuncian despidos y deficiencias de seguridad', available at http://www.diarioinformacion.com/alicante/2010/01/10/vigilantesatuneros-denuncian-despidos-deficiencias-seguridad/968129.html.
5. See for example *Diagonal* (8 January 2009, No. 93), 'Los nuevos mercenarios "made in Spain"'; *El Mundo* (18 October 2009), 'Ex soldado se ofrece por 10.000 euros'; *La Voz de Galicia* (4 November 2009), 'La única empresa de mercenarios en España se ofrece para proteger barcos'; *Tiempo* (29 January 2010), 'Blackwater a la española', available at http://www.tiempodehoy.com/espana/blackwater-a-la-espanola; Laborie Iglesias (2010).
6. See Zamora Media and Losada Díaz (2010); *El Confidencial* (19 November 2009), 'El "Alakrana"' desquicia al Gobierno y deja muy tocadas a De la Vega y Chacón'; *ABC* (22 November 2009), 'La crisis del "Alakrana" hunde al Gobierno a mes y medio de la Presidencia de la UE'; *El País* (4 February 2011), 'Un marinero del "Alakrana": "El Gobierno hizo una puñetera chapuza"', available at http://elpais.com/elpais/2011/02/04/actualidad/1296811036_850215.html.

References

ABC online (2009), 'Los armadores piden extender la misión "Atalanta" de la UE, que cumple un año', *ABC*, 9 November.

Abrisketa, J. (2009), 'Regular y controlar la actividad de las Compañías Militares y de Seguridad Privadas: ¿es necesario?', in F.A. Cuervo-Arango and J. Peñaranda Algar, eds., *Dos Décadas de Posguerra Fría, Actas de las I Jornadas de Estudios de Seguridad de la*

Comunidad de Estudios de Seguridad 'General Gutiérrez Mellado', Tomo III. Madrid: Instituto Universitario General Gutiérrez Mellado IUGM, pp. 473–501.

Aixalà i Blanch, A. (2005), 'La política exterior española ante los retos de su politización: del consenso a la legitimidad', *Revista CIBOD d'Afers Internacionals*, no. 69, pp. 89–105. Available at http://dialnet.unirioja.es/servlet/articulo?codigo=1212787

Armada Española (2012), *Piratería*. Madrid: Ministerio de Defensa.

Arteaga, F. (2011), 'La lucha contra la piratería en Somalia: el problema persiste a pesar del esfuerzo militar', Análisis del Real Instituto Elcano 52/2011, 14 March. Madrid: Real Instituto Elcano.

Bacas Fernández, J.R., Bordas Martínez, F., Gil Pérez, J., Regueiro Dubra, R., Sepúlveda Muñoz, I., and Vega Fernández, E. (2009), 'La participación europea en la lucha internacional contra la piratería en el cuerno de África: la operación Atalanta', in J.R. Bacas Fernández, eds., *Crisis somalí, piratería e intervención internacional*. Madrid: Instituto Universitario General Gutiérrez Mellado IUGM, pp. 153–178.

Barbé, E. (2011), 'Interacción entre política exterior española y política exterior europea: normas europeas, intereses españoles y condicionantes internacionales', in J.M. Beneyto and J.C. Pereira, eds., *Política exterior española: Un balance de futuro*, Vol. 1. Madrid: Biblioteca Nueva, pp. 93–120.

Beneyto, J.M. (2011), 'La política exterior española en el nuevo escenario mundial', in J.M. Beneyto and J.C. Pereira, eds., *Política exterior española: Un balance de futuro*, Vol. 1. Madrid: Biblioteca Nueva, pp. 19–59.

Bürgin, A.C. (2011), *Privatisierung von Sicherheit und Frieden?* Bern: Peter Lang.

Calafell Ferrá, V.J. (2009), 'Cortes Generales y misiones militares en el exterior: la autorización del Parlamento para envíar tropas españolas al extranjero', in I. Sepúlveda, ed., *España en las operaciones internacionales de pacificación, III Congreso Internacional de historia de la Defensa*. Madrid: Instituto Universitario General Gutiérrez Mellado IUGM, pp. 379–92.

Cerrada, P. (2010), 'Vigilantes de los atuneros denuncian despidos y deficiencias de seguridad', *Información*, 10 January.

Congreso (2009), *Diario de Sesiones del Congreso de los Diputados, Año 2009, IX Legislatura, no. 58, Miércoles 21 January 2009*. Madrid: Congreso de los Diputados.

CRS Congressional Research Service (2011), 'Piracy off the Horn of Africa', Congressional Research Service Report for Congress R40528, Washington, DC.

Dirección General de la Policía (2012), 'Organización Central. Comisaría General de Seguridad Ciudadana'. Available at http://www.policia.es/org_central/seguridad_ciudadana/seguridad_privada/seguridad_privada.html, accessed 6 March 2012.

DCAF (2008), *Democratic Control of Armed Forces, DCAF Backgrounder. 05/2008*. Geneva.

EFE (2008), 'Los armadores piden el envío de una fuerza naval para luchar contra la piratería en Somalia', *EFE online*, 3 November.

EFE (2012), 'Euskadi mantiene la ayuda a los atuneros vascos con 1,4 millones para 2012', *EFE online*, 17 July.

Ehrhardt, H. and Petretto, K. (2012), 'The EU and Somalia: counter-piracy and the question of a comprehensive approach', *Study for the The Greens/European Free Alliance*. Hamburg: European Free Alliance.

Ehrhardt, H., Petretto, K. and Schneider, P. (2010), 'Security Governance als Rahmenkonzept für die Analyse von Piraterie und maritimem Terrorismus – Konzeptionelle und Empirische Grundlagen', *PiraT-Arbeitspapiere zur Maritimen Sicherheit*. Hamburg: PiraT.

Ejército del aire (2012), *Atalanta (Yibuti)*. Available at http://www.ejercitodelaire.mde.es, accessed 6 March 2012.

EU NAVOR Somalia (2009), *Alakrana*. Available at http://www.eunavfor.eu/tag/alakrana/, accessed 6 March 2012.

Europa Press (2010), 'Los armadores agradecen a Chacón sus compromisos contra la piratería pero piden mayor esfuerzo internacional', 25 November.

Eurostat (2011a), *Fischereiflotte, Gesamttonnage*. Brüssel: Europäische Kommission.

Eurostat (2011b), *Gesamte Fischereierzeugung – Fanggebiete, insgesamt*. Brüssell: Europäische Kommission.

MARITIME TERRORISM AND PIRACY IN THE INDIAN OCEAN REGION

Fontán Aldereguía, L. (2010), 'Lucha contra la agresión en el ámbito marítimo. Una aproximación europea', in M. Requena and D. de Revenga, eds., *Luces y Sombras de la Seguridad Internacional en los Albores del Siglo XXI*. Madrid: Instituto Universitario General Gutiérrez Mellado IUGM, pp. 279–288.

Gobierno de España (2011), *Estrategia Española de Seguridad. Una responsabilidad de todos.* Madrid: Gobierno de España.

Herranz Surrallés, A. (2008), 'El Congreso de los Diputados y las políticas europeas de seguridad: ¿cuánto (des)control parlamentario?' in E. Barbé, ed., *España en Europa 2004–2008*. Barcelona: Institut Universitari d'Estudis Europeus. Available at http://www.iuee.eu/pdf-publicacio/127/Yvmfs0PJWOoyLiSLgwmg.PDF

Ibáñez, J. (2009), *Personal de seguridad privada para la protección de buques españoles en aguas internacionales y zonas declaradas de alto riesgo por el Consejo de Seguridad de la ONU como complementario y subordinado a la seguridad pública y a las fuerzas armadas*. Available at http://www.belt.es/expertos/HOME2_experto.asp?id=4588, accessed 6 March 2012.

IMB (2011), *Piracy and Armed Robbery Against Ships. Report for the Period of 1 January – 30 June 2011*. London: ICC international Maritime Bureau.

IMB (2012), *Piracy and Armed Robbery Against Ships. Report for the Period of 1 January – 31 December 2011*. London: ICC international Maritime Bureau.

Jiménez Redondo, J.C. (2006), *De Suárez a Rodríguez Zapatero: La política exterior de la España democrática*. Madrid: Diles.

Kirchner, E.J. (2006), 'The challenge of European Union security governance', *Journal of Common Market Studies*, Vol. 44, no. 5, pp. 947–968.

König, D. and Salomon, T.R. (2011), 'Private Sicherheitsdienste auf Handelsschiffen – Rechtliche Implikationen', *PiraT-Arbeitspapiere zur Maritimen Sicherheit*. Hamburg: Institut für Friedensforschung und Sicherheitspolitik an der Universität Hamburg.

Krahmann, E. (2003), 'Conceptualizing security governance', *Cooperation and Conflict*, Vol. 38, no. 5, pp. 5–26.

Kupferschmidt, F. (2010), 'Multinationales militärisches Engagement', in S. Mair, ed., *Piraterie und maritime Sicherheit*. Berlin: Stiftung Wissenschaft und Politik, pp. 70–78.

Laborie Iglesias, M.A. (2010), 'La controvertida contribución de las empresas militares y de seguridad privadas (EMSP) a la resolución de conflictos', in Ministerio de Defensa, eds., *Los actores no estatales y la seguridad internacional: Su papel en la resolución de conflictos y crisis*. Madrid: Instituto Español de Estudios Estratégicos, pp. 77–138.

La Moncloa (2008), 'España y Francia firman un acuerdo histórico que duplica la interconexión eléctrica entre ambos países'. Available at http://www.lamoncloa.gob.es/ActualidadHome/2008/270608AltoNivel.htm?galv2r=0, accessed 6 March 2012.

La Moncloa (2010), 'Subvenciones excepcionales para seguridad privada en buques atuneros que operan en el Índico'. Available at http://www.lamoncloa.gob.es/ConsejodeMinistros/Enlaces/081010-buques.htm, accessed 6 March 2012.

La Moncloa (2011), 'Government of Seychelles to authorise use of larger calibre weaponry to increase security for Spanish tuna fishermen in the Indian Ocean'. Available at http://www.lamoncloa.gob.es/IDIOMAS/9/Gobierno/News/09092011Seychelles.htm, accessed 6 March 2012.

La Voz de Galicia (2009), 'Los piratas intentaron ayer asaltar otro barco con gallegos a bordo, el tercero en menos de una semana', *La Voz de Galicia*, 10 September.

MARM (2011), *Estadísticas Pesqueras, Octubre 2011*. Madrid: Ministerio de Medio Ambiente, y Medio Rural y Marino.

Marrero Rocha, I.C. (2007), *La participación de las fuerzas armadas españolas en misiones de paz*. Madrid: Plaza y Valdés.

Mayntz, R. (2004), 'Governance im modernen Staat', in A. Benz, eds., *Governance – Regieren in komplexen Regelsystemen*. Wiesbaden: VS Verlag für Sozialwissenschaften, pp. 65–77.

MDE Ministerio de Defensa (2012), 'Vigilantes del Índico'. Available at http://www.defensa.gob.es/Galerias/areasTematicas/misiones/fichero/indico12.pdf, accessed 26 July 2012.

Nieves, G. (2010), 'Seguridad Marítima: lucha contra amenazas reales en un espacio sin fronteras físicas', *Atenea*, 01 February.

Puertas Cristóbal, E. and Fernández Alles, J.J. (2010), 'Fundamentos jurídicos y sociales de las operaciones de paz en España', *Entelequia Revista Interdisciplinar*, no. 12, pp. 41–55.

Ramos, F. (2012), 'PSOE y PP han intentado siempre marginar la voz del andalucismo', *Huelva Información*, 16 March.

Rosenau, J. (1992), 'Governance, order, and change in world politics', in J. Rosenau and E. Czempiel, eds., *Governance Without Government: Order and Change in World Politics*. Cambridge: Cambridge Studies in International Relations, pp. 1–29.

Ruesta Botella, J.A. (2009), 'Seguridad marítima: tendencias y retos', in Instituto Español de Estudios Estratégicos, eds., *Impacto de los riesgos emergentes en la seguridad marítima.*, pp. 79–116.

Sobrino Heredia, J.M. (2008), *Piratería y terrorismo en el mar*. Bilbao: Argitalpen Zerbitzeua Servicio Editorial, pp. 82–147.

Teleprensa (2009), 'Defensa traslada a Seychelles a los agentes de seguridad privada que embarcarán en los pesqueros españoles', *Teleprensa*, 13 November.

Torreblanca, J.I. (2005), 'Ideas, preferences and institutions: explaining the europeanization of Spanish foreign policy', *ARENA Working Paper*, WP 01/26.

Venice Commission (2008), 'Report on the democratic control of the armed forces', 74th Plenary Session. Venice: Council of Europe, March.

Zamora Media, R. and Losada Díaz, J.C. (2010), 'The strategic communication of hijackings: Some lessons from how the Spanish government managed the crisis of the Alakrana', IPSA Paper, IPSA-Research Committee for Political Communication RC22, 4–5 November 2010, Leicestershire, UK.

German maritime security governance: a perspective on the Indian Ocean Region

Patricia Schneider

Institute for Peace Research and Security Policy at the University of Hamburg (IFSH), Germany

Besides the high number of attacks by Somali pirates, terrorists have threatened to disrupt Western maritime trade and oil and gas supplies in the Indian Ocean Region. This case study of German maritime security governance aims to examine these threats faced by Germany, and German countermeasures and preparedness. The German economy relies heavily on its international sea trade and Germany is home to the world's biggest container shipping companies. On one hand, authorities and stakeholders have been eager to improve risk assessment and implement international agreements. On the other hand, the different interests of ship-owners, seafarers and insurers, as well as a lack of agreement between the different ministries, are major challenges for German maritime security governance. Germany chooses to act within the international context concerning maritime security, but generally not in a leading role. However, maintaining a secure Indian Ocean region is paramount to ensuring its own economic security.

1. Introduction

Piracy and maritime terrorism can broadly be classified as maritime violence, although each describes different concepts. The main differences between terrorism and piracy concern their motives: politically-driven terrorism and by and large profit-oriented piracy. The 'maritime' in 'maritime terrorism' indicates its definition according to where the act takes place, just as a differentiation is made between air and sea piracy.[1] Yet, both use similar approaches and tactics. The hijacking of a ship with the intention of financing terrorist operations can, for example, be described as an act of political piracy (Eklöf Amirell 2006). Likewise, Somalia's Islamists' interest in the ransom generated by their pirate counterparts has come under close scrutiny, as it heightens the prospect of dangerous nexus between terrorism and piracy. (In some cases an exchange of hostages has been reported as well). In February 2011, for example, Al Shabaab captured several pirates because they refused to give them a fifth of the revenue. Al Shabab is allegedly collecting large sums of money from the pirates, in the range of 30% of the ransom in 2010 alone (Kolb, Salomon and Udich 2011, pp. 113–115).

German security governance initiatives have so far put in place a large number of coordinating structures and mechanisms in order to limit the risks of maritime terrorism and piracy.[2] This paper examines those German initiatives, the actors and policies, with respect to the Indian Ocean Region, as a case study to analyse the challenges of national and international regimes concerning maritime security governance.

At its core, this paper strives to answer the following research question: why is Germany not taking the initiative and acting as a leading figure in maritime (trade) security related to the Indian Ocean Region (IOR)? Answering this main question requires addressing a few others: is the often-asserted importance of maritime trade in the IOR for Germany and Europe overstated? How relevant is maritime security in the IOR for Germany and how is this reflected in domestic German politics? Which key actors are involved and how do they relate to one another? How do they act on the international level? Is this mélange of actors and interests the major challenge towards adequate security governance or are other factors relevant?

It became evident during the course of this study that information pertaining to the roles, tasks and competences of relevant German actors was not easily accessible. There are only a few open sources that describe the roles and tasks of German actors in sufficient depth. Moreover, the situation is currently in flux. It was thus necessary to complement the secondary literature and limited primary documents with anonymised interviews with stakeholders (by phone, mail or in person, conducted in spring 2012).

After discussing the significance of maritime trade for German and EU economies, this article will address the relevance of maritime security for Germany, offer an overview of the involved German actors in maritime security, and assess the involvement of key German stakeholders in international maritime security governance. The article will also consider other possible factors for Germany's deliberate restraint before concluding with a summary and conclusions.

2. Relevance of maritime trade for the German and European economy

The relevance of maritime trade for Germany's export-oriented economy and global trade is often described as tremendous. But how important is German and European maritime trade, especially with the IOR?

A glance at the statistics seem to confirm the often-asserted significance of sea trade for Germany: about 90% of world commerce, 95% of Europe's foreign trade and almost 70% of German exports and imports are carried out through international sea trade. There are 419 German shipping companies and ship-owners, making Germany the third in the world in transporting bulky goods, with 3716 merchant ships altogether. German-controlled container ships are the largest and encompass 1776 container ships, with 32.1% of world-wide container capacity. However, only 297 of these ships fly the German flag (German Fleet Command 2011a, p. 53; German Fleet Command 2011b, p. 2). The three countries that have the largest merchant fleets are developed countries, namely Greece, Japan and Germany. Cumulatively, they account for 41% of the world's deadweight tonnage (UNCTAD 2011, p. 148).

German maritime cross-border traffic quantitatively increased in past years. The import of (energy) raw material plays a vital role, and the IOR is an important source and/or conduit of these raw materials. On the export side, security of trade routes is of central importance for the export-oriented industries (automobile, machine-production, chemical and pharmaceutical industry; Engerer 2011, p. 27; DIW 2012). The UNCTAD Line Shipping Connectivity Index (LSCI) reveals that Germany, along with Hong Kong SAR and Singapore, is the second most connected country in the world next to China (UNCTAD 2011, p. XVI).

With a total area of approximately 70 million square kilometres, the Indian Ocean is the third largest, after the Pacific and Atlantic. Historically, its geographic position at the southern periphery of Eurasia has determined its central economic importance: it lies at the intersection of resource-rich coastal regions and interna-tional sea routes between the Red Sea, the Arabian Gulf and the western Pacific. The Indian Ocean contains large amounts of natural resources, including nearly 40% of global oil and gas reserves, as well as large amounts of mineral resources. The Indian Ocean has overtaken the Atlantic and Pacific in terms of international trade, with a large proportion of oil exports from the Middle East transitioning it, while economic globalisation has led to an increased use of seaways and promoted the development of export-oriented coastal regions (Arz 2012).

While two recently-published studies estimate the direct and indirect global costs of piracy at about US\$7 billion for the year 2010 (Oceans Beyond Piracy 2010; One Earth Future Foundation 2012), and while another study examines the human cost of Somali piracy (ICC/OBP 2012), there are no such comprehensive studies on the costs of maritime terrorism. One could assume that some of the included costs, such as additional security measures on board and the use of military forces, could also help in the case of political violence.

Among many things, however, maritime terrorism can cause time-delays and thus disrupt maritime trade. Germany and other EU members agreed about EU's dispatching of a military mission (Operation Atalanta) for this precise reason. Trade interests constituted part of the member states' motivations to approve the mission. As matters of trade are a supra-nationalised competence of the EU, member states are more comfortable in agreeing to an EU military mission that protects highly relevant maritime routes for their own trade.

Any attempt to determine the economic impact of maritime violence on Germany should be approached cautiously, as not all sectors in the economy are affected to the same extent – apart from the maritime industry – because some sectors depend more on imports or exports than others. Moreover, the option of a substitute route or port usually exists. It is also important to assess whether trade routes pass through high-risk areas of piracy and political violence. For European countries, intra-European trade is of higher importance than that with third countries. The most important trade partners for the EU are the states of North America, while the Mediterranean neighbours are second. Over the past few years China has become a vital trading partner for Germany, even more so than North America. Considering the value of transported goods, there is a difference: the share of imported goods from Asia has grown (from 8% in 2000 to 15% in 2008) and so has the use of security relevant seaways as a route of transport (DIW 2012, p. 11). At the same time, there are opportunities for substituting potential losses in the shipping and other industries through higher revenues in other sectors, e.g. the use of insurance companies or private security businesses.

The importance of sea trade for Germany and Europe is therefore not overstated. Nevertheless, not only does it not affect all sectors of the economy alike, but economic factors are only half of the picture. The following section discusses threat assessments at the political level.

3. Relevance of maritime security for Germany

Since 2008, Somali piracy has been a pressing problem for ship-owners, seafarers and insurers. But the threat of maritime terrorism world-wide remains controversial. While there is wide-ranging agreement on the catastrophic consequences of several scenarios, there is little consensus about the likelihood of such attacks, the associated risk level, or appropriate countermeasures. For example, Operation Enduring Freedom (OEF) was launched four weeks after the terrorist attacks of 11 September 2001. The operation later included a maritime component, responsible for the security of sea routes. Germany participated in conducting surveillance in the area around the Horn of Africa to prevent the trade and transport of drugs, weapons and ammunition. The last mandate expired on 15 December 2010. The German government announced in June 2010 that they would withdraw the military from international counter terrorism deployment. The minister of defence at the time, Karl-Theodor zu Guttenberg, justified the decision, declaring that it was 'due to the low terror threat in the area of sea around the Horn of Africa' (*Tagesspiegel* 2010). The German Navy participates in European Union Naval Force (EUNAVFOR) Atalanta, initiated in December 2008; its tasks are the protection of vessels of the World Food Programme (WFP), the protection of vulnerable vessels, the deterrence, prevention and repression of acts of piracy and armed robbery, and the monitoring of fishing activities (Reininghaus 2011). The German Navy also participates in the United Nations Interim Force in Lebanon-Operation (UNIFIL), to prevent the smuggling of weapons to Lebanon via seaways. Germany's involvement in the 'fight against terror' lies in the deployment of forces in the Mediterranean Sea led by NATO forces in 'Operation Active Endeavour' (OAE).

Regarding terrorism, the last noticeable terror attack in the IOR was a July 2010 bomb detonation on the Japanese oil tanker *M Star* in the Strait of Hormuz, causing only minor damage to the ship. The perpetrators were the 'Abdullah Azzam Brigades', an affiliate of al-Qaeda (Winter 2011, pp. 890–891). However, due to the attack, the German *Bundeskriminalamt* (BKA, Federal Criminal Police Office) stated in its report on Sea Security in 2010 that potential targets for maritime terrorism were the Suez Canal, the Red Sea and the Gulf of Aden, and mentioned the Arabian Peninsula in the 2011 report. Germany lies in the focus of terrorist groups due to its latest engagement in Afghanistan; German merchant shipping is thus subjected to the threat, as are cruise ships and port facilities. But since then there have been no indications of any concrete planned attempts in the maritime domain (BKA 2011, pp. 5–9). Table 1 gives an overview of terror attacks in the IOR in 2000–2010 and illustrates that this threat played a role in the recent past and continues to be a risk in the future.

According to International Maritime Bureau (IMB) data, while world-wide attacks by pirates have increased continually in the last few years (first decline in 2011 with a further drop occurring in 2012), pirates became less successful in hijacking ships, relative to previous years. Piracy has also increased economic

MARITIME TERRORISM AND PIRACY IN THE INDIAN OCEAN REGION

Table 1.   Attacks by perpetrators in the IOR in 2000–2010.

Perpetrator	Country	International target	Number of attacks
Abu Sayyaf Group (ASG)	Malaysia [(2), 2005, 2010]	50%	2
Al Qaeda	Yemen [(2), 2000, 2002], Jordan [(1), 2005], Somalia [(1), 2007], Oman [(2), 2010]	100%	6
Al-Shabaab al-Islamiya	Somalia [(7), 2007, 4 × 2009, 2 × 2010]	29%	7
CPI-Maoist	India [(1), 2010]	50%	1
Free Aceh Movement (GAM)	Indonesia [(6), 2000, 2001, 2002, 3 × 2005], Singapore & Malaysia [(1), 2003]	29%	7
Free Papua Movement	Indonesia [(1), 2009]	0%	1
Hezbollah	Israel [(1), 2003]	100%	1
Islamic Courts Union	Somalia [(1), 2008]	100%	1
Islamic Jihad	Israel [(1), 2002]	0%	1
Jama'at al-Tawhid	Iraq [(2), 2004]	100%	2
Liberation Tigers of Tamil Eelam (LTTE)	Sri Lanka [(17), 4 × 2000, 2 × 2001, 2 × 2003, 2005, 2 × 2006, 2 × 2007, 2 × 2008, 2 × 2009]	24%	17
Unknown	Bangladesh [(2), 2000], Indonesia [(2), 2002, 2004], Iraq [(1), 2005], Somalia [(5), 2006, 2 × 2009, 2 × 2010], Thailand [(2), 2006, 2007], Australia [(1), 2009], Pakistan [(1), 2010]	–	14
Total			60

Source: generated by the author using the pirate database, see Schneider (2011).

damage by raising ransom demands for fewer ships. Lastly, the use of force by pirates has had a tendency to increase (Joint Research Project PiraT 2011; ICC – IMB/OBP 2012).

German-owned ships are often affected by piracy. The Federal German Police states, according to IMB reports in 2011, that

> there were a total of 439 cases of piracy against ships. German companies and Singaporean companies, having respectively faced 64 (14.5%) and 65 incidents (14.8%), are worldwide the most affected by pirate raids. With a share of only 7% of world trade, German shipping companies are significantly overrepresented. (BPOL See 2012, p. 20, translation by author)[3]

However, data from the Piracy Prevention Centre shows a different result when comparing the numbers in relation to the number of passages: the Federal German Police (BPOL See) keeps records in the Piracy Prevention Centre of all pirate incidents in the high risk area, which in 2011 encompassed the Gulf of Aden, the Red Sea, the Arabian Sea and the Indian Ocean, as far as the Indian coast and Mozambique Channel. Sources in the Federal German Police reveal a slightly different result on how affected German ships are relative to the number of ships that pass through the area: 16% of the incidents involving pirate attacks had a German connection and German ships total about 15% of all ship passages in this high risk area (Interview, BPOL See, 2012),[4] indicating a consistency between the number of German ships affected by pirate attacks and their traffic volumes in that area. Contrary to the claim above, Germany would therefore not be disproportionally more affected. This argument is supported by the fact that there is hardly any evidence that ships with a German connection are systematically targeted.

A piracy attack is registered in an existing alarm system, and the structures of the Federal Crisis Response Task Force, working under the Foreign Ministry, are activated. This occurs whenever German interests are affected (dubbed above as a 'German connection'), for example when:

(1) a German-flagged ship is involved;
(2) German nationals are onboard; or
(3) the ship is owned by a German natural or legal person.

Table 2 shows the number of German ships hijacked by Somali pirates in the IOR. As only two of them actually flew a German flag, it might have made it more difficult for ship-owners to lobby for state-vessel protection teams, as they are only responsible for ships flying the national flag. The fact that four of the 16 hijackings were resolved in less than a week (25%) and the remaining 12 lasted between three to four weeks or more than seven months serves as an explanation as to why public pressure on state authorities was not as extensive as in other cases (e.g. in Spain). The German Ship-Owners Association (*Verband Deutscher Reeder*, VDR) also noticed that public awareness was much higher when oil or gas tankers were involved, as these cases immediately stimulated the debate on rising energy costs. This occurred in only two of the 16 cases (12.5%), none of which flew a German flag.

It is unknown how many ships employ Private Security Companies (PSCs) on board, since there is no obligation to report; hence information only exists when incidents are reported. According to the Piracy Prevention Centre, 42% of the ships attacked in high risk areas in 2011 had private security personnel. There is an even higher rate of attacks against German affiliated ships, as 53% of attacks were directed at them. In comparison to 2010, when only 8% of the attacked ships employed private security personnel, this displays a sharp increase. These numbers may be misleading, because private security personnel are believed to be deployed only on ships facing a high risk (e.g. slow ships with a low freeboard), according to the Best Management Practice (BMP4) Handbook (interview, BPOL See, 2012).

In the aforementioned cases of 2011, according to the Piracy Prevention Centre only one German-flagged ship had a PSC on board. This is due to the complicated treatment of German-flagged ships; coastal states want flag-state certification, indicating that the deployed PSC is certified. Such a certification from German authorities has until now not been issued. On German-flagged vessels, the use of PSCs is not prohibited, but neither is their use actively supported. (It is a similar case in Greece, but contrary to, for example, the Netherlands). The procedures of certification and regulation of PSCs are only now being developed, modelled on International Maritime Organization (IMO) recommendations (interview, BPOL See, 2012). The fact that it is not formally unlawful to hire PSCs on German-flagged

Table 2. Piracy incidents involving German vessels in the Indian Ocean Region.

	Name of vessel	Duration	Location	German connection	Ransom
1	Amiya Scan Dry Bulk Carrier	24 May – 25 June 2008 (33 days)	Gulf of Aden	German owner	Unknown
2	Lehmann Timber Cargo ship	28 May – 8 July 2008 (41 days)	On the way from the Indian Ocean to Suez Canal	German flag	US$0.75m
3	BBC Trinidad Freighter	21 August – 11 September 2008 (21 days)	Indian Ocean off the coast of Somalia	German owner	US$1.1m
4	Longchamp Gas tanker	29 January – 29 March 2009 (60 days)	Gulf of Aden	German owner	Unknown
5	Hansa Stavanger Container ship	4 April – 3 August 2009 (122 days)	400 miles off the coast of Somalia	German owner	US$2m
6	Patriot Freighter	25 April – 15 May 2009 (21 days)	Gulf of Aden	German owner	Unknown
7	Victoria Freighter	5 May – 18 July 2009 (75 days)	On the way to Jeddah/Saudi Arabia	German owner	Unknown
8	Charelle Freighter	12 June – 3 December 2009 (175 days)	60 miles from Sur (Oman)	German owner	Unknown
9	Taipan Container ship	5 April – 5 April 2010 (1 day)	500 miles east of Somalia	German flag	No ransom
10	Marida Marguerite Chemical tanker	8 May – 27 December 2010 (234 days)	Indian Ocean off the coast of Somalia	German owner	US$5.5m
11	Magellan Star Container ship	8 September – 9 September 2010 (2 days)	On the way from Bilbao to Singapore	German owner	No ransom
12	Beluga Fortune Liquefied gas tanker	24 October – 25 October 2010 (2 days)	1200 miles from the Kenyan port city Mombasa	German crew	No ransom
13	MCL Bremen Multipurpose cargo ship	27 November – 28 November 2010 (2 days)	1000 miles from the Horn of Africa	German owner and German crew	No ransom
14	Ems River Cargo ship	27 December 2010 – 1 March 2011 (65 days)	280 km north-east of the port city Salala in the Arabian Sea	German owner	Unknown
15	Beluga Nomination Multipurpose heavy lift project carrier	22 January – 13 April 2011 (82 days)	361 miles north of the Seychelles in the Indian Ocean	German owner	US$5m
16	Susan K Cargo ship	8 April – 16 June 2011 (70 days)	In the Arabian Sea 40 miles south of the coast of Oman	German owner	US$5.7

Source: own table based on: BKA (2008, 2009, 2010, 2011) and press reviews: stern.de (18 July 2009, 24 October 2010), FAZ (9 July 2008, 25 October 2010), spiegel.de (12 June 2009, 29 January 2011, 17 June 2011), and wikipedia.org (List of ships attacked by Somali pirates 2008, 2009, 2010, 2011).

vessels seems to be less a problem of international and domestic law than one of communication between the authorities and the practitioners.

The federal government stated that complete protection for all German ships by soldiers or policemen is logistically, financially and operatively impossible (BReg 2011, p. 9). It is also unconstitutional: the police can only be deployed for internal affairs and the military is not allowed to protect civilian vessels. Moreover, the change in thinking toward the certification of PSCs could be a consequence of ship-owners registering under different flags. The fact that it is not illegal to hire PSCs seems contradictory in this regard. It may well be that in order to avoid potential legal problems due to the uncertainty of a perceived grey-zone and in order to be able to hire PSCs without doubting the legality of their doing so, ship-owners still opt to register under foreign flags. This takes place even though they would prefer that either police or naval personnel be employed to protect their ships. In this respect it is important to consider that of the 3654 mercantile ships currently registered in Germany, only 495 fly the German flag (BSH 2012). The discrepancy is not only due to potentially difficult PSC regulations, but the perceived legal grey zone of PSCs in Germany is also relevant to ship-owners. (A further reason for changing flag is due to the comparatively high social insurance costs involved). Germany desires that ships fly the German flag for a number of reasons, among them the increased visibility of the flag state when sailing in international waters and commensurate influence in IMO deliberations. This would also give Germany greater control of ship safety and environmental standards. Although ship-owners dispute the last point by claiming that it is sufficiently ensured by international standards, flying the German flag makes their customers believe that they deliver a better quality of service (interview, VDR, 2012).

Private Security Companies are proud that no ship under their protection has ever been successfully hijacked, that crews will not travel in high risk areas without protection and that insurance companies will reduce premiums when PSCs are employed. A faster passage through high risk zones leads to higher fuel costs, which, according to PSCs, make their deployment more attractive. According to the IMO, however, the use of PSCs does not replace the need to implement its Best Management Practices. Vulnerable ships are, therefore, increasingly employing PSCs for self-protection. As of now, British and US firms dominate the market, but German firms are discovering a market focus for their services, especially for German customers. The certification procedures with interim provisions are expected in late 2012, and if they do as planned, Germany would become a role model and be at the forefront of setting international standards.

There is an ever-present fear of a 'black sheep' in the industry, because the responsibility for all actions taken onboard a ship rests on its master. According to König and Salomon (2011), captains fear criminal charges and responsibility if PSCs use excessive force and/or cause injury to innocent people (fishermen), as was most recently the case on the Italian *Enrica Lexie* by navy personnel: 'her armed security guard fired at a fishing boat believing that they were being approached by pirates' (*Navaltoday* 2012).

There had been some hesitation on how to regulate PSCs while it was unclear whether sovereign powers would protect vulnerable vessels by providing escort teams. The idea to use state forces was eventually dismissed due to capacity limitations. Targeted procedures imply official approval of (German and foreign) companies under specified standards. This approach is also supported by the security sector, as this may increase the confidence of potential customers in the capabilities and reliability of PSCs. PSCs are suspected to pursue their business interests instead of trying to make a sustainable contribution to solving the problem. It is thus of utmost importance to identify serious and competent service providers and to establish effective control mechanisms.

Piracy remains a volatile issue for maritime trade in the next years, at least concerning the hijacking of ships and hostage-taking of crews. However, terrorist activities in the maritime arena continue to be rare (for detailed empirical analysis, see Schneider 2011). This view was also reflected in a survey taken by German shipping and insurance companies (Engerer and Gössler 2011, p. 11, 13–14; Verbundprojekt PiraT 2011). The potential vulnerability of shipping and dependence on trade flows nonetheless demand a thorough analysis of potential risks. The differing natures of piracy and maritime terrorism, as well as the divergent motives of the perpetrators, make further investigation necessary. The effectiveness of any security governance measures, especially those with long-term minimisation of risks, should be taken into account.

4. Mix of actors involved in German security governance

Which key players (ministries, administrative bodies and associations) are involved in maritime security governance relevant to the IOR and what is their relation to one another?

It has been difficult to distinguish between the roles of safety and security, as only one word, *Sicherheit*, exists in German for both concepts. Because there are numerous institutions involved, it was decided that the focus would be toward authorities that have core tasks related to security. Hence, only the security-related tasks of ministries and administrative bodies will be mentioned.

The Federal Republic of Germany is divided into 16 federal states (*Länder*, singular *Land*), with a clear delineation of powers between the Federal and *Länder* governments. The Federal-*Länder* structure is also evident in the security domain and it is not different from other similarly-structured domains. Maritime security tasks are accordingly carried out by the *Länder*'s Interior Ministers' Conference (IMK 2009).

The responsibilities of the Federation and the *Länder* in the field of maritime defence are intricately defined by the German Constitution (*Grundgesetz*). The Federal Government assigned enforcement tasks to a multitude of authorities. The preservation of maritime security is thus, according to Hess (2011, pp. 90–91), not effectively and efficiently pursued, due to this complicated division of competences.

The federal structure determines the responsibilities for the coast and sea. They are divided between the *Länder* and federal police forces, following a territorial principle: the *Länder* are responsible for the area 12 nautical miles off the coast, while the Federal German Police (*Bundespolizei See*), excluding border protection, are responsible for the waters beyond that zone. The coastal *Länder*'s division of responsibility for the 12 nm coastal waters have never been put to the test, because no incidents of political violence have thus far taken place there (interview, WSP Hamburg, 2012). Currently, the main responsibilities for maritime security are confined to the German Navy, Federal Criminal Police Office and Federal German Police. These three institutions do cooperate with one another.

Police leadership, at the *Länder* and federal levels, has committed itself to managing maritime threats and major incidents, including, but not limited to, situations such as hostage-taking, acts of piracy and terrorism, occurring possibly on the coast or out at sea. The response capacities of the police are limited because they lack the required resources to effectively prevent a large ship from continuing its journey. In order to guarantee maritime security, according to Hess (2011, p. 93), each analysis oriented towards the asymmetrical threat of international terrorism must conclude that policing services must be allocated the required resources.

In 2007 the coastal *Länder*, along with the federal government, established a Maritime Safety and Security Centre (*Maritimes Sicherheitszentrum*, MSZ) in Cuxhaven, with the Joint Emergency and Reporting Assessment Centre (*Gemeinsames Lagezentrum See*, GLZ See) constituting its operational core, in order to improve cooperation in securing the German coast, including the main shipping lanes of all German commercial ports. The Waterways Police of the coastal *Länder* are brought together in the MSZ, in addition to all other relevant federal administrative bodies, while maintaining each one's separate legal responsibilities and status (IMK 2009, p. 49). Synergy should thus be utilised without having to change the federalist make-up. The MSZ was founded due to perceived threats following 9/11 and primarily serves as a forum for information exchange. It was created with the intention of integrating different responsibilities within a single institution.

In safety- and security-related emergency situations, German-flagged ships located beyond German territorial waters can contact the 'Point of Contact' at the Maritime Safety and Security Centre (MSSC/MSZ) in Cuxhaven, including incidents of piracy and maritime terrorism. German ship-owners are also able to consult the *Bundespolizei*'s Piracy Prevention Centre in Neustadt/Holstein for their crew training on how to react to piracy attacks (Joint Research Project PiraT 2011). In a comparative study with other coordinating authorities, Renner (2011, pp. 295–296) concludes that the establishment of the MSZ, irrespective of the hesitant establishment of the necessary physical and technical infrastructure, contributed to the effectiveness of security proceedings with a maritime connection. General expansions for the facilities and participation in EU Common Information Sharing Environment for the surveillance of the EU maritime domain (CISE) are planned by 2014 (BMVBS 2012). This is due to a drive to coordinate civilian and military capabilities of the EU and its member states. The objective of CISE is to create a situational awareness of activities at sea that impact maritime safety and security (Ehrhart and Petretto 2012, p. 11). Thiele (2011, p. 19) points out that there are several governmental, business and military organisations that collect information, but that those sets of information are not integrated to offer a shared situational awareness about maritime security.

The Federal Ministry of Defence (*Bundesministerium der Verteidigung*, BMVg) deploys the German Navy in the framework of mandated operations. So far the protection of merchant ships by the German Navy only occurs when partaking in missions such as Operation Atalanta. German forces have until now been active in the eastern Mediterranean and in the seas around the Horn of Africa, collecting surveillance and securing operations of other forces (Hess 2011, pp. 88–89).[5]

The Federal Ministry of Interior (*Bundesministerium des Inneren*, BMI) is responsible for all policing measures. Likewise, the BMI (with its Department of Public Security, Maritime Security Branch/*Abteilung Öffentliche Sicherheit, Referat Seesicherheit*) is tasked with defining SOLAS (International Convention for the Safety of Life at Sea)[6] security levels and the designation of the covered areas. This is done in consultation with the Federal Ministry of Transport, Building and Urban Development (*Bundesministerium für Verkehr, Bau und Stadtentwicklung*, BMVBS). The BMVBS is tasked with overseeing the passive protection (self-protection) of merchant vessels, defining emergency response plans for ships and ensuring adherence to safety regulations (BReg 2011, p. 15). The subordinate authority that publishes security levels and hazard notices is the Federal Maritime and Hydrographic Agency (*Bundesamt für Seeschifffahrt und Hydrographie*, BSH).

The Federal Ministry of Economics and Technology (*Bundesministerium für Wirtschaft und Technologie*, BMWi) plays a special role: its parliamentary state secretary, Hans-Joachim Otto, was appointed the 'Federal Government Coordinator for the Maritime Industry' or, in short, 'Maritime Coordinator'. His tasks include arranging the National Maritime Conference and developing a process for the approval of Private Security Companies. Plans do exist for the Federal Office of Economics and Export Control (*Bundesamt für Wirtschaft und Ausfuhrkontrolle*, BAFA) to be the responsible authority in this process, in cooperation with other authorities, such as the Federal German Police (*Bundespolizei*; interview, BAFA, 2012).

The Inter-ministerial Working Group for Maritime Security (*Arbeitskreis Maritime Sicherheit*, AK MarSi) was established due to a danger of losing sight of the many overlapping initiatives and forums that, on national and above all international levels, occupied themselves with maritime surveillance or coast guard functions. Additionally, this hampered the ability of representatives of the Federal Government to speak with one voice (interview, BMVBS, 2012). At its inauguration it was described most briefly: 'it will be a working group for "maritime security" that will regularly meet to share information' (BMVBS 2006). The AK MarSi involves all departments concerned with coast guard duties, including the BMVg, in order to agree on and represent consistent German positions in EU-wide and other initiatives, and in projects developed for maritime surveillance (interview, BMVBS, 2012).

There are a dozen people from five ministries represented (two from the BMVBS and BMF, one from the BMI, BMLEV (Federal Ministry of Food, Agriculture and Consumer Protection/*Bundesministerium für Ernährung, Landwirtschaft und Verbraucherschutz*) and BMVg, and a representative from each of the five coastal *Länder*). They perform necessary coordination work. It is eye-opening that this same circle represents the steering group for the MSZ. The AK MarSi is therefore a pragmatic Federal-*Länder* Working Group, which concerns itself with maritime matters that must be regulated, regardless of whether they fall under the scope of 'safety' or 'security'. This also comprises the agreement concerning the external representation of the Federal Republic of Germany in expert committees (interview, BMVg, 2012). The working group does not generally engage with themes of organised crime, piracy and terrorism (interviews, BMVBS, 2012; BMVg, 2012).[7] Piracy is handled by the coordinator as a by-product, especially with regard to the certification of PSCs. The related economic aspects take on only a secondary role for the AK MarSi. Here, it is almost solely fixated on German territorial waters and the

Exclusive Economic Zone (EEZ). For piracy there are always further non-institutionalised, departmental reviews, in which not the *Länder* but the BMWi and the Foreign Office (AA) are represented, and again the BMVBS has the leading role (interview, BMVg, 2012).

As mentioned above, the Ministry of Interior (BMI) is responsible for all policing matters, with the help of its administrative bodies. For example, the Federal German Police – Sea (*Bundespolizei See*) handles cases of piracy, if there is German involvement, while the Federal Criminal Police Office (BKA) handles hostage takings of German nationals outside territorial waters; inside the 12 nm zone, the *Länder* authorities are legally responsible, regardless of the nature of the situation (political, economic or otherwise). However, in hostage situations involving German citizens, the AA, with its Crisis Response Centre (*Krisenreaktionszentrum*, KRZ), takes the leading role (interview, BKA, 2012).

Concerning law enforcement, piracy cases are usually abandoned because perpetrators can often not be investigated, as in cases of catch-and-release or no catch at all (interview, WSP HH, 2012). So far there is only one (still ongoing) court proceeding against 10 Somali piracy suspects in Hamburg, Germany.

When it comes to hostage situations involving German nationals, coope-ration with other authorities (Federal Intelligence Service/*Bundesnachrichtendienst*, BND and the German Armed Forces/*Bundeswehr*) occurs under the framework of the KRZ. There can be case-based cooperation, inter alia, between intelli-gence and policing services, albeit only if a concrete threat is perceived (interview, BKA, 2012).

Figure 1 provides an overview of German state actors' roles and jurisdictions within maritime security. It partially summarises aforementioned facts, naming the most relevant authorities, and details their most important tasks in security structures across five categories: risk analysis, preventive measures, regulation, operative measures/active defence and criminal prosecution. However, the categories are not always ideal as there can be overlaps, such as between active defence and prevention, for instance in the case of border protection.

The Federal German Police (Piracy Prevention Centre/BPOL See), along with the Criminal Investigation Offices of the respective *Länder* (*Landeskriminalämter*), cooperates with the private sector (such as associations) in combating piracy. The economic and private actors are experts in their business segments and engage in lobbying activities. The German Ship-Owners Association (VDR) for instance, seeks to underline their position, both nationally and internationally, regarding the issue of piracy. They work towards an appropriate and practical implementation of regulations, such as the PSC certification process. There are also other forms of cooperation: ship-owners provide vessels for the Police or Navy to use for exercises and training (interview, VDR, 2012).

Only a few German companies specialise in the protection of ships at sea, but the market is expanding. Survey results (Joint Research Project PiraT 2011) amongst insurers and ship-owners show that ship-owners use Private Security Companies as a promising form of protection, even though they would prefer staff from the German authorities, at least for German-flagged vessels. The German government was oblivious to this opinion, which is meanwhile willing to contribute to multilateral naval operations but not to provide vessel protection teams for all merchant ships. Ship-owners should provide security on their ships, which could

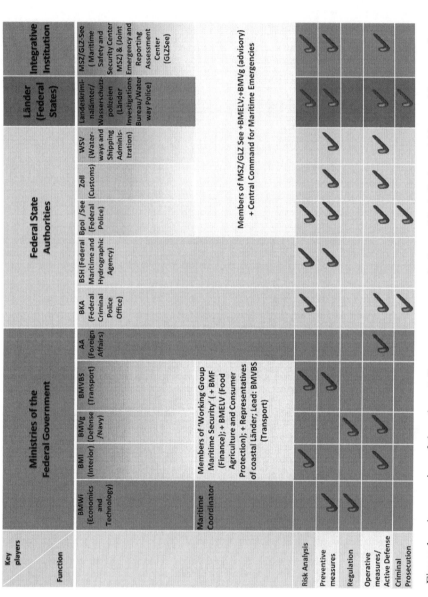

Figure 1. An overview of the relevant German state actors' roles and jurisdiction within maritime security. Source: own illustration.

include hiring PSCs. In the survey, ship-owners showed a lot of insecurity in the assessment and handling of PSCs. As by German law it is not forbidden to hire PSCs for this purpose (see König and Salomon 2011), but it is not explicitly supported either, an ambiguity that is expected to change with the above-mentioned planned certification procedures.

5. Germany's key players and their involvement in international maritime security governance

How do the key players involved in national maritime security governance act on the international level? And how does Germany's involvement in international mechanisms connect with national mechanisms?

The responsibility for international agreements is always dependent on its character. Fundamentally, the AA is responsible for this. Yet, in policing matters, the BMI is responsible, and with customs-related agreements the Ministry of Finance (*Bundesministerium für Finanzen*, BMF) takes responsibility. Everything security and maritime traffic related is devoted to the BMVBS. Therefore the BMVBS acts as a representative at the IMO. It is supported by the BMI with expertise regarding policing measures. Germany has signed up to many international agreements under UN, NATO and EU frameworks. Germany, however, often fails to successfully apply international regulations to domestic law which is not oriented on practical implementation (Hess 2011, p. 94). Additionally, Germany has maintained a very low profile on the international stage, in both IMO meetings and Contact Group on Piracy off the Coast of Somalia (CGPCS) meetings. It seems that this restraint has been deliberately planned. Germany did not provide an answer to the IMO-questionnaire that surveyed the port/coastal policy on armed guards (MSC-FAL.1/Circ.2). Hence, there is no (bilateral) cooperation between Germany and the IMO at this level (interview, IMO, 2012).

Various international measures were adopted with regards to harbour and ship protection. Likewise, counter-terrorism policies are used to legitimise naval missions. The international defensive measures against maritime terrorism (as outlined in Schneider 2011) can be summarised as follows: the ISPS-Code, focussing on port and ship security; the Container Security Initiative (CSI), tasked with customs security (24 Hour Rule); Customs-Trade Partnership Against Terrorism (C-TPAT); and Authorised Economic Operator (AEO), facilitating cooperation between commercial enterprises and public authorities, with the Port Security Initiative (PSI) focusing on inter-state cooperation. Various direct measures, such as the various military missions (OEF, GMP, CMF, CTF 150/151/152) and inter-state naval and air patrol cooperation MALSINDO (Malaysia, Singapore, Indonesia), are also evident.

Thus, these initiatives, led mainly by the US but less so by the IMO and EU, create international networks of cooperation, whether legally binding or not (ISPS/CSI/C-TPAT/AEO): firstly, the increased rights of harbour authorities to verify and access cargo (ISPS/CSI); secondly, the increased focus on preventive risk management through education and readily available information (ISPS/CSI); thirdly, the national harmonisation and improvement of trade security (PSI); and lastly, the cooperation of navies (OEF/OAE/GMP/CMF/CTF). German Armed Forces are, inter alia, part of NATO and took action, for instance, in the first naval operation within the framework of the Common Security and Defence Policy (CSDP) of the European Union – EUNAVFOR Atalanta.

The *Marineschifffahrtleitstelle* (MSLtSt, Naval Control of Shipping) is responsible for ensuring the protection of merchant shipping in times of conflict and crises. Therefore it establishes Shipping Cooperation Points (SCP). The two SCPs of the German Navy in Bremerhaven and Hamburg are controlled by the German Fleet Command. They conduct, amongst other things, operational training in NATO procedures and provides personnel. It follows the guidelines of NATO's 'Naval Co-operation and Guidance for Shipping' (NCAGS n.d.) programme. Naval forces are able to provide protection for merchant shipping in dangerous situations by clearing mines, escorting convoys or providing boarding teams for the enforcement of embargos and monitoring of ships. In these courses, naval officers and embargo liaison officers are trained together. The current restructuring of the *Bundeswehr* also has ramifications for the Navy. The German Fleet Command and the Naval Office will be joined and restructured starting 1 October 2012 to create the Navy Command based in Rostock. The MSLtSt should continue undertaking sub-tasks (interview, MSLtSt, 2012). To perform the aforementioned tasks, the Federal Criminal Police Office (BKA) is designated to liaise also with international bodies such as EUROPOL and INTERPOL, and bilaterally with third countries (interview, BKA, 2012).

Many associations in the maritime sector, belonging to an umbrella organisation, cooperate with international organisations as well. For example, the Organisation of German Shipmasters and Ship Officers (*Verband Deutscher Kapitäne und Schiffsoffiziere*, VDKS) is connected to the International Federation of Shipmasters' Associations (IFSMA) and are, at the European level, linked to the Confederation of European Shipmasters' Association (CESMA). In the International Union of Marine Insurance (IUMI) there is a delegate from the German Insurance Association (GDV).

The VDR is participating in the process of revising the current version of the 'Best Management Practices for Protection against Somalia Based Piracy' (BMP) (BReg 2011. p. 15). This is taking place within international federations, which includes the International Chamber of Shipping (ICS) along with the International Shipping Federation (ISF; see www.marisec.org). Also, various navy forces such as EUNAVFOR and other industrial associations are supporters of the BMP.

The influence of the International Chamber of Commerce (ICC) is based on their worldwide network of members. Internationally-active German companies are, along with chambers of trade and industry, umbrella organisations and professional associations, members of the German National Committee (ICC Germany). There is a connection to the International Maritime Bureau (IMB) and its Piracy Reporting Centre, as it forms part of the ICC. Figure 2 offers a brief overview of key German players in the international maritime domain.

6. Other possible factors explaining Germany's deliberate restraint

There are always different topics of national interest competing with each other for public and political attention and seeming more relevant for Germany, hence taking priority (e.g. the financial crisis, Arab Spring etc.). German abstention in the UN Security Council to mandate the use of force against the Gaddafi Regime in Libya

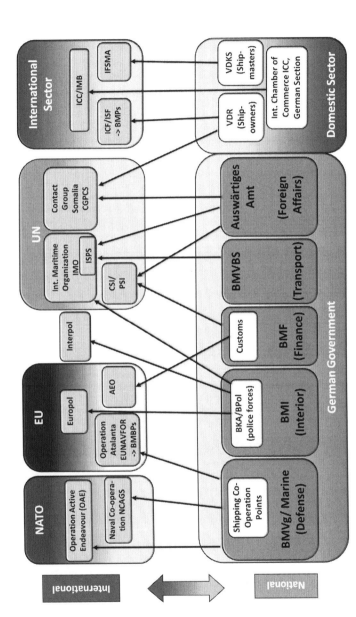

Figure 2. A select overview of key German players in the international maritime domain. Source: own illustration.

was heavily criticised and many called for stronger leadership. However, Germany took a leading role in the almost two-year ongoing debate over the European debt crisis. Germany, being the most heavily populated and strongest economy in the EU, took the lead role, with the support of France, in managing the financial crisis. This is in the very interest of Europe, because European integration, which is essential for European economic and political development in a globalised world, is at stake (Müller-Brandeck-Bocquet 2012).

This competition with other priorities is particularly strong for maritime piracy and terrorism, because the overall effects of the two remain low. However, there has been media attention due to the attractiveness of reporting on piracy-related issues. Even more so when a national ship is attacked or when readers feel they can link their knowledge about commercial pirate films to press reports or when fears about the piracy-terrorism nexus or energy supply and related rising costs are raised. The proceedings against 10 Somali pirates in Hamburg are also closely followed by the press, as it is the first such of cases tried in Germany for about 600 years.

Germany is known historically to be a land power with strong armed forces but little naval capability due to short coastline compared to its size. This is a different case in historically-seagoing nations, as for example Great Britain, the Netherlands or Spain. However, even though Germany has a small navy, marine facilities and shipyards are an integral part of Germany's economy, as Germany still constructs special custom-made ships, cruise liners, navy vessels and leading-edge technology (i.e. air-independent propulsion conventional) submarines.

7. Conclusion

The economic impact from maritime piracy and terrorism against German ship-owners has been relatively low and a big share of the economic risk is insurable. Hence there does not seem to be a necessity for the German government to be more active than its current involvements in international initiatives. However there can be severe human costs as a result of piracy and maritime terrorism in the IOR, which would not be covered sufficiently by insurance. The potential impact of maritime terrorism and repeated threats that endanger strategic trade routes stress the importance of the need for effective governance in this field, and in other fields of crime governance.

The reason for Germany's restraint from taking leadership roles in security governance regarding maritime (trade) security can be explained as follows: due to the large number of authorities involved, the ability to achieve consensus is hampered and bureaucratic politics form an element of decision making that limit state policies in a modern, federal state. The most important reasons for the exceptionally complicated German structures are fourfold: the federal structure, the rivalries between the ministries, the competition with more pressing economic and political priorities, and the historical strict separation between the police, the armed forces and in part the intelligence services.

The delimitation of competences between the federal organs, and between the Federal government and the coastal *Länder* is complicated. Political responsibility within this fragmented system remains unclear. This could hamper effective and efficient protection against threats at sea. There are several arguments for reforming responsibilities in Germany. While there are problems with coordination and communication, where appropriate mechanisms could be used to improve the situation, the real issue could lie in a lack of sufficient leadership necessary in crisis situations (Hess 2011, p. 95).

A change in the ways of thinking about these issues is highlighted by the multitude of international maritime security initiatives that exist today (Hess 2011, p. 1). The high number of these efforts leads to the necessity for limited but improved coordination procedures for administrative action on the national level, as has been shown in the German case. The MSZ cooperation network indicates an effort for compromise: it coordinates bodies that 'are the appropriate administrative instruments of political action in order to attain an improved overall performance of involved authorities, without interfering in the existing division of competences' (Renner 2011, p. 298, translation by author).

Leadership in this sphere is unlikely to improve because of the competing rivalries between the different ministries. While preserving performance with the achieved level of cooperation is possible, this will be tested should budgets be tightened or its effectiveness possibly questioned following a terrorist attack. The latter could, for example, serve as a political catalyst or a successful piracy incident, involving a German-flagged vessel in the IOR with severe human costs or other impact like an accident, being set alight, an oil spill or the like, with no assistance readily available from an international military mission.

However, the participation of Germany in EU and NATO missions and in diverse coordination mechanisms proves its ability to act. In addition, whereas the establishment of the Piracy Prevention Centre by the Federal Police is one of a kind, the BMPs are co-developed and implemented in close cooperation with the German ship-owners association. In sum, more has been done on the piracy issue than on the maritime terrorism issue, which reflects the different perceptions of risk, piracy being perceived as a more acute threat to the shipping industry and terrorism just being a latent danger. Germany even led the Atalanta mission for several six-month terms and provided a big share of the ships and Long Range Maritime Patrol and Reconnaissance Aircraft (LR-MPRA) for the mission for a time. Nevertheless, an inter-agency action strategy is still missing (Joint Research Project PiraT 2011).

The inability to consolidate the responsibilities of German authorities has hindered the creation of a maritime security strategy, which could otherwise enable this process. Alternatively, another perception is possible: there is no maritime security strategy because a consolidation of efforts would be the precondition for creating the necessary consensus for a maritime strategy. In Germany strategies are generally unpopular; currently the country lacks even an overall security strategy. Furthermore, the share of maritime business in the German economy compared, for example, with Denmark with its ship-owner Maersk, is much lower. That could explain why Denmark has a maritime strategy with Maersk lobbying for it and Germany does not; German ship-owners do not have such a strong influence. The already planned procedures for the regulation of private security companies could set international standards if reached in time and would therefore present a more active role for Germany, with a role model function in the international community.

Gupta has argued that if a nation lacks 'the power to govern the sea', the country may not have 'the ability to do or act in national interest and, if called upon, in national defence' (Gupta 2010, p. 265). For Gupta, the only remedy is to be found in the firm establishment of 'the political will to be able to act or function at sea in a manner of governing in control' (Gupta 2010, p. 266). The political will to devote resources and to cooperate with allies is necessary for Germany and other nations to develop governance solutions to issues that either emanate from or take place in the Indian Ocean waters.

People may not be aware of the importance of sea trade (this phenomenon is often called 'maritime blindness') and are too focused on issues that occur on land. However, there is not only a threat of violence by non-state actors (either terrorists or pirates), but there is also a growing geo-strategic importance of the sea, and the IOR in particular, that touches on many areas of international relations: it becomes the focus for a new era of economic exploitation, sustainable transportation and inter-state rivalry. A high number of security initiatives and other regulations indicate that a new security architecture, which reflects current challenges, might be needed. Due to the importance of maritime trade for Germany, it is advisable to further contribute to these initiatives. However, Germany's deliberate restraint on the (inter)national stage in the maritime domain could result in its partners not perceiving Germany as reliable or predictable. However, Germany's economic security interests make it imperative to help maintain a secure Indian Ocean Region.

Acknowledgements

The author would like to thank the three anonymous reviewers for their valuable comments and suggestions. I also thank Andrew C. Winner, Awet T. Weldemichael, Tim Salomon, Sascha Pristrom, Heinz-Dieter Jopp, Kerstin Petretto, Hans-Georg Ehrhart and Johann Schmid for their useful feedback.

Notes

1. In the following, a working definition for this article is presented: the main characteristics of maritime terrorism include the ultimate political, ideological or religious goals of its perpetrators. The threat or exertion of violence by non-state actors, contrary to the rules of international law, is aimed at enforcing political and/or social change or the political-ideological interests of the actor. Such effects are achieved by generating fear, disrupting public order and the people's faith in their government, or by directing the media to focus attention on their cause, culminating in political pressure. Attacks can be targeted against civilians or the government, including military targets. If the attacks occur in a maritime area, the phenomenon is called maritime terrorism; this includes attacks launched from the sea or land against ships or maritime infrastructure, such as oil rigs, their passengers or personnel. Any type of ship can be targeted, for instance cargo ships, warships or passenger boats and cruise liners. Port cities, maritime facilities or coastal cities can also be targeted.
2. Following Hans-Georg Ehrhart, 'security governance can be provisionally defined as the collective furnishing of security by a variety of state and non-state actors, in a non-hierarchical relationship with one another and using different means, instruments and methods to reach a common goal on the basis of common norms, values and/or interests' (Ehrhart, Petretto and Schneider 2010, p. 10). For an overview of the development and meaning of the concept of Security Governance, see Ehrhart, Petretto and Schneider (2010, pp. 10–23).
3. The PiraT data bank of maritime terrorism is comprised of information taken from a number of other databases (RAND, GTD and WITS) and summarises a number of findings drawn from these. There were, however, problems with the state of the data available (see Schneider 2011).
4. The high risk area was extended, rendering the data from 2011 incomparable to 2010. The Federal German Police gathers information, for example, through radio communications

from naval units. Whereas accurate and concrete information is available for German-flagged ships, other numbers have to be estimated by help of other indicators.

5. 'The German Armed Forces have the task to provide national security and defence against any threat from outside enemies. In accordance with a recent Supreme Court ruling concerning the Aviation Security Act, protection against imminent terrorist attacks may be considered as grave threats to security and the Armed Forces may act to prevent such threats in accordance with the German Constitution (Art. 35). In particular it is the task of the German Armed Forces to monitor all German Air and Water Space and to support other agencies in exercising sovereign rights. Rescue operations, evacuation operations and surveillance missions are also within the scope of tasks of the German Armed Forces' (European Commission 2007, p. 17). However, the employment and jurisdiction of the German Navy to protect merchant ships remains debatable and 'raises fundamental questions relating to [German] constitutional law' (Wahlen 2012, p. 34, translated by author). Similarly, while König notes that, theoretically, any navy can be deployed for protection purposes to stop any given ship suspected of piracy (König 2010, pp. 224–225), she also points to 'dispute issues of [German] constitutional law' (König 2010, p. 231, translated by author).

6. Though it has to be noted that responsibilities within SOLAS XI/2 are split, as the convention differentiates between ship security and port security. For ship security, the flag state government is responsible. Thus for defining the ship security levels of all ships flying the German flag, the BMI, *Referat Seesicherheit*, is responsible. The responsibility for publication lies with the *Bundesamt für Seeschifffahrt and Hydrographie* (BSH). For port security, the port state government is in charge of setting the security level for all territorial port facilities. This responsibility was referred to the German *Länder*, thus Germany has decentralised the responsibility and currently seven *Länder* have the responsibility to set security levels and publish these for their territorial port facilities (IMO 2011).

7. A predecessor, with varied composition, amongst other things, with the involvement of the Foreign Office (*Auswärtiges Amt*, AA), got together to achieve agreements regarding the Proliferation Security Initiative.

References

Arz, W. (2012), 'Krisenregion Indischer Ozean'. Available at http://www.eurasischesmagazin. de/artikel/drucken.asp?artikelID=20120405, accessed 5 April 2012.

Bundesamt für Seeschifffahrt und Hydrographie (BSH) (2012), 'Bestand der deutschen Handelsflotte ab BRZ 100 der letzten 12 Monate, 2011–2012, Version: July 2012'. Available at http://www.bsh.de/de/Schifffahrt/Berufsschifffahrt/Deutsche_Handelsflotte/Statistik_Handelsflotte.pdf, accessed 13 August 2012.

Bundeskriminalamt (BKA) (2008), *Lagebild Seesicherheit 2007*, jährlicher Bericht des Bundeskriminalamtes/Wirtschaftsfassung, Version: March 2008 (reporting period 1 January 2007–31 December 2007).

Bundeskriminalamt (BKA) (2009), *Lagebild Seesicherheit 2008*, jährlicher Bericht des Bundeskriminalamtes/Wirtschaftsfassung, Version: March 2009 (reporting period 1 January 2008–31 December 2008).

Bundeskriminalamt (BKA) (2010), *Lagebild Seesicherheit 2009*, jährlicher Bericht des Bundeskriminalamtes/Wirtschaftsfassung, Version: March 2010 (reporting period 1 January 2009–31 December 2009).

Bundeskriminalamt (BKA) (2011), *Lagebild Seesicherheit 2010*, jährlicher Bericht des Bundeskriminalamtes/Wirtschaftsfassung, Version: April 2011 (reporting period 1 January 2009–31 December 2010).

Bundesministerium für Verkehr, Bau und Stadtentwicklung (BMVBS) (2006), *Maritime Surveillance. Vermerk der Ressortbesprechung vom 18.10.2006*. Report available on request.

Bundesministerium für Verkehr, Bau und Stadtentwicklung (BMVBS) (2012), *Projekt Küstenwache /Martimes Sicherheitszentrum aus Sicht des BMVBS*, 7 February 2012. Report available on request.

Bundespolizei See (BPOL See) (2012), *Pirateriebericht der Bundespolizei See – 4. Quartal 2011/ Jahresbericht 2011*. Neustadt in Holstein: Bundespolizei See.

MARITIME TERRORISM AND PIRACY IN THE INDIAN OCEAN REGION

Bundesregierung (BReg) (2011), *Maßnahmen im Kampf gegen Piraterie, Drucksache 17/6715, Antwort der Bundesregierung auf die Kleine Anfrage der Abgeordneten Uwe Beckmeyer, Dr. Hans-Peter Bartels, Heinz-Joachim Barchmann, weiterer Abgeordneter und der Fraktion der SPD Drucksache 17/6381*. Berlin: Bundesregierung.

Deutsches Institut für Wirtschaft (DIW) (2012), 'Indikatoren zur Darstellung wirtschaftlicher Aspekte von Piraterie', Beitrag des Deutschen Instituts für Wirtschaftsforschung zum Verbundprojektgemeinsamen Arbeitspapier, forthcoming.

Ehrhart, H.-G. and Petretto, K. (2012), 'The EU and Somalia: counter-piracy and the question of a comprehensive approach', Study for the Greens/European Free Alliance. Available at http://www.greens-efa.eu/the-eu-and-somalia-5416.html, accessed 24 March 2012.

Ehrhart, H.-G., Petretto, K. and Schneider, P. (2010), 'Security Governance als Rahmenkonzept für die Analyse von Piraterie und maritimen Terrorismus - Konzeptionelle und Empirische Grundlagen', PiraT Working Paper on Maritime Security No. 1. Available at www.maritimesicherheit.eu, accessed 9 December 2011.

Eklöf Amirell, S. (2006), 'Political piracy and maritime terrorism: a comparison between the straits of Malacca and the southern Philippines', in G.G. Ong-Webb, ed., *Piracy, Maritime Terrorism and Securing the Malacca Straits*. Singapore and Leiden: Institute of Southeast Asian Studies (ISEAS)/International Institute for Asian Studies (IIAS), pp. 52–67.

Engerer, H. (2011), 'Piraterie und maritimer Terrorismus – Entwicklung und Bedeutung des Seehandels', PiraT Arbeitspapier zur Maritimen Sicherheit Nr. 3. Available at http://www.maritimesecurity.eu/fileadmin/content/news_events/workingpaper/PiraT_Arbeitspapier_Nr3_2011_Engerer.pdf, accessed 21 November 2011.

Engerer, H. and Gössler, M. (2011), 'Maritimer Terrorismus und Piraterie aus Sicht der deutschen Versicherungswirtschaft – Ergebnisse einer Befragung deutscher Transportversicherer'. PiraT Arbeitspapier zur Maritimen Sicherheit Nr. 12. Available at http://www.maritimesecurity.eu/fileadmin/content/news_events/workingpaper/PiraT_Arbeitspapier_Nr12_2011_DIW_Versicherer.pdf, accessed 18 November 2011.

European Commission (2007), 'Integrated Maritime Policy for the EU', Working Documents on Offshore Activities of Coastal EU Member States and Cross Border Cooperation, DG Fisheries and Maritime Affairs/Maritime Policy Task Force.

Frankfurter Allgemeine (2008), 'Entführtes Frachtschiff wieder frei', 7 July. Available at http://www.faz.net/aktuell/gesellschaft/kriminalitaet/somalia-entfuehrtes-frachtschiff-wieder-frei-1663242.html, accessed 16 October 2012.

Frankfurter Allgemeine (2010), 'Flucht in den "Panikraum" bringt die Freiheit', 25 October. Available at http://www.faz.net/aktuell/politik/beluga-fortune-wieder-frei-flucht-in-den-panikraum-bringt-die-freiheit-1573336.html, accessed 16 October 2012.

German Fleet Command (2011a), *Jahresbericht 2009 Fakten und Zahlen zur maritimen Abhängigkeit der Bundesrepublik Deutschland*. Glücksburg: Marine. Available at www.marine.de, accessed 21 March 2012.

German Fleet Command (2011b), *Kennzahlen zur maritimen Abhängigkeit der Bundesrepublik Deutschland*. Glücksburg: Marine. Available at www.marine.de, accessed 21 March 2012.

Gupta, M. (2010), *Indian Ocean Region: Maritime Regimes for Regional Cooperation*. Heidelberg: Springer.

Hess, S. (2011), 'Seesicherheit: Abwehr des Terrorismus in nationalen Gewässern und auf Hoher See', in H.-J. Bücking, ed., *Streitkräfte im Nachkriegsdeutschland*. Berlin: Duncker & Humblot, pp. 93–98.

International Chamber of Commerce (ICC) – International Maritime Bureau (IMB)/Oceans Beyond Piracy (OBP) (2012), 'The human cost of Somali piracy 2011'. Available at http://oceansbeyondpiracy.org/sites/default/files/hcop_2011.pdf, accessed 9 August 2012.

IMK – Ständige Konferenz der Innenminister und -senatoren der Länder (2009), *Programm Innere Sicherheit, Fortschreibung 2008/2009*. Berlin: Bundesrat. Available at www.bundesrat.de, accessed 7 December 2011.

International Maritime Organisation (IMO) (2011), 'IMO security measures'. Available at http://www.imo.org/OurWork/Security/Instruments/Pages/SecurityInstruments.aspx, accessed 14 August 2012.

Joint Research Project PiraT (2011), 'Verbundprojekt PiraT: Ergebnisse der Fragebogenaktion und Kommentierung'. Available at http://www.maritimesecurity.eu/fileadmin/content/Publications/PiraT–Ergebnisse-der-Fragebogenaktion-Nov-2011.pdf, accessed 9 August 2012.

König, D. (2010), 'Der Einsatz von Seestreitkräften zur Verhinderung von Terrorismus und Verbreitung von Massenvernichtungswaffen sowie zur Bekämpfung der Piraterie: Mandat und Eingriffsmöglichkeiten', in S. Hobe, E.A. Kieninger, D. König, T. Marauhn, K. Odendahl, K. Schmalenbach, K. Thorn, and A. Zimmermann, *Moderne Konfliktformen*. Heidelberg: C.F. Müller, pp. 203–248.

König, D. and Salomon, T.R. (2011), 'Private Sicherheitsdienste auf Handelsschiffen – Rechtliche Implikationen', PiraT Arbeitspapier zur Maritimen Sicherheit Nr. 2, Hamburg. Available at http://www.maritimesecurity.eu/fileadmin/content/news_events/workingpaper/PiraT_Arbeitspapier_Nr2_2011_Koenig-Salomon.pdf, accessed 9 August 2012.

Kolb, A.S., Salomon, T.R. and Udich, J. (2011), 'Paying danegeld to pirates – humanitarian necessity or financing jihadists', *Max Planck Yearbook of United Nations Law*, Vol. 15, pp. 113–115.

Müller-Brandeck-Bocquet, G. (2012), 'Deutschland – Europas einzige Führungsmacht?', *Aus Politik und Zeitgeschichte*, Vol. 62 (10/2012), pp. 16–22.

Naval Cooperation and Guidance for Shipping NCAGS within NATO (n.d.), 'Concept for cooperation with merchant shipping in crisis and conflict management to enhance the safety of participating merchant ships and support military operations'. Available at www.shipping.nato.int, accessed 20 March 2012.

Navaltoday (2012), 'Italian cargo vessel Enrica Lexie stays at coast of Kochi for further investigation', 17 February. Available at http://navaltoday.com/2012/02/17/italian-cargo-vessel-enrica-lexie-stays-at-coast-of-kochi-for-further-investigation/, accessed 13 August 2012.

Oceans Beyond Piracy (2010), 'The economic costs of maritime piracy', One Earth Future Working Paper. Available at www.oneearthfuture.org, accessed 28 February 2011.

Petretto, K. (2011), 'Diebstahl, Raub und erpresserische Geiselnahme im maritimen Raum: Eine Analyse zeitgenössischer Piraterie', PiraT Working Paper on Maritime Security No 8, 2011. Available at http://www.maritimesecurity.eu, accessed 18 November 2011.

Renner, R. (2011), *Sicherheit in See- und Luftfahrt*. Frankfurt: Verlag für Polizeiwissenschaft.

Schneider, P. (2011). 'Maritimer Terrorismus: Tätergruppen und Anschlagstypen – Eine empirisch-analytische Bestandsaufnahme'. PiraT-Arbeitspapier zur Maritimen Sicherheit Nr. 13, Hamburg. Available at http://www.maritimesecurity.eu/fileadmin/content/news_events/workingpaper/PiraT_Arbeitspapier_Nr13_2011_Schneider.pdf, accessed at 9 August 2012.

Spiegel Online (2009), 'Piraten entführen "MV Charelle"', 12 June. Available at http://www.spiegel.de/panorama/justiz/containerschiff-piraten-entfuehren-mv-charelle-a-630231.html, accessed 16 October 2012.

Spiegel Online (2011a), 'Tödliches Feuergefecht um gekaperte "Beluga Nomination"', 29 January. Available at http://www.spiegel.de/panorama/justiz/entfuehrtes-deutsches-schiff-toedliches-feuergefecht-um-gekaperte-beluga-nomination-a-742360.html, accessed 16 October 2012.

Spiegel Online (2011b), 'Piraten geben "Susan K" frei', 17 June. Available at http://www.spiegel.de/panorama/frachter-deutscher-reederei-piraten-geben-susan-k-frei-a-768976.html, accessed 16 October 2012.

Stern.de (2009), 'Jede fünfte Reederei bereits Piraten-Opfer', 9 July. Available at http://www.stern.de/wirtschaft/news/maerkte/ueberfaelle-vor-somalia-jede-fuenfte-reederei-bereits-piraten-opfer-705841.html, accessed 16 October 2012.

Stern.de (2010), 'Piraten kapern zwei Schiffe mit Deutschen an Bord', 24 October. Available at http://www.stern.de/panorama/entfuehrungen-vor-somalia-und-kenia-piraten-kapern-zwei-schiffe-mit-deutschen-an-bord-1617021.html, accessed 16 Octobre 2012.

Tagesspiegel (2010), 'Antiterroreinsatz wird beendet', 23 June. Available at http://www.tagesspiegel.de/politik/nachrichten-nachrichten/1867096.html, accessed 9 August 2012.

Thiele, R.D. (2011), *Building Maritime Security Situational Awareness*. Köln: Politisch-Militärische Gesellschaft e.V., forthcoming.

Wahlen, D. (2012), *Maritime Sicherheit im Bundesstaat*. Berlin: Duncker&Humblot.

Wikipedia (2012), 'List of ships attacked by Somali pirates'. Available at http://en.wikipedia.org/wiki/List_of_ships_attacked_by_Somali_pirates, accessed 13 October 2012.

Winter, L. (2011), 'The Abdullah Azzam Brigades', *Studies in Conflict and Terrorism*, Vol. 34, no. 11, pp. 883–895.

Yemeni security-political dynamics and maritime security in the Indian Ocean Region

Stig Jarle Hansen

International Relations Programme, University of Life Sciences, Ås, Norway

When analysing maritime security issues and Yemen, emphasis tends to be on the state weakness of Yemen and its '4.5' conflicts. While keeping the conflicts in the analysis, this article changes focus and argues that Yemen's position along two maritime highways and situated in two regional 'cold wars' should not be neglected.

Yemen in security analyses

Yemen has often been seen as a security threat because of its weakness. It has dwindling oil resources, a capital that is expected to run out of ground water before 2017 and a weak state apparatus (Staff writer 2010). Weak states are often associated with security threats (Stewart 2011, p. 7) and logically Yemen is among the more important of them. If Yemen's security issues transforms into maritime security threats, it could potentially disrupt one of the major waterways of the world: the maritime highway going through the Suez, passing along the Yemeni coast. In her briefing paper for United States Congress in 2008, Liana Sun Wyler (2008) suggests that weak states might be problematic for several reasons, dividing modern security threats into Terrorism, International Crime, Weapons Proliferation and Regional Instability. Policy-makers like Condoleezza Rice had been arguing the point, declaring that weak states are a problem for security, and the CIA had even mapped out 50 weak states, to know where to put in resources (Stewart 2006). The weakness of the Yemeni state is also connected to the various conflicts in the country; the '4.5' conflicts that Yemen struggles with.

The first conflict is the conflict between Al-Qaeda in the Arab Peninsula and its local Islamist umbrella organisation, Ansar Al-Sharia (Phillips 2010, p. 107). The international focus of Al-Qaeda might explain why this conflict gains attention. Although the territories controlled by Ansar and Al-Qaeda are limited, it remains important for scholars' analytical focus, even when writing on issues of Yemeni maritime security (Hartkorn 2011, p. 28).

The second conflict is between the loose movements of southern activists called Al-Hiraak, some of whose members want to re-create the old southern Yemeni republic which merged with north Yemen in 1990. The union was troublesome and southern politicians fought northern forces in a civil war in 1994. As for the Hirak activists today, some want a separation between north and south Yemen, while others just want more autonomy (International Crisis Group 2011).

The third conflict is the so-called Saadah rebellion, where Shia political activists face the government in a (at the time of writing still peaceful) standoff, although five rounds of fighting have flared up in the past (International Crisis Group 2009).

The fourth conflict is tribal in nature, and refers to the tribes in the Yemeni countryside attacking each other as well as the government (Dresh 1989). This conflict dimension is often highly ritualistic and less violent than many believe. Some tribal conflicts have been ongoing for more than 40 years with few casualties. Tribal conflicts do however present an obstacle to the Yemeni state and its ability to implement its policies.

The 'half' conflict is basically the aftermath of the 'Arab Spring', where the Gulf Cooperation Council (GCC) brokered a transition between the old presidency of Ali Abdellah Saleh and a new coalition government, led by the old Vice President Hadi and members of the Sanaa-based opposition.

The '4.5' serves as a common focus for most of the maritime security assessments. The examples are many. Siris Hartkorn (2011), for example, explores the rise of Al-Qaeda in Yemen when analysing maritime threats, as does Atle Mesøy (2010). Both of them focus on 'the first' conflict and examine the possibility of Al-Qaeda in the Arab Peninsula (AQAP) launching large-scale attacks on maritime targets. Al-Qaeda has done so before: in 2000 on USS *Cole* and USS *The Sullivans*, and in 2002 against the French tanker *Limburg*. As expressed by both Hartkorn and Mesøy, AQAP has stated that attacks against maritime targets, especially disruption of oil transportation and US naval ships, are a part of its strategy and that it can attack maritime targets (Hartkorn 2011, p. 28). Hartkorn discusses the 'second conflict' and the possibility of southern secession. However, the Southern Movement, or al-Harakat al-Ganubiyyat (Hirak) was born and led, loosely, by members of the Military Retirees' Co-ordination Council, a group of retired southern officers, some of whom had fought as allies of the North in 1993–1994. The movement has by and large been pacifist, with some notable localised exceptions. It quickly gained strength in southern Daliha and Radfan in Lajh, and these areas are today more or less outside government control. However, the fragmented nature of the movement ensured that there were few alternatives to government institutions. By the summer of 2009, there were efforts to co-ordinate the movement more closely, through the creation of the so-called Council of the Peaceful Southern Revolution on 12 June 2009. Led by retired General Hassan Ahmed Baoom, the group incorporated old jihadists such as Tareq Al Fadhil. Many notable and popular southern leaders are outside this organisation. This means that they are fragmented. While southern cessation thus remains highly unlikely, riots in port cities such as Aden do present a threat to ships using the port facilities.

As for Al-Qaeda, the examples of attacks against ships are old. The often-stated examples are the attacks on USS *The Sullivans* and USS *Cole* in 2000, and the *Limburg* in 2002. However, Al-Qaeda's international organisation has been severely weakened since 11 September 2001, and was almost destroyed in 2004. Al-Qaeda in Yemen today is the creation of the 2006 prison break in Sanaa, and is in many ways a new organisation. Some observers were rightly concerned that Al-Qaeda may exploit the Arab Spring to expand its holdings in Yemen (Castro e Almeida 2012). Moreover, in 2011, an Al-Qaeda-affiliated local umbrella organisation, Ansar al-Sharia, seized parts of the Abayan province, including the capital of Zinjbar, as well as several other cities. By May 2012, however, the government went on the counter offensive, and it does not seem like Al-Qaeda is on the verge of establishing an off-shore capacity capable of staging maritime terrorist attacks, as predicted by several analysts in the wake of 9/11 (Castro e Almeida 2012). This does not mean that the Al-Qaeda in Yemen will refrain from attacking maritime targets. Onshore Yemeni oil installations are especially tempting targets. But maritime targets have proven much harder to hit than expected and maritime operations are tactically more challenging.

It should be kept in mind that the near future will most likely see a re-strengthening of the central power in Yemen. The army, which split over the issue of the Arab Spring into an Ali Abdellah Saleh fraction and a fraction supporting the opposition, is slowly re-integrating. This process has been riddled with problems, but has enabled the army to concentrate enough resources against e.g. Al-Qaeda and oust it from most of the cities it conquered under the Arab Spring. Possibly, these developments could stop and Saleh loyalists within the army could create conflict, however, at the time of writing, both ex-President Saleh's nephew Mohammed Abdullah (Republican Guard's 3rd Brigade) and air-force commander Mohammed Saleh al-Ahmar, the half-brother of the president, have stepped down. While there might be obstacles in the future, the reconciliation agreement in the capital seems to be relatively on track, with the major weakness of failing to deal with the Houthi and the southern conflicts completed in the negotiations. The effect is nevertheless that the pressure will mount more strongly on Al-Qaeda. On one hand, this will lead to less resources for Al-Qaeda attacks on third parties; on the other hand, the losses in the battlefield might inspire Al-Qaeda to mount relatively small 'terrorist attacks', such as the militants' April 2012 attacks on the pipelines, or the suicide attack in Sanna of 21 May and, perhaps the most successful of the attacks, the killing of Brigadier Salim Ali Qatan, the commander of the anti Al-Qaeda operations in the south. However, it should be understood that the focus will most likely be onshore, as the infrastructure needed for offshore operations becomes harder and harder to get when the anti-Al-Qaeda offensive in the south mounts, and tactical considera-tions, leading to strikes directly at Yemeni government personnel, become more pressing.

The '4.5' conflicts are relevant for the security landscape but it seems that maritime manifestations will be rare. All of the above conflicts are important in their own ways, but too much attention on them removes other, more structural, issues from our focus. Modern security studies have been successful in asking new questions: who the security is for; who defines the threats against security; indeed, who defines what security is? (Williams 2008, pp. 7–10). It might just be that our habitual focus challenges our ability to see several other security challenges intervening and interacting with the '4.5'. Yemen is centrally located in global trade and emigration patterns and non-state networks, and neighbouring states heavily influence its security landscape, as do the region's natural resources. These factors provide underlying structures of future conflicts while exacerbating the existing ones.

1. The two maritime highways

Yemen's maritime security is influenced by its geographical position in the world and its two gates: the 'Gate of Tears' (Bab el Mandeb) and its 'Gate to Fortune'. These two gates are indeed symbolic points on two maritime highways. The first maritime highway is the way through the Red Sea and past the Bab El Mandeb strait, through which an estimated 3.2 million barrels per day (bbl/d) flowed in 2009 alone (Cutler 2011). It is a major maritime highway, important for global trade. In this sense Yemen's importance becomes elevated, thus Yemeni security issues have direct relevance for faraway maritime countries like Norway and Greece, and Yemeni problems will have increased global effects because of Yemen's strategic importance.

Yemen is also situated in the middle of another maritime highway, the 'Gate to Fortune'. Yemen ties together the rich Gulf and even Europe to economically poorer East Africa. Yemen is the staging point for human traffickers, smuggling Somalis, Ethiopians and others out of Bosasso (Somalia) or Obock (Djibouti) before they are transported further into Saudi Arabia, the Gulf States or Europe (Jeureidini 2010). It serves as a gate to the hope of a new life for many. The Yemeni position on the two maritime highways means that it attracts the attention of crime syndicates capable of weakening the fabric of the Yemeni society itself.

Recent works in security studies have correctly highlighted the potential consequences of unregulated popular routes. They can weaken existing power structures, threaten social cohesion and identity, and can generate income for crime syndicates (Bali 2008, p. 471). At the same time, human trafficking across the Gulf of Aden has major impacts on the smuggled themselves, with smugglers trafficking humans in small and dangerous ships and at times killing their passengers when suspecting that they can be caught. In Yemen, many of the refugees from Somalia will face a challenging life in the refugee camps, while Ethiopian refugees will be returned (Human Rights Watch 2009).

In the Gulf of Aden, human smugglers have established elaborate organisations, often involved in arms trafficking and at times in piracy. One of the most prominent smugglers, the Somali Mohamed Bari Bari, for example, combines his business with piracy (Hansen 2012). Human smuggling ties in with arms smuggling, in general going from Yemen to Somalia as well as armed groups in Ethiopia and Eritrea (Hansen 2012). Many of the operatives are corrupt Yemeni officials, especially from the army, and profit from the lucrative trade contributions in exchange for corruption (Hansen 2012). Indeed, the Yemeni coastguard stresses that smuggling and human trafficking are some of its major challenges (Hansen 2012).

In this sense, insecurity in Yemen's regional surroundings contributes to its insecurity. Moreover, organised crime cartels in the region present a challenge to the international merchant fleets that seek to avoid being involved in trafficking and arms smuggling, and learn what to do when facing pirates or boats with human cargo on the verge of sinking. Importantly, these criminal networks create a black economy that further destabilises the governments in the region, including the Yemeni government. They are directly connected with onshore conflicts and, in the case of Yemen, with the '4.5' conflicts (Hansen 2012). One example is the Yemeni businessman, Fares Mohamed Hassan Manaa, accused by the United States of the massive smuggling of arms to Somalia, but also of supplying the northern

Houthi rebels with arms inside Yemen (The Council of the European Union 2011). Manaa is currently the governor for the Houthis in Saadah (Staff writer 2011).

The full extent of transnational maritime crime networks is hard to establish, but their reach seems to run high up in Yemeni elite circles. They exacerbate the '4.5' conflicts, corrupting the Yemeni governance structures and creating real dilemmas for maritime actors. In the Yemeni maritime landscape, livelihood security can also influence more traditional forms of security. It should be noted that Yemen is a fishing nation. Protection of its fishermen is high on the Yemeni agenda. Unfortunately, Yemen's neighbours also want to increase the role of their fishing industry. Fishing was an important element in the 1996 clash between Yemen and Eritrea over the Hanish islands. Although the issue was solved peacefully in 1998, tensions have lingered on and there have been frequent clashes between Yemeni and Eritrean coast guards and fishermen. As recently as March 2011, four Yemeni boats were boarded by Eritrea (Staff writer 2012a). This is perhaps also due to the fact that the 1998 agreement between the two countries recognised the rights of traditional fishing. After clarifications by the court it was indicated that this enabled Eritreans to fish in Yemeni waters, however, controversially, Yemen also maintained that the recognition of the traditional fishing rights enabled them to fish in Eritrean waters (Kwiatkowska 2000).[1]

It should be noted that traditional fishing habits in the region in many instances transcend maritime borders; indeed in many cases fishing patterns are older than the states in question, and in as many cases fishermen do not know where the maritime borders are. While there is a détente between Yemen and Eritrea and there are fishing agreements between Yemen and Somaliland, the problems have not been fixed and can be taken advantage of by leaders who need an excuse to rally local support. It should be mentioned that even 2012 saw serious incidents, including the kidnapping of an Eritrean soldier by Yemeni fishermen (Staff writer 2012b). There has been very limited interest on the part of the international community to solve these problems for the last 10 years, perhaps due to Eritrea's pariah status, Somaliland's lack of recognition and the unstable state of Somalia. However, if Somalia stabilises, a new Somali government should be expected to pursue more strongly the monitoring of Yemeni fishing as well as border demarcation, which may in turn lead to more tension. Adding to this are the region's un-demarcated maritime borders, as are the Somali-Yemeni borders.

It should further be noted that several of the Red Sea/Gulf of Aden nations have fishers who carry arms out of tradition, enabling small fishing conflicts to flare up into something larger. Yemeni fishermen have had serious problems with Eritrean fishermen, as well as Somaliland and Puntland's. The corruption of Yemeni officials, the weakness of Yemen's maritime capacities, both naval and coast guard, as well as the lack of cooperation between various Yemeni services, increase the opportunity for illegal fishing. Opportunities for illegal fishing are also created by the weakness of Yemen's neighbours, Eritrea, Djibouti and Somalia/Somaliland, which have larger problems with patrolling their waters. Many ships, especially Egyptian, Spanish, North Korean and Thai-registered vessels take advantage of the situation and attempt to exploit Yemeni resources, sometimes fully illegally, sometimes paying too little in fees, instead paying overheads to corrupt officials. This in turn spurs rumours, creating tension. The presence of Somali pirates, as well as armed guards hired for anti-pirate duties, also add to this situation. Pirates attack Yemeni and international ships, often hijacking Yemeni dhows and using them as mother ships. As armed guards and counter-pirate measures become ever more prominent amongst many of the wealthier shipping agencies, the poorer Yemeni coastal traffic became an increasingly common target for pirates during the spring of 2012, while ill-trained security guards shoot at Yemeni fishermen.[2]

2. The two 'great games' of the region

In addition to being positioned on two maritime highways, Yemen is also situated in the middle of two regional rivalries. The regional rivalry between Saudi Arabia and Iran has left its mark on the '4.5' and on maritime relations. Saudi Arabia and Iran have, over time, supported different allies in Lebanon, Bahrain, Syria and most probably in Yemen too. Saudi Arabia also keeps an eye on potential Iranian moves to support Saudi Arabia's own Shia population. It should not be assumed that the relationship is one of full hostility for there is also Iranian-Saudi cooperation, but the perception of rivalry – clearly present at many occasions – creates effects of its own, even in cases where it is not there (Wehrey *et al.* 2009).

This Saudi-Iranian rivalry is especially important in Yemen's third conflict, the Houthi rebellion. The rebellion broke out in 2004 in the Saadah district on the Saudi border, which is still its stronghold. The Houthis, manly hailing from the Shia Islamic tradition, maintain that they are fighting against Yemen's partnership with the United States as well as Saudi supported anti-Shia religious activism. Anti-Wahhabism also constitutes a crucial part of the Houthi agenda (International Crisis Group 2009). The rebels claim that Saudi Arabia has intervened already in 2004, by bombing a Houhti village. But matters did not come to a head until 2009, when Houthi rebels allegedly killed a Saudi security officer in a cross-border attack. The rebels took control of a mountainous territory inside Saudi Arabia's border region of Jabal al-Dukhan and occupied two villages inside Saudi territory (Staff writer 2009). This prompted a Saudi response: first aerial bombing, followed by the deployment of the Army.

Iran has often been accused of supporting the Houthis, although the exact degree of Iranian involvement is unknown (Smith and Worth 2012). However, it should be noted that the Zayidi Shiism of the Houthi rebels is closer to the forms of Yemen's Sunni Islam than it is to Iran's Shiism (Ali 1996, p. 9). There are important differences between the Zayidi form of Shiism and the Iranian Ja'afari Shiism. However, allegations of connections between Iran and the Houthis occur frequently (Smith and Worth 2012). Rumours of Iranian support for Eritrea-based efforts to resupply the Houthis were used as a justification for a Saudi naval blockade of the coast of Yemen. The fighting thus had direct maritime consequences (Smith and Worth 2012). Piracy also exacerbates Iranian-Saudi rivalry, as Iran deploys naval units in the Gulf of Aden and the Red Sea to fight pirates and could have contributed to the Saudi decision to block the Yemeni coastline. The keywords are tensions and the security dilemma as stated by realist scholars; fear is equally important in creating tension as facts and false rumours of engagement by one party could lead to very real counter-measures by another party. In itself, it is unlikely that Iranian-Saudi rivalry will trigger direct conflict; it can however further complicate existing conflicts, of which there are many.

The first regional rivalry also feeds into the second regional rivalry, as Eritrea frequently has been accused of gaining Iranian support. Again, the validity of these accusations can be doubted. It does however illustrate that the Eritrean-Ethiopian conflict still influences security dynamics in Yemen's vicinity. Ethiopia and Eritrea fought in 1998–2000 and Ethiopia attempted to isolate Eritrea by enlisting the support of Yemen and Sudan in a military alliance, claimed to target 'terrorists' but widely believed to target Eritrea (Staff writer 2003). However, from 2010 onwards Eritrea was steadily breaking out of diplomatic isolation and, despite the fishing issues with Yemen, the two countries formed a détente.

3. Conclusion

The '4.5' conflicts are important for Yemeni security and thus also for maritime security in the north-western Indian Ocean. Admittedly, there could be scenarios where these conflicts could have maritime ramifications. Yemeni tribes might, for example, kidnap maritime officers on leave in order to pressure the government for some concession, following old traditions of using foreigners to pressure the government into concessions. The Saddah conflict will have maritime implications if arms are smuggled across the sea to Yemen by Iranian vessels. If this happens, we could see a repetition of the Saudi maritime blockade; the larger the effort of Iran, the larger the blockade. Al-Hirak can create havoc in southern Yemen, perhaps enabling pirate cartels to launch attacks from there because of the lack of Police forces that could be deployed against such groups due to local anarchy. Al-Qaeda can attack maritime targets if regaining operative capacity or refocusing their efforts. However, too strong a focus on these conflicts, especially on Al-Qaeda activities, tends to overshadow some very important maritime security issues that are under–researched, and the trends are not pointing towards an increased importance of these conflicts. The existence of clandestine maritime criminal networks of gunrunners and human traffickers are possibly the most important; these networks and their trade fuel conflicts in Yemen and the Horn of Africa. Furthermore, they contribute to corruption and hamper Yemen's ability to deal with its internal problems. Another commonly neglected topic is the various fishing conflicts and maritime border demarcation issues that Yemen could face in the future. Yemen is also influenced by regional rivalries between Saudi Arabia and Iran and between Ethiopia and Eritrea.

The questions surrounding Yemen's maritime security should not focus solely on the '4.5', since new actors such as criminal networks warrant serious attention, as do new questions like whose security we are talking about and what a security issue can be sparked by. Moreover, Yemen's strength could also spark conflict should it seek to unwisely use its favourable geographic position or aggressively exploit disputed fishing resources.

Notes

1. For a description of the Yemeni view see Bin Sallam (2012).
2. MARISK statistics. Available at http://www.marisk.dk/index.php, accessed 15 May 2012.

References

Ali, A. (1996), *Islamic Dynasties of the Arab East: State and Civilization During the Later Medieval Times*. New Delhi: M.D. Publications Pvt. Ltd.

Bali, S. (2008), 'Population movements', in P.D. Williams, ed., *Security Studies, An Introduction*. London: Routledge, pp. 486–480.

Bin Sallam, M. (2012), 'First deputy minister: Yemen intends to demarcate borders with Somalia (Part II)', *Yemeni Times*, 12 March.

Castro e Almeida, M. (2012), *Al-Qaeda After Bin Laden*. Dubai: Al Mesbahr Publications.

Cutler, D. (2011), 'Fact box – some facts on the Bab al-Mandab shipping lane', *Reuters*, 4 June.

Hansen S.J. (2012), 'Yemen, regional political security issues', Noref briefing paper. Oslo: Noref.

Human Rights Watch (2009), 'Hostile shores', *HRW REPORT 1-56432-581-4*.

International Crisis Group (2009), 'Yemen, defusing the Sadaa time bomb', Middle East Report No. 86.

International Crisis Group (2011), 'Breaking point? Yemen's southern question', Middle East Report No. 114.

Jeureidini, R. (2010), 'Mixed migration flows, Somali and Ethiopian migration to Turkey', Report from the Centre for Migration and Refugee studies, American University of Cairo. Prepared for the Mixed Migration Task Force. Available at http://www.drc.dk/fileadmin/uploads/pdf/IA_PDF/Horn_of_Africa_and_Yemen/Mixed%20Migration%20through%20Somalia%20and%20across%20Gulf%20of%20Aden%20-%20Background%20study.pdf, accessed 1 August 2012.

Kwiatkowska, B. (2000), 'The Eritrea/Yemen arbitration: landmark progress in the acquisition of territorial sovereignty and equitable maritime boundary delimitation', *IBRU Boundary and Security Bulletin 2000*.

Mesøy, A. (2010), 'Holy war on the Horn: Al Shebab and Al-Qaeda on the Arabian peninsula', *Strategic Insights*, Vol. 5, no. 28, pp. 8–11.

Phillips, S. (2010), 'What comes next in Yemen', Carnegie Endowment Paper No. 107, March.

Smith, E. and Worth, R.F. (2012), 'With arms for Yemen rebels, Iran seeks wider mideast role', *New York Times*, 16 March.

Staff writer (2003), 'Horn "anti-terror alliance"', *BBC*, 13 January.

Staff writer (2009), 'Riyadh continues air raids on northern Yemen', *Press TV*, 24 December . Available at http://www.presstv.ir/detail.aspx?id=114578&sectionid=351020206, accessed 29 December 2009.

Staff writer (2010), 'YEMEN: capital city faces 2017 water crunch', *IRIN*, 23 March.

Staff writer (2011), 'Sadaa, a cry for help', *Yemen Post*, 6 November.

Staff writer (2012a), 'Eritrean foreign minister arrives in Sanaa, holds talks with Yemeni official', *Yemen Post*, 31 March.

Staff writer (2012b), 'Yemeni fisherman captures Eritrean soldier', *Yemen Post*, 19 March.

Wehrey, F., Karasik, T.W., Nader, A., Ghez, J.J., Hansell, L. and Guffey, R.A. (2009), *Saudi-Iranian Relations Since the Fall of Saddam: Rivalry, Cooperation, and Implications for U.S. Policy*. Santa Monica, CA: RAND Corporation.

Williams, P.D. (2008), *Security Studies, An Introduction*. London: Routledge.

Wyler, L.S. (2008), 'Weak and failing states: evolving security threats and U.S. policy', International Crime and Narcotics Foreign Affairs, Defense, and Trade Division, USA.

The abundant sea: prospects for maritime non-state violence in the Indian Ocean

Martin N. Murphy

Security Studies Program, Georgetown University, Washington, DC, USA

Maritime violence perpetrated by non-state actors is a feature of the Indian Ocean. This includes the piracy, which has occurred most prominently off Somalia but also in the waters of Bangladesh, India and Indonesia, and terrorism perpetrated by al-Qaeda, the Tamil separatist movement in Sri Lanka, the Liberation Tigers of Tamil Eelam (LTTE), and the Pakistani Islamist group Lashkar-e-Taiba (LeT) against the Indian city of Mumbai. This paper aims to chart why opportunities for non-state actors to use violence to advance their interests may continue across the region.

1. Introduction

The Indian Ocean is an ocean of abundance. The energy resources lying under the waters off East Africa promise to transform the lives of the people on the coast. Mineral deposits in international waters are being explored. Although its higher-value fisheries have been depleted, fish stocks overall remain high. Most importantly, the Indian Ocean is returning to its rightful role as the crossroads of world trade. But the Indian Ocean region (IOR) – its coastal states and hinterland states such as Afghanistan and Ethiopia – is populated by some countries where governments are fragile and others that are amongst the world's most unstable. States such as Kenya, marred by political corruption, have found managing the forces unleashed by rapid economic change difficult. Somalia, broken by clans struggling for control of scarce resources, and Pakistan, nearly broken by the machinations of political extremism, have exported their domestic troubles to others. One medium for that transfer has been the Indian Ocean itself.

Piracy, maritime terrorism and other illicit activities at sea arise out of opportunity driven by several factors, including geography, jurisdictional disagreement and the availability of the skills necessary to operate in the unforgiving marine environment. The most salient are the absence of effective security and the presence of reward for criminals and targets for terrorists. This combination of factors has been most propitious around the coast of South East Asia and the area which is the subject of this investigation, the Indian Ocean. This paper is not a jeremiad; it does not conclude that violent disorder will be the inevitable outcome of greater wealth and consequent competition between newly enriched states. Given, however, that piracy is thriving in the region and that three of the most successful examples of maritime terrorism have occurred around its shores, it would be myopic to assume that the Indian Ocean rim will not witness more criminally- and politically-inspired disorder at sea in the future.

Economic promise and political uncertainty

World commercial maritime traffic is expected to grow from around 22,000 billion ton-miles in 2000 to around 74,000 billion ton-miles by the mid-century. The Indian Ocean's centrality to this trade is unquestionable: more than 80% of the world's trade in oil crosses its waters, the bulk entering it through the Strait of Hormuz and leaving it eastwards through the Strait of Malacca (35%) and westwards via the Bab el-Mandeb (8%) on its way to the Suez Canal. India is expected to be the world's largest energy importer by 2050. The security of this trade, particularly the eastward movement that feeds the major economies of China, Korea and Japan, is especially sensitive. In addition, the ocean is transited by some 50% of the world's container traffic and one-third of the world's trade in non-oil bulk cargoes, agglomerating to some 100,000-ship movements annually (Michel and Sticklor 2012, pp. 9–12; DeSilva-Ranasinghe 2012).

Illegitimate goods are also being moved. The Indian Ocean is over-shadowed by the world's two most significant opium producing regions: the Golden Crescent, which embraces parts of Pakistan and Afghanistan, and the Golden Triangle, stretching across part of northern Myanmar and Thailand. Much of their output travels overland, but an unknown portion travels by sea depending upon the viability of the overland routes. While narcotics may stimulate the greatest concern, other smuggling networks move arms, migrants, traffic in human beings and engage in illegal, unregulated and unreported (IUU) fishing, all of which present serious problems. One of the great ironies of Somali piracy is that the abundant fishing grounds off the country's coast, whilst they have been the target of predatory fishing fleets from around the world, remain viable for the moment. But how they will fare if and when piracy is suppressed successfully remains an open question.

When it comes to undersea resources, around 40% of global offshore oil production comes from the Indian Ocean Region (IOR) already – primarily from the Arabian Gulf – but this could be added to substantially by supplies from East Africa, where a fault line which runs from Somalia to Madagascar is believed to constitute one of the planet's last remaining unexplored oil and gas provinces. Estimates suggest that Somalia alone might have oil reserves larger than those of Kuwait (UPI 2012). China's eagerness for minerals has led it to secure a license from the International Seabed Authority (ISA) to explore for polymetallic sulphide deposits in a 10,000 square kilometre block in the south-western Indian Ocean, a move that has alarmed India (Varma 2011).

The IOR, which is made up of 36 littoral and 14 adjacent hinterland states, is populated by 2.6 billion people, 40% of the global total. Its political context is one of inter-state competition and intra-state instability. The two sharpest inter-state contests are, first, the attempt by the United States to limit Iran's regional and nuclear ambitions; and second, between India and China, which share a common border through the Himalayas and fought a war as recently as 1962 that left India with deep scars. Each is vying for influence around the ocean's rim and amongst its smaller island nations as they advance their growing trade and natural resource interests.

When it comes to intra-state instability, 11 of the Indian Ocean region's 50 states are regarded as amongst the world's most unstable: Afghanistan, Burma, Burundi, Ethiopia, Iraq, Kenya, Pakistan, Somalia, Sudan, Yemen and Zimbabwe. Even India, a democracy that is regularly predicted to become one of the twenty-first century's great powers, is affected by the long-lasting Naxalite insurgency that troubles some 80 districts across nine states (down from 180 districts in 2009). These countries' instability has already created problems regionally or even destabilised their neighbours. All but four have coastlines.

At the same time, the complexion of the world's naval power is changing. Barring major war, the outcome of which is by its very nature unpredictable, the United States Navy (USN) is likely to remain pre-eminent globally. The character and location of the challenges it faces are, however, changing. The equivalent of fleet-on-fleet engagement will no longer take place only at sea. The development of long-range coastal-based missile forces, using aerial and space-based surveillance and targeting assets, means that expeditionary forces must now be prepared to engage and defeat well-protected and well-resourced land-based and sub-surface defences intent on denying navies access to their littoral areas (an intent known as anti-access/area denial or A^2/AD in military parlance), out to distances potentially in excess of 1000 nautical miles. Both the land- and sea-based elements of this developing competition are technologically demanding and therefore hugely expensive.

The United States believes it is confronted by two such challengers: China and Iran. Although there is a substantial technological disparity between the two, overcoming either one gives rise to unique and formidable military and political difficulties. Matching each one geographically means that the USN is concentrating its resources in the western Pacific and Persian Gulf, a move that has been labelled a 'pivot to Asia'. Competing with them technologically (and affordably) means that it is focusing its investment on fewer ships armed with more capable war-fighting systems. The USN's presence outside these areas of concentration is becoming less (although it will not be absent altogether) while the deployment of its hugely capable platforms on lesser missions such as maritime security is becoming harder to justify. Its principal allies will follow it down this path to the extent that they can.

The likely consequences of these changes are plain. For the USN, maritime security will be limited increasingly to the protection of the sea lines of communications (SLOCs) connecting its areas of concentration. Maritime security outside these corridors is likely to be covered by aerial assets not ships. This will not mean that the resources devoted to maritime security – to deterring and if necessary defeating political and criminal non-state threats – will necessarily decline overall. On the contrary, they may well increase. China and India, for example, have both embarked on extensive naval ship-building programmes, although most of the investment is going into hulls and systems designed for regional power confrontations or, in the case of the Chinese Navy, into platforms that can also contribute to the anti-access/area denial (A^2/AD) capabilities. Even smaller regional navies are acquiring relatively high-end capabilities. Malaysia, for example, is buying French-built Scorpene-class submarines (SSKs), which have limited utility against low-end threats.

The pattern of naval activity in the Indian Ocean is consequently likely to become more diverse, revoling around several potential risk factors, the most prominent of which are arguably:

- the US-led confrontation with Iran and its aftermath;
- the competition for regional influence between India and China;
- the clash of wills between India and Pakistan, which may become more unpredictable if Pakistan's internal politics and therefore stability comes under increasing strain; the collapse of all or part of the Pakistani state – which would inevitably draw in Afghanistan, India and Iran – could ignite a hybrid conflict involving state and non-state actors made more dangerous by the presence of nuclear weapons;
- competition for secure access to African land-based natural resources and oceanic sub-sea resources, by China particularly; this competition could become dangerously complicated if the conflicts that have marred such competition in West Africa were to be replicated in the east (Gilblom 2012); and
- the ever-present prospect of state failure, which for the moment is focused on the Horn of Africa and across the Gulf of Aden in Yemen.

More naval vessels will be active in the Indian Ocean – including ships suitable for maritime security operations – but the demands of inter-state competition and the possibility of navy-on-navy engagement may lessen the focus on maritime security. The assumption, in other words, that maritime security addresses a concern that all states share and which can therefore bring them together to find solutions to a common problem – one that underlies the US Navy's *Cooperative Strategy for 21st-Century Seapower* (Department of the Navy 2007) and has been suggested by India's former foreign minister Shivshankar Menon (2009) – will be put to the test and maybe found wanting. States, moreover, that are attracted to China's authoritarian economic model might, depending on whether or China succeeds in its East and South China Sea claims, attempt a similar 'territorialisation' of their adjacent waters.[1]

2. The pirate opportunity

Piracy arises as a consequence of economic dislocation on land, not at sea. What occurs on the water is merely its most visible manifestation. It cannot occur just anywhere. Ships carrying items whose value, relative to the risk, exceeds whatever is available to the perpetrators on land must pass by at an acceptable range from the coast; the shape of the coast must provide safe anchorages and launching points, ideally ones that require detailed local knowledge to navigate safely; political authority on land must be incapable or unwilling to take suppressive action either because it is absent or because it connives in what is taking place; the police must therefore be limited in their ability to respond effectively; conflict and disorder can be conducive but not if it forces gangs to take disproportionately expensive security measures to protect their bases on land (Murphy 2009, p. 28). The existence of an experienced maritime community – usually fishermen – is generally essential, but as the Somali example has demonstrated, this base need neither be large nor long-established provided it can be supplemented by specialist training; in 2001 a cadre of about 300 men were trained in ship-boarding and other fishery protection techniques by a private security company and when its contract was prematurely terminated they turned to piracy (Murphy 2011b, p. 22).

In fact, Somali pirates are not inheritors of a tradition, but they just might be starting one. The Indian Ocean is no stranger to pirate activity. However, apart from piracy in the Strait of Malacca, where it has persisted over centuries, most piracy elsewhere in the ocean and its connected waters has generally been small-scale. What is occurring today in the Malacca Strait, off Bangladesh and off India, fits that pattern; the magnitude of the current outbreak off Somalia is unprecedented. Historically-speaking it is probable that only the activities of the Red Sea Men, British and American pirates displaced from the Caribbean, who raided ships out of a base in Madagascar between 1693 and 1721, can match it in importance.[2]

Despite claims to the contrary, piracy does not spread easily to other localities. Local outbreaks have local causes. If outbreaks are not confined to their point of origin, however, they can range widely, although the Somali pirates' achievements have been exceptional. They have used 'mother ships' to operate thousands of miles from their bases – compared to about 100 nautical miles for South China Sea pirates in the 1990s, who were previously considered to be the most mobile – and taken on fuel and supplies at distant ports and from remote islands.

The Somali business model, moreover, will be hard to replicate in its entirety: no other pirates in modern times have been able to hold ships hostage for months without fear of recapture or to operate freely without fear of arrest. This is due partly to the nature of Somali clan relationships and the resulting close connections between the pirates and the country's various political leaders, in the north-eastern territory of Puntland particularly (Reuters 2012). However, it also owes much to the reluctance of naval powers to intervene on land in time-honoured counter-piracy fashion. To a degree this reluctance arises out of the United States' experience in Mogadishu between 1993 and 1995, and especially to the events recounted by Mark Bowden in his book *Black Hawk Down* (2000). It is also because of the nature of the modern state system, which privileges state sovereignty over state responsibility; within its own borders a state can treat or mistreat its population almost with impunity.

Nonetheless, parts of the model may be adopted in areas where economic disequilibria are matched similarly to political failure. Even in states with less complicit political leadership and more effective policing than Somalia, it is demonstrably possible to hold small numbers of high-value crew-members hostage for as long as it takes to obtain ransom; this is the model used by South American kidnappers against commercial executives and Nigerian gangs against oil company employees. This monetisation of hijacked crews could present the next generation of pirates with rick-pickings if the anticipated East African oil bonanza triggers social tensions similar to those that have emerged in other African oil provinces.

3. Piracy-terrorism nexus

The fear has been expressed regularly that pirates and terrorists might find common cause. Each, however, is motivated differently: the first broadly criminal, the second broadly political, such that it appears unlikely this coming together will occur unless they are driven to it by some policy miscalculation, such as an undifferentiated bombing campaign. Pirates have shown no inclination to form any sort of common front with insurgents or terrorists, although this has not precluded either side from striking opportunistic deals when the need arose.

Looked at in practical terms neither side needs the other. Terrorists do not need pirate help to achieve what they want. The contacts that do occur are often the result of the two groups occupying the same physical, not conceptual, space. Contacts between pirates and al-Shabaab in Somalia, which have included the payment of 'taxes' and the use of the al-Shabaab-controlled port of Kismayo as a supply base, have been little more than acts of convenience based often on clan connections, and do not represent anything approaching an alliance.

4. The terrorist temptation

It is striking that three of the most successful maritime terrorism campaigns have been conducted in the IOR region, and while each one may ultimately have failed, they all achieved noticeable tactical success. The three campaigns are those conducted by al-Qaeda around the Arabian Peninsula, which attacked energy targets and launched one attack on a navy ship, the Liberation Tigers of Tamil Eelam (LTTE), which created a sophisticated naval arm to support its land-based insurgency on Sri Lanka, and the Lashkar-e-Taiba (LeT) attack on prestige targets in Mumbai, India's commercial capital.

Al-Qaeda

In 2000 al-Qaeda mounted first an unsuccessful attack and then a successful attack against US warships refuelling in Aden harbour, Yemen. Both targets were Aegis-equipped destroyers of the Arleigh Burke class, first the USS *Sullivans* and secondly the USS *Cole*. The second attack killed 17 and wounded 39 US servicemen. The ship did not sink but images of its badly-damaged hull as it was lifted back to the United States for repair symbolized US weakness in the face of two determined men willing to face death in order to place a 500lb device close to a well-armed warship.

This attack caused consternation around the world and led to substantial changes in vessel protection protocols whenever a US – or indeed any other western warship – visited a foreign port. However, despite the considerable publicity it generated, al-Qaeda did not repeat the feat and because of the heightened level of security that now accompanies warship visits and transits it is unlikely they will be able to use the same tactic in the future (BBC News 2012).

In 2001 Khalid Sheik Mohamed, the mastermind behind the 9/11 aircraft attacks, planned to sail a mother ship loaded with high explosive into the crowded shipping lanes passing through the Strait of Hormuz. Small raiding craft would have been lowered over the side and launched against high value targets such as oil tankers or warships. Once these boats had either detonated their charges or been destroyed, the mother ship would have been maneuvered close to a significant target and its massive explosive charge triggered. The operation was cancelled for fear that its discovery would compromise the much more important 'planes operation' against New York and Washington.

Subsequent attacks were designed to disrupt global energy supplies. The immediate fruit of the targeting switch was the 2002 attack on a VLCC, the *Limberg*, which, like the attack on the USS *Cole*, was launched from Yemen. In 2004 the al-Qaeda affiliate in Iraq (AQIM) mounted a coordinated boat attack against two oil terminals located off Basra through which the bulk of the country's oil exports were shipped. Three US servicemen lost their lives but the terminals were largely unharmed. In 2010 an obscure al-Qaeda affiliate tried to sink a tanker, the *M Star*, in the Straits of Hormuz, but it escaped with only minor damage (Worth 2010). Several attacks were also attempted on various land-based oil facilities and refineries with little success.

All these attacks fitted into an al-Qaeda economic strategy, which has been known about since the mid-2000s (Hunt 2007, pp. 14–17). The fact that the raid on Bin Laden's Abbottabad compound revealed that he still regarded this strategy – and attacks on oil tankers in particular – as viable despite the setbacks, the acknowledged practical difficulties and the fact that so little had been achieved was perhaps surprising (Johnson 2011; Stevens 2011).

Liberation Tigers of Tamil Eelam

The Tamil Tigers created what many observers consider to be the twentieth century's most effective non-state navy, designed to protect the land-based insurgency's seaward flank and the supply routes upon which the insurgency depended. It did this by conducting traditional sea control and sea denial operations, and by mounting amphibious assaults on government positions. It also conducted water-borne suicide missions using domestically-manufactured 'stealth' craft, launched bomb attacks against Sri Lankan Navy (SLN) recruits and other personnel, in a campaign that came close to breaking the navy's morale, and deployed a range of effective home-produced naval mines and water-borne improvised explosive devices (WBIEDs). Before its demise it was looking to build its own submarines and had established links to Columbian drug cartels, possibly to exchange information on the design, manufacture and operation of submersibles. The Sea Tigers' primary mission, however, was the protection of supply ships. The LTTE created an international network that raised money from amongst expatriate communities overseas and conducted criminal activities that included drug smuggling, which fed the organisation's hugely effective arms and equipment purchasing organisation. Using techniques to hide beneficial ownership that the Iranian state now uses to hide its ownership of its oil tanker fleet, these purchases were conveyed to drop-off points close to Sri Lanka, where they were trans-shipped at sea into fast moving delivery craft which then ran to the coast covered by heavily-armed gunboats that fought – and for the most part won – running battles with SLN vessels (Rosett 2012). It was only once the SLN was able to locate and track Tamil Tigers provisioning ships beyond the range of the Sea Tigers' gunships that it was able to cut the insurgency's supply lines. Once the Tigers could no longer replace their material losses the Sri Lankan Army was able to exploit a split in the Tigers' ranks and bring the rebellion to an end in 2009.

It is perhaps too early to tell whether or not the greater autonomy that the Tamils fought for will be achieved through negotiation. If they once again resort to arms they will not succeed without a maritime arm. The Tigers were defeated because they were wedded to the territory they held between 2002 and 2006. When the government rearmed and renewed the conflict the Tamils fought the subsequent war conventionally in defence of that territory rather than returning to the guerrilla tactics that had won it for them. In the face of more heavily-armed SLN boats available in greater numbers, and the adoption by the SLN of tactics that mirrored their own, the Sea Tigers found they had nowhere to hide.

Regional political interests had also turned against them. India, which had originally regarded Sri Lanka with hostility, after 2006 provided the Sri Lankan government with the military advice and help it needed, partly because of the Tigers' own political ineptitude, but also to counter the help China was also providing and its growing regional influence. Only if India or China achieves a position of influence on the island that the other finds intolerable and sees utility in supporting renewed Tamil violence is it likely that an armed Tamil insurrection will find success in the future (Murphy 2006, pp. 6–10; Murphy 2009, pp. 310–321; Povlock 2011).

Lashkar-e-Taiba

Assaults on land-based targets from the sea are not new, but the scale of the 2008 attack on Mumbai (Bombay), which focused on popular and historical sites in India's commercial and media capital resulting in at least 172 deaths, was extraordinary (Binnie and La Miere 2008; Rabasa *et al.* 2009). LeT, which is held responsible for the attack and the 2001 assault on the Indian parliament building, is a substantial Islamist militant group. Based in Pakistan, it supposedly has close links to the Pakistani intelligence organisation Inter-services Intelligence (ISI). Indeed, while some have suggested that LeT may have managed the assault on its own, it is hard to envision how a group without previous maritime experience could have managed the complexity of the maritime domain, which included leaving Karachi in a cargo vessel, navigating a course over 500 miles, intercepting and capturing an Indian fishing vessel at roughly the mid-point of the voyage, making a second cross-deck transfer to small inflatable boats close to Mumbai, followed by a surreptitious approach to the busy port, without experienced naval training. Palestinian raiders, intent on striking Israel, failed on more than one occasion to complete less complex voyages.

The most probable motive for the attack was to increase tensions between India and Pakistan. While Muslim militants regard this as a desirable end in itself, the more specific reason could have been to relieve pressure on militant encampments along the Afghan-Pakistan border by forcing the Pakistan Army to relocate units to the Indian frontier to counter possible reprisals. Consequently, the fact that cool heads prevailed in Delhi after the attack is to be applauded. While the move might appear to offer Pakistan few advantages, and indeed prejudice its own national security, many outside observers believe ISI is not entirely under the control of Pakistan's government and acts in support of militant Islamist organisations on its own initiative. That the leader of LeT had not been questioned by the Pakistani authorities nearly four years after the attack raised questions about what possible links may have existed between them (Lieby 2012).

The attackers' use of firearms rather than explosives might be explained by the added media coverage; the July 2006 railway bombing killed over 200 people but yielded far less attention. It might also explain why the group chose to approach the target by boat. A considerable quantity of weapons and ammunition was required to mount the attack, both of which could be transported readily by sea. The desire to maintain unit cohesion might be another reason; if the raiding party had been intercepted the raid would have failed immediately, but once they arrived together the attack proceeded according to the plan. Poor navigation, a fault that marred more than one Palestinian assault, could have forced the group to have improvised its attack on the basis of inadequate knowledge; that accurate navigation was not an issue reinforces the impression that the group had experienced naval guidance. Poor weather during the voyage or at the landing point could also have disrupted the operation, as it similarly affected the Palestinians, but again careful planning minimised the risk. The length of time at sea, which increased the possibility of interception, would appear to have been a risk, except we now know how poor Indian coastal security was, something about which the Pakistani authorities would have been aware. The use of communications at sea could have raised suspicions about a suspect approach, and indeed a questionable transmission was intercepted but unfortunately ignored.

Using the sea to attack coastal targets undoubtedly presents any potential group with difficulties. This may be outweighed by the defender's problems which are potentially much larger; the surveillance and response resources required to protect a coastline as long as India's are considerable (Pushpita 2011; Sharma 2011). Concerns about possible future attacks have apparently forced the Indian Navy to withdraw several of the ships it had deployed on counter-piracy missions off Somalia closer to its own coast.

5. Implications

Somalia's pirates have revealed a weakness that the world appears reluctant to recognise: that maritime security is an orphan. This, arguably, has two causes. The first is one of nomenclature: maritime security is not solely maritime, it is littoral. The security of offshore waters is linked inextricably with security on land. In places where landward security is not assured, seaward insecurity is a real or potential problem. Neither neighbours nor maritime states have proved keen to intervene in cases of state failure, in some cases because they lack the resources to do so but more often because they are unwilling to risk the political capital needed to break the norm of non-intervention. States have demonstrated that breaking this norm is hard, even in cases of genocide such the Balkan conflicts of the 1990s, Rwanda and East Timor; it has proved much harder where the stakes are lower and, given that much of what happens at sea is beyond the purview of most people, the stakes in maritime security are amongst the lowest. The second cause is the confusion over whether maritime security is driven primarily by politics or economics. The answer for the past century has been economics. While this era has witnessed two titanic naval struggles, the exploitation of the sea has continued generally without interruption outside the areas immediately affected. The economic rationale for maritime security was gradually reinforced by the decline in national flags and the rise in open registers which have flourished because they offer lower financial and compliance outlays. In an age when the pressure on transportation costs as a proportion of a good's final price has been relentless and shipping industry margins have consequently been squeezed sometimes to the point of imperceptibility, any opportunity to reduce expenditure has been welcomed.

This is not to deny that states have jealously guarded their legal rights at sea. Some, such as the Philippines and Indonesia, have seen these rights in almost patrimonial terms. Nonetheless, in countries where budgets were tight and where coastal territories were not under substantial threat, economic arguments prevailed and practical protective measures such as coast guards and navies have been starved of investment. Neither Indonesia nor Nigeria, for example, felt it necessary to make substantial investments in coastal forces despite increasing numbers of pirate incidents in their waters.

This emphasis on economics faced no serious opposition from the United States Government or the US Navy. Lacking a merchant marine of its own, and in the absence of a legal or economic link with the commercial shipping of other nations, it has not seen trade protection as anything other than exceptional, for example during the Iran-Iraq 'Tanker War' between 1984 and 1988 when US Navy ships protected Kuwaiti tankers reflagged as US vessels. Mostly, it has viewed the international shipping network as a robust and self-sustaining system, guided by a 'hidden hand', that needs and benefits from the lack of anything more than limited technical guidance from bodies such as the International Maritime Organisation (IMO).

Certainly US attitudes about maritime security changed following 9/11. Measures were taken to prevent terrorist abuse of the international container system and US domestic legislation establishing a monitoring regime for its home ports was adopted almost word-for-word by the IMO and implemented at other ports around the world. While these measures imposed an expensive supervisory layer onto international trade – the efficacy of which remains the subject of debate – the US did not try and change the substance of the international system. It had no desire to, as the physical realisation of free market principles was its system.

The Somali pirates have provided a salutary reminder that maritime security has a political dimension. Piracy may be a product of economic dislocation in the country or region in which it occurs, but responses to it are essentially political. In the zero-sum world of mercantilism, everyone understood that one state's gain was another's loss;[3] in the more economically-enlightened era of free markets this linkage has been diluted but not submerged entirely as status, influence and ultimately power flows to states that are seen to secure trade most effectively. Despite this, summoning the political will to suppress piracy has never been easy because of the immense cost of naval construction and operations. Today it appears to be harder than ever. The most capable naval states no longer have adequate numbers of ships appropriate to the task, while the injection of human rights concerns have changed the way perpetrators are viewed and dealt with. States prepared to surmount these obstacles must see some larger political advantage. In this they are no different from their historical predecessors. When the Roman general Pompey suppressed the Cicilian pirates in 67BC he did so on the way to defeating a more substantial foe, King Mithridates of Pontus (Murphy 2012).

Similar patterns of state behaviour can be observed off Somalia today: China has a genuine interest in protecting its seafarers, but without the excuse of piracy it would have found it harder to justify an Indian Ocean presence including, quite possibly, an operating base in the Seychelles, nor been able to learn valuable lessons that will aid future long-range, deep-water deployments (Page and Wright 2011; Singh 2011). The same could be said for India, Russia, Iran and the European Union; concerns larger than piracy have drawn them to the vast spaces of the Arabian Sea.

What the navies have *not* achieved is piracy suppression. The number of incidents was reduced but the pirate infrastructure within Somalia remains intact and the motivation to use it remains strong. The navies can claim to have contributed to this decline but not to have brought it about alone. The adoption of self-protection measures by ships, including the employment of armed guards, has been more influential. Legal restrictions have made many western states reluctant to arrest and prosecute pirate suspects, but the over-arching problem was that the US and other western navies in particular were operating in the absence of a coherent political policy for engagement with political, social, business and religious groups within Somalia who could help solve the piracy problem.

The United States arguably had the most to lose from this policy failure. The most damaging effect the Somali pirates have achieved is to show up shortcomings in US maritime leadership. Somali pirates were *allowed* to achieve what they have because of US distraction or indifference. The US Navy's failure, in tandem with its coalition partners, to curb their activities raises doubts about America's willingness to devote the political resources necessary to make maritime security a reality; doubts that raise questions about its position as the 'natural leader' of global or regional maritime security regimes. The United States is the ultimate guarantor of maritime security. It is a role loosely analogous to the dollar's position as the world's reserve currency; it gives the United States a huge advantage, one that the US should fight to retain (Murphy 2011a).

The rationale for the reassertion of US maritime leadership is compelling. In the Somali context this begins with a coherent *political* strategy for those parts of Somalia that are willing and able to engage in a productive dialogue because, as Wess Mitchell and Jakob Grygriel (2009) have pointed out, failed states 'are not only a source of domestic calamities; they are also potentially a source of great power competition' and that 'America's global rivals are doing what aspirant powers have done at moments of transition for millennia [...] probing the top state on the outer limits of its power commitments [...] reading America's responses to gauge how much latitude they have to make low-cost revisions to the system in their favor' (Mitchell and Grygiel 2011). Somalia and the presence of rival navies justified rhetorically by a common need to suppress piracy fits these descriptions well.

One beneficiary of these hesitations has been the private security industry. There were about 10 maritime private security companies (PSCs) in the world half a decade ago, and now there are more than 160, drawn from around the globe, although most are American and British. Shipping companies are turning to private contractors because, having waited for the major western navies to come to their aid off Somalia, they have realised they are not coming. Instead, they need to take defensive measures, including the deployment of armed guards, to defend their ships in much the same way oil companies off Nigeria and elsewhere now employ them to defend fixed offshore installations and vulnerable offshore supply vessels. The continuing growth of offshore extractive industries, including the development of East African oil and gas fields, is likely to ensure that maritime PSCs will grow in size and influence. Supposedly, the introduction of these companies will free navies to concentrate on the high-intensity conflict that will be fought with high-technology weapons on, below and above the sea. An alternative reading is that any navy that fails to protect trade has forgotten its roots. It has taken pirates to show us that modern navies lack the resources to fulfil missions that have been theirs for 200 years. The relentless cost of modern war has concentrated more powerful weapons in fewer hulls, so that modern high-technology navies are more like those of Elizabethan

England and post-Revolutionary America, except that instead of depending on privateers they are now coming upon private contractors for the fulfilment of some combat missions.

The final group is the terrorists who have observed what the pirates have achieved (Lia 2007, p. 401; Biyokulule Online 2008). The increasing economic abundance on, below and around the Indian Ocean – and the competition and conflicts to which this may give rise – offers plentiful targets for their malevolence. Given, furthermore, that India, Pakistan, China and possibly Iran are nuclear powers, and given also the disparity in conventional military power between, for example, India and Pakistan or the United States and Iran, states may choose to advance their interests using non-state actors (Barnes 2012). Superficially, at least, all the elements are in place for this to happen.

Experience suggests that either outcome – violence perpetrated by non-state actors for political ends either autonomously or as a state proxy – is easier to imagine taking place in the maritime domain than to perform successfully. The sea is not a happy hunting-ground for terrorists: there are few people to kill; just as few to watch them being killed; seafarers are not people who the world's population identifies with easily and therefore their deaths or perils elicit little sympathy; worthwhile economic targets are generally large and robust; and, finally, oceans and coastal seas are unforgiving environments, the mastery of which requires special skills and equipment.

The most likely terrorist methods have already been tried and the factors that make them successful revealed. Terrorist attacks carried out in the maritime domain can achieve local effects; attacks carried out by the LTTE in Sri Lanka and the various 'Moro' groups in the Philippines demonstrated this. However, once the effects achieved a scale which attracted the interest of major powers, the counter-vailing skills and resources they were able to bring to bear were usually sufficient to curtail or terminate the rebellion; in the case of the Philippines the US initiated the Joint Special Operations Task Force – Philippines (JSOTF-P) (Joint Special Operations Task Force n.d.), while India and China came to the assistance of the Sri Lankan Government (Smith 2010, pp. 40–44). These attacks and the effectiveness of the responses provide another lesson: these were island-based insurgencies whose critical *dependence* upon access to the sea for supplies could be used against them.

The strategy of attacking economic targets, pursued to a degree by al-Qaeda, remains unfulfilled. The focus on shipping appears to be wrong-headed. The world is too dependent upon oil to be concerned by one-off attacks. Terrorist groups must demonstrate that they can inflict overwhelming damage repeatedly and at will before they can achieve anything close to their aims. The difficulties of closing a strait such as Malacca or Bab el-Mandeb are immense and would provoke a strong naval response. In this sense terrorists should be looking across Africa to what the politico-criminal group MEND and its criminal successors have achieved off Nigeria: repeated attacks on offshore oil infrastructure and large-scale thefts from oil pipelines on land have moved the world oil price upward. Despite this, however, they have not moved it enough to cause a crisis. Only attacks on the scale possibly achievable by Iran against shipping in the Strait of Hormuz could turn an oil shortage into a weapon (Hodge 2012). As the century progresses and US domestic production of 'tight' oil increases, American vulnerability will decrease. Chinese and Indian dependence, however, may well move in the other direction.

The demanding nature of the maritime domain suggests that state support can be an important enabler for sea-borne terrorist operations; it was undoubtedly critical to the success of the Mumbai atrocity which was carried out with military precision. The evidence points strongly to Pakistani authorship and it is highly likely that the raiders were trained by Pakistani serving or retired Special Operations Forces (SOF) and supported by ISI intelligence. The group's command of small boat handling was highly impressive. Attacks on this scale and over this distance require military-quality planning and execution. Even this, however, may not be sufficient: the Palestinian groups received foreign military assistance but this did not prevent several of their raids going seriously wrong (Murphy 2009, pp. 290–297).

6. Conclusion

The Indian Ocean Region is embarking on a period of strong economic growth. That growth and the social disruption that accompanies it will heighten tensions within already fragile states and between neighbouring states. Whenever that instability spills across borders – as it has most recently in the Horn of Africa – external powers will intervene in pursuit of their own interests. The disorder will create opportunities for pirates and, because of the fragmentation in naval power and the often orphan status of maritime security, will encourage the rise of private security providers to protect the world's trade and the resource-extractive infrastructure that the world's economy depends upon.

These changes will incite terrorist interest. They will share the sea with smugglers and occasionally with pirates, and may behave like both these groups in support of their own land-based operations. The use they make of the sea as an attack medium will depend on circumstances and technology. If terrorists view the use of the maritime medium as a necessary and viable option then, providing they can assemble the necessary skills and equipment, they will use it. But unless exploitation of the maritime domain is essential to their entire operation they will abandon it as soon as less risky options present themselves.

Arguably they will only be successful if they benefit from state support such that they can mount effective land assaults from the sea as they did against Mumbai, or if they are given access to land-based stand-off weapons with adequate over-the-horizon (OTH) surveillance assets capable of acquiring targets, which does not necessarily imply pilotless aircraft (UAVs) or other aerial assets, but could be something as simple as fishing boats with satellite phones. State actors may alternatively prove willing to provide them with light-weight precision-guided munitions (PGMs) capable of being fired in numbers from swarms of small vessels or from coastal locations. The presence of states in the IOR with both these resources and the political will to render this assistance should not be under-estimated. Until that happens, however, maritime terrorism will remain latent but rarely realised, as it has been for the past half-century.

Notes

1. The most comprehensive analysis of this issue is by Kraska (2011). For further reference see also Oxman (2006).

2. Ritchie (1986) gives probably the most rounded account of this period. The piracy perpetrated by the Qasimi tribe off what is now the UAE is also of interest. The fullest account is by Davies (1997).
3. One is reminded here of Gore Vidal's quip: 'It's not enough to succeed. Others must fail'.

References

Biyokulule Online (2008), 'Jihadist website commentary argues "maritime terrorism" strategic necessity'. Available at http://www.biyokulule.com/view_content.php?articleid=1156, accessed 28 August 2012.

Barnes, J.E. (2012), 'US says Iran plans to disrupt oil trade', *Wall Street Journal*, 19 July. Available at http://online.wsj.com/article/SB10000872396390444097904577537221896965492. html?mod=WSJ_World_LeadStory, accessed 24 August 2012.

BBC News (2012), 'US Navy ship fires on boat in Gulf', 16 July. Available at http://www.bbc.co.uk/news/world-middle-east-18862480, accessed 24 August 2012.

Binnie, J. and La Miere, C. (2008), 'In the line of fire: could Mumbai happen again?', *Jane's Intelligence Review*, posted 11 December.

Bowden, M. (2000), *Black Hawk Down: A Story of Modern War*. New York: Penguin Books.

Davies, C.E. (1997), *The Blood-Red Arab Flag: An Investigation into Qasimi Piracy, 1797–1820*. Exeter: University of Exeter Press, 1997.

Department of the Navy (2007), 'A cooperative strategy for 21st century seapower'. Available at http://www.navy.mil/maritime/Maritimestrategy.pdf, accessed 28 August 2012.

DeSilva-Ranasinghe, S. (2012), 'The Indian Ocean Region and Australia's national interests', *Future Directions International*, 29 May. Available at http://www.futuredirections.org.au/files/sap/may/FDI_Strategic_Anlaysis_Paper_-_29_May_-_Fact_Sheet_-_The_Indian_Ocean_Region_and_Australias_National_Interests_1.pdf, accessed 1 July 2012.

Gilblom, K. (2012), 'Kenya, Somalia border row threatens exploration', *Reuters*, 20 April. Available at http://www.futuredirections.org.au/files/sap/2012/FDI_Strategic_Analysis_Paper_-_17_August_2012.pdf, accessed 14 August 2012.

Hodge, N. (2012), 'In war against Iran, US firepower would vie with guerrilla tactics', *Wall Street Journal*, 17 April. Available at http://online.wsj.com/article/SB1000142405270230417710457731444082569820.html, accessed 14 August 2012.

Hunt, M. (2007), 'Bleed to bankruptcy: economic targeting tactics in the global jihad', *Jane's Intelligence Review*, January, pp. 14–17.

Johnson, K. (2011), 'Al Qaeda considered attacking oil tankers', *Wall Street Journal*, 21 May. Available at http://online.wsj.com/article/SB10001424052748704083904576335440434649646.html, accessed 24 August 2012.

Joint Special Operations Task Force (n.d.), 'Joint Special Operations Task Force – Philippines (JSOTF-P)'. Available at http://www.globalsecurity.org/military/agency/dod/jsotf-p.htm, accessed 26 August 2012.

Kraska, J. (2011), *Maritime Power and the Law of the Sea: Expeditionary Operations in World Politics*. Oxford: Oxford University Press.

Lia, B. (2007), *Architect of Global Jihad: The Life of Al-Qaida Strategist Abu Mus'ab al-Suri*. London: Hurst & Co.

Lieby, R. (2012), 'Pakistani militant rallies supporters, defying US bounty', *Washington Post*, 6 April. Available at http://www.washingtonpost.com/world/asia_pacific/pakistani-militant-rallies-supporters-defying-us-bounty/2012/04/06/gIQAGuZYzS_story.html, accessed 24 August 2012.

Menon, S.S. (2009), 'The evolving balance of power in Asia', remarks to the IISS 7th Global Strategic Review on 13 September. Available at http://www.iiss.org/conferences/global-strategic-review/global-strategic-review-2009/plenary-sessions-and-speeches-2009/fifth-plenary-session-shiv-shankar-menon/, accessed 14 August 2012.

Michel, D. and Sticklor, R. (2012), 'Maritime security policy challenges', in D. Michel and R. Sticklor, eds., *Indian Ocean Rising: Maritime Security and Policy Challenges*. Washington, DC: Stimpson Center.

Mitchell, A.W. and Grygiel, J. (2011), 'The vulnerability of peripheries', *The American Interest*, March-April. Available at http://www.the-american-interest.com/article.cfm?piece=923, accessed 26 August 2012.

Murphy, M.N. (2006), 'Maritime threat: tactics and technology of the Sea Tigers', *Jane's Intelligence Review*, Vol. 18, no. 6, pp. 6–10.

Murphy, M.N. (2009), *Small Boats, Weak States, Dirty Money: Piracy and Maritime Terrorism in the Modern World*. New York and London: Columbia University Press/Hurst.

Murphy, M.N. (2011a), 'Somali piracy: why should we care?', *RUSI Journal*, Vol. 156, no. 6, pp. 5–11.

Murphy, M.N. (2011b), *Somalia the New Barbary? Piracy and Islam in the Horn of Africa*. New York and London: Columbia University Press/Hurst.

Murphy, M.N. (2012), 'Counter-piracy in historical context: paradox, policy and rhetoric', *Journal of Conflict and Terrorism*, Vol. 35, nos. 7–8, pp. 507–522.

Oxman, B.H. (2006), 'The territorial temptation: a siren song at sea', *The American Journal of International Law*, Vol. 100, no. 4, pp. 830–851.

Page, J. and Wright, T. (2011), 'Chinese military considers new Indian Ocean presence', *Wall Street Journal*, 14 December. Available at http://online.wsj.com/article/SB100014240 5297020351840457709626106155053 8.html, accessed 14 August 2012.

Povlock, P.A. (2011), 'A guerrilla war at sea: the Sri Lankan civil war', *Small Wars Journal*, 9 September. Available at http://smallwarsjournal.com/jrnl/art/a-guerilla-war-at-sea-the-sri-lankancivil-war, accessed 14 August 2012.

Pushpita, D. (2011), 'Why India's coastal security arrangement falters?', *Institute for Defence Study and Analysis Comment*, 26 August. Available at http://www.idsa.in/idsacomments/WhyIndiasCoastalSecurityArrangementFalters_pdas_260811, accessed 14 August 2012.

Rabasa, A.M., Blackwill, R.D., Chalk, P., Cragin, K., Fair, C.C., Jackson, B.A., Jenkins, B.M., Jones, S.G., Shestak, N. and Tellis, A.J. (2009), 'The lessons of Mumbai', RAND Occasional Paper. Santa Monica, CA: RAND. Available at http://www.rand.org/pubs/occasional_papers/2009/RAND_OP249.pdf, accessed 14 August 2012.

Reuters (2012), 'Somali kingpins enjoy "impunity" – UN experts', 17 July. Available at http://www.reuters.com/article/2012/07/17/us-somalia-un-piracy-idUSBRE86G0ZN20120717, accessed 26 August 2012.

Ritchie, R.C. (1986), *Captain Kidd and the War against the Pirates*. Cambridge, MA: Harvard University Press.

Rosett, C. (2012), 'How Iran steams past international sanctions', *Wall Street Journal*, 12 July. Available at http://online.wsj.com/article/SB10001424052702303919504577522431458614636.html, accessed 24 August 2012.

Sharma, R. (2011), 'India boosts coastal defence', *The Diplomat*, 10 August. Available at http://thediplomat.com/indian-decade/2011/08/10/india-boosts-coastal-defence/, accessed 20 September 2012.

Singh, M. (2011), 'China base a threat to India navy?', *The Diplomat*, 17 December. Available at http://the-diplomat.com/2011/12/17/china-base-a-threat-to-india-navy/?all=true, accessed 14 August 2012.

Smith, N.A. (2010), 'Understanding Sri Lanka's defeat of the Tamil Tigers', Joint Force Quarterly, No. 59, pp. 40–44. Available at http://www.ndu.edu/press/understanding-sri-lanka.html, accessed 19 August 2012.

Stevens, W.S. (2011), 'Oil tanker terror hijacks easy, attacks complex', *USA Today*, 21 May. Available at http://www.usatoday.com/news/world/2011-05-21-terror-plot-oil-tankers_n.htm, accessed 20 September 2012.

UPI (2012), 'East Africa hits it big in oil, gas boom', 29 February. Available at http://www.upi.com/Business_News/Energy-Resources/2012/02/29/East-Africa-hits-it-big-in-oil-gas-boom/UPI-28311330532003/, accessed 11 August 2012.

Varma, K.J.M. (2011), 'China to explore Indian Ocean, India worried', *Rediff News*, 3 August. Available at http://www.rediff.com/news/report/china-to-explore-indian-ocean-india-worried/20110803.htm, accessed 13 August 2012.

Worth, R.F. (2010), 'Tanker damage caused by attack, inquiry finds', *New York Times*, 6 August. Available at http://www.nytimes.com/2010/08/07/world/middleeast/07tanker.html, accessed 19 August 2012.

Maritime security and port state control in the Indian Ocean Region

Sam Bateman[a,b]

[a]Australian National Centre for Ocean Resources and Security, University of Wollongong, Australia; [b]Maritime Security Programme, S. Rajaratnam School of International Studies, Nanyang Technological University, Singapore

This paper evaluates the effectiveness of the Port State Control (PSC) regime in relation to ensuring the safety and security of international shipping against threats of piracy and maritime terrorism in the Indian Ocean Region (IOR). Responsibility for ensuring compliance with required international standards of safety and security rests primarily with the flag states of vessels, but in practice, effective compliance is verified mainly through the system of Port State Control (PSC). However, PSC appears ineffective in the IOR, including around the Horn of Africa, where acts of piracy and armed robbery against ships are prevalent. Significant numbers of sub-standard ships operate in this region. These vessels are more likely to be successfully attacked or involved in illegal activity than quality ships. This situation could be symptomatic of wider problems in international shipping that throw doubt on the effectiveness of current regional regimes for ship safety, security and marine environmental protection, including measures to prevent maritime terrorism and illicit trafficking in weapons of mass destruction (WMD) and related materials.

1. Introduction

Shipping in the Indian Ocean Region (IOR)

The Indian Ocean is a busy waterway for international and regional shipping. In geo-political terms, the Indian Ocean is assuming greater importance as it becomes 'centre stage' for the twenty-first century (Kaplan 2009). This is partly because of the crucial strategic significance of the trade routes that criss-cross it. These are vital to the economies both of the extra-regional countries, which are dependent on the rich resources of the Indian Ocean Region (IOR), and to the countries within the region itself.

Two-thirds of the world's seaborne trade in oil, 50% of the world's seaborne container traffic, one-third of the world's seaborne bulk cargo and the world's highest tonnage in the seaborne transportation of goods are reported to transit through the Indian Ocean each year (DeSilva-Ranasinghe 2012). It is not just the extra-regional traffic from the Suez Canal and ports in the Middle East to destinations in East Asia, North America and Europe that is important, but also the intra-regional trade within and between various sub-regions of the IOR: East Africa, the Gulf, the Indian sub-continent and Southeast Asia. Seaborne trade is vitally important to the economic development of countries in these regions. Because the land transport infrastructure is not well developed in these regions, coastal and local shipping carries the vast majority of intra- and inter-regional trade in the IOR. The ships involved include many smaller product tankers, chemical tankers and general cargo vessels that, as this paper later discusses, are more vulnerable to pirate attack and hijacking than larger vessels of the same types.

Seaborne trade around the Horn of Africa has a particularly long history with the traditional trading routes between south-western Asia and East Africa, facilitated over the centuries by the monsoon system that prevails in this part of the Indian Ocean (McPherson 1995, p. 45). This trade continues to the present day both in traditional trading dhows and smaller merchant ships. While larger ships are occasionally hijacked by Somali pirates, the smaller vessels in the local trade provide the 'bread and butter' targets and steady income for the pirates. The income comes not only from the ransoms received for the release of hijacked vessels, but also possibly from protection money received for not hijacking vessels. There is nothing new to this. Piracy has been endemic to the Indian Ocean for centuries, with the coast of East Africa from Somalia south to Mozambique once being so unsafe that it was referred to as the Pirate Coast (Kaplan 2010, p. 299).

Maritime security

The IOR has experienced several incidents of maritime terrorism, notably the attacks on the American destroyer USS *Cole* in Aden in 2000 and on the French oil tanker *Limburg* off Yemen in 2002, as well as the sea-launched terror attacks on Mumbai in 2008. Terrorist threats associated with shipping and seaborne trade include shipping being used to smuggle terrorist materials or personnel into a country, and a ship being hijacked either to raise funds to finance terrorist activities or to use directly as a weapon.

Global solutions to problems of maritime security and dealing with the threats of piracy and maritime terrorism have been pitched at several levels, including the physical security of ships and ports, operational cooperation at sea, the tracking of vessels, the integrity of container cargo and enhancing seafarer identity documentation. They include new measures by the IMO, particularly the International Ship and Port Facility Security (ISPS) Code, other amendments to the 1974 Safety of Life at Sea (SOLAS) Convention, such as the mandatory fitting of ship-borne Automatic Identification Systems (AIS), and amendments to the 1988 Convention for the Suppression of Unlawful Acts against the Safety of Maritime Navigation (SUA Convention) and its Protocol covering offshore facilities.

Evidence from recent shipping accidents points to the human element as a key cause of accidents, suggesting that standards of crew training and efficiency are not what they should be. This trend is of security concern because it is the seafarers who are ultimately responsible for the standards of safety and security onboard ships. Evidence further suggests that the 'checks and balances' to ensure that commercial ships are operated safely and securely are not working effectively. As a consequence, sub-standard ships that do not meet the required standards of safety and security are still operating around the world, particularly in regions where the 'checks and balances' are ineffective.

This paper looks in particular at the effectiveness of the Port State Control (PSC) regime in reducing the number of sub-standard ships in the IOR. Sub-standard ships are ones that fail to meet the required standards of safety and seamanship as laid down in relevant international conventions. These vessels pose risks to maritime security and to the lives of their crew. Sub-standard ships are more likely to be successfully attacked by pirates, and more likely to be involved in illegal activities at sea, including trafficking in destabilising military equipment and narcotics. A sub-standard ship is most likely to be the vessel involved in support of terrorist activities or to convey a weapon of mass destruction (WMD) or associated materials rather than a more respectable vessel operated by law-abiding owners or ship operators. Enhancing PSC has been identified as probably the most effective method of combating a wide variety of maritime crime, including trafficking (Griffiths and Jenks 2012, p. 33).

Sub-standard ships are also more frequently involved in accidents at sea and pose serious risks to maritime safety and the marine environment. In an example of the problems that can occur, the Panama-flag bulk carrier *Rak*, laden with 60,000 tonnes of coal, inexplicably sank off Mumbai in August 2011, potentially leading to a major ecological disaster (NDTV 2011). The *Rak* was old, having been built in 1984, with a poor PSC record, having been detained once in 2010 for serious safety deficiencies (EMSA, *Equasis*). Shipping accidents tend to carry very high economic costs, due to the large asset values and the high operational risks associated with shipping, particularly the risks associated with a marine pollution incident (Knapp, Bijwaard and Heij 2011).

2. International shipping

Nature of the industry

International shipping is the classic globalised industry, with ships often under the flag of one country, owned by a company in another country, which in turn might be a subsidiary of a company in yet another country, and crewed by seafarers of many different nationalities. Cargo owners might come from other countries, and the various insurance policies required to be held by a ship might represent the interests of a range of other countries. It is a highly-competitive industry, with ship owners under continual pressure to reduce costs. Many opportunities exist for disreputable practices, including corruption, false certification and the abuse of the seafarers that crew ships engage in international trade (Couper 1999). An unscrupulous ship owner can follow a 'cheap-skate' policy of attempting to get a quick profit by buying and operating a ship cheaply, skimping on maintenance and safety measures and, in a worst-case scenario, when repairs become too expensive, abandoning the ship and its crew in some obscure port from which the owners cannot be easily traced (Goss 2008, p. 143).

Ship ownership and registration

Greece remains the world's largest ship owning nation. As at early 2011, owners from Greece controlled an estimated 16.2% of the world's deadweight tonnage, followed by Japan (15.8%), Germany (9.2%) and China (8.6%; UNCTAD 2011, Table 2.5, p. 43). The size of the Greek fleet in 2010 was a record amount, equating to more than 202 million deadweight tons (dwt). In terms of vessel numbers, owners from Germany, Japan and China have more ships than Greek owners, mainly because, in the case of China and Japan, these countries have large domestic fleets, including relatively small vessels. In terms of nationally-flagged and nationally-owned tonnage, the Greek fleet continues to be by far the world's largest, accounting for 65 million dwt, followed by the Chinese-owned and -flagged fleet, which accounts for 46 million dwt.

Using a flag of convenience – also called an open registry (OR) – offers benefits by avoiding heavy tax liabilities and expensive labour standards in the ship owner's own country. Major ship owning countries, such as Greece, Japan, the United States and China, have a high percentage of their fleets registered with ORs. Some ORs have excellent safety records, while some closed registers have poor ones (Llacer 2003, p. 521). Some countries, including Norway, operate international registries catering mostly for owners from their respective countries, albeit under conditions that are more favourable than those of the more classic national registries, which, for example, place stricter limitations on the employment of foreign seafarers (UNCTAD 2011, p. 49).

OR flags are extensively used by ships trading around the Horn of Africa and, as a consequence, figure prominently in ship hijackings. Of the 54 commercial ships (i.e. vessels other than dhows, fishing vessels and yachts) hijacked by Somali pirates in 2010 and 2011, 33 were under OR flags (IMB 2011 and 2012). Of these, 12 (or about 36% of the total) flew the flag of Panama. This is a much higher percentage than is suggested by Panama's 7.7% of the world fleet by ship numbers (shown in Table 1).

Table 1 shows the largest flags of ship registration at 1 January 2011. However, the flag of a ship is no indication of the true nationality of its owners. In 2011, more than 68% of the world's tonnage was registered under a foreign flag (UNCTAD 2011, p. 46). Eight of the top ten ship owning countries use foreign flags for more than half of their tonnage. During 2010, the 10 major open and international registries further increased their combined market share, reaching 56.1% of dwt in January 2011. Their highest market share is among dry bulk carriers (61%), followed by oil tankers (56%).

Table 1. Ten largest flags of registration (as at 1 January 2011).

Flag	No. of vessels	Share of world total (no. of ships)	DWT '000 dwt	Share of world total (dwt)	% growth dwt 2010–2011
Panama	7986	7.7	306,032	21.9	6.0
Liberia	2726	2.6	166,246	11.9	16.0
Marshall Is.	1622	1.6	98,757	7.1	26.9
China Hong Kong SAR	1736	1.7	91,733	6.6	23.0
Greece	1433	1.4	71,420	5.1	5.6
Bahamas	1384	1.3	67,465	4.8	5.2
Singapore	2667	2.6	67,287	4.8	9.1
Malta	1724	1.7	61,294	4.4	9.1
China	4080	3.9	52,741	3.8	16.8
Cyprus	1014	1.0	32,321	2.3	3.2

Source: UNCTAD 2011, Table 2.7, p. 47.

Among the remaining registries, the share of developed countries decreased by 0.94%, reflecting the long-term trend towards greater ship ownership in developing countries (UNCTAD 2011, p. 48).

In January 2011, there were 103,392 seagoing commercial ships in service, with a combined tonnage of 1396 million dwt (UNCTAD 2011, p. 36). Most ships in service by number are general cargo ships (33%) followed by tankers (25%), dry bulk carriers (14%) and container ships (12%). Table 2 shows the breakdown of the world shipping fleet by type of vessel and dwt. Dry bulk carriers have continued to dominate deliveries in 2011. During the first quarter of the year, the dry bulk fleet grew by 2.7%, resulting from the delivery of 222 new vessels and the demolition of only 67 (UNCTAD 2011, p. 51). As the time lag between ordering a vessel and having it delivered is two to three years, this increased delivery of new bulk carriers reflects the optimistic expectations of ship owners prior to the onset of the downturn in international shipping following the global financial crisis (GFC).

Downturn in international shipping

The currently depressed market for shipping has been an under-appreciated factor in explaining the surge in acts of piracy and armed robbery over the past four or five years, with more ships laid up, including in areas at risk of attack, unemployed ships at sea and ship owners possibly taking 'short cuts' with safety and security measures as they seek to reduce ship operating costs (Bateman 2009). There is an ongoing glut in international shipping largely caused by an over-supply of shipping, as ships ordered during the boom years in shipping prior to the GFC enter service, and insufficient numbers of older vessels are scrapped. Shipping markets remain in the doldrums, with depressed freight and charter rates for most classes of vessel, surplus shipping capacity, ships laid up and more unemployed seafarers.

There are both direct and indirect implications for maritime security of the downturn in international shipping. Direct implications flow from increased numbers of unemployed seafarers and larger numbers of laid up ships, possibly in anchorages that are prone to armed robbery, as well as from the possibility that

Table 2. World fleet by principal vessel types, 2010 (ships 100 GRT and above).

Vessel type	% world fleet by tonnage	'000 DWT	% change from 2005
Oil tankers	34.0	474,846	5.5
Dry bulk carriers	38.1	532,039	16.5
General cargo	7.8	108,971	0.7
Container ships	13.2	183,859	8.7
Gas carriers	3.1	43,339	6.6
Chemical tankers	0.5	5,849	−20.5
Passenger ships and ferries	0.4	5,649	1.1
Offshore supply	2.4	33,227	34.7
Other	0.5	3,450	−43.7
Total	100.0	1,305,743	9.4

Source: UNCTADRMT 2013, Table 2.1, p. 37.

ship owners may take 'short cuts' with safety and security measures as they seek to reduce ship operating costs. This could lead to a fall in the levels of social responsibility in shipping, with greater abuse of the rights of seafarers and increased risks of pollution. Indirect implications include possibilities of increased criminal activity at sea, greater concentration of ship ownership and increased risks of environmental pollution arising from various sources, such as more ships being broken up and the possibility that ships may become less well maintained and operated.

3. Sub-standard shipping

Ship vulnerability

Most assessments of the vulnerability of ships to the threats of piracy and armed attack are generalised appreciations based on absolute numbers of ships and attacks. This is a misleading approach that can lead to incorrect policy recommendations. Much more attention should be paid to the circumstances of attack and the vulnerability of individual ships (an assessment of the vulnerability of the different types of ship using the Malacca and Singapore Straits may be found in Bateman, Ho and Mathai 2007). For example, any ship might be attacked while in port or at anchor if precautions are not taken against attack, but the vulnerability of a ship while underway depends on factors such as ship's size, speed, freeboard and size of crew, as well as on whether or not appropriate measures are in place to secure the vessel against attack. The flag of registry of a ship and the type of vessel have been found to be significant factors in determining the likelihood of a successful piracy attack (Mejia, Cariou and Wolff 2009). The IMO 'has frequently drawn attention to the number of "sub-standard" ships engaged in the bulk trades, often operating within complex, multinational structures that obscure the relationship between individual ships and their ultimate owners' (King 2005, p. 242).

Evidence from ship hijackings by Somali pirates suggests that sub-standard ships are more likely to be successfully hijacked than quality vessels. Well-operated and maintained vessels will follow the best management practice (BMP) guidelines to avoid attack recommended by the IMO and ship owner associations, but poor quality vessels are less likely to do so. Table 3 shows that of the 54 commercial vessels hijacked by Somali pirates in 2010 and 2011, 23 vessels, or about 42% of the total hijacked, could be assessed as being sub-standard either by virtue of age and their PSC record.

Ship age

As older ships are regarded by PSC regimes as having higher risk factors, age may be taken as an indication of a possible sub-standard ship. While there will be exceptions, with some older ships operated safely and efficiently, nevertheless, an older ship is more likely to be sub-standard and operated by a less well trained and motivated crew than a newer vessel. A ship may start her life with a reputable company, but over the years, she may change her name and flag, progressively ending up with less responsible owners. The independent ship vetting system, RightShip, has recently introduced a requirement that dry bulk carriers in the range 8000 dwt aged 18 years

MARITIME TERRORISM AND PIRACY IN THE INDIAN OCEAN REGION

Table 3. Ships hijacked by Somali pirates 2010–2011.

	2010	2011	Total
Total hijackings	51	28	79
Fishing vessels	9	6	15
Dhows	5	1	6
Yachts	1	3	4
Commercial vessels of which:	36	18	54
Good ships[a]	8	5	13
Fair ships[b]	13	5	18
Poor ships[c]	15	8	23
Total	51	28	79

Sources: International Maritime Bureau (IMB) Piracy Reports and *Equasis* data base (EMSA).
Notes: [a]Good ships have had few, if any, deficiencies at recent inspections. [b]Fair ships have had some deficiencies at recent inspections. [c]Poor ships have had numerous deficiencies and/or have been detained after recent inspections. They were all older ships (i.e. more than 25 years old).

and above will require an annual acceptable RightShip inspection as part of its vetting programme. This change has come about due to the correlation between vessel age, associated casualties and PSC deficiencies and detentions (Knapp, Bijwaard and Heij 2011). It is significant that, as shown in Table 3, 23 of the commercial vessels hijacked in 2010 and 2011 were more than 25 years old.

A recent study by the Stockholm International Peace Research Institute (SIPRI) investigated ships reported to be involved in transporting destabilising military equipment, dual use goods and narcotics (Griffiths and Jenks 2012). The study found that ships involved in trafficking in destabilising commodities when the owner, commercial operator or ship's officers appear to have been complicit in the activity had an average age of more than 27 years with poor PSC records. They were vessels repeatedly identified as poor performers in PSC inspections carried out by European or North American authorities for at least seven of the past eleven years (Griffiths and Jenks 2012, p. 29).

Older ships are more likely to fall below the standards of the more respected classification societies, port state controls and flag States in areas such as safety and pollution. This makes them more likely to sail under certain flags of convenience (which tend to recognise a wider range of classification societies) and to ply routes via ports where controls are less rigorous, such as around the north-western Indian Ocean. Furthermore, some flag States will not register ships over a certain age. Older ships tend to have worse safety and pollution records and may be subject to higher levels of port state control inspection as a result (Griffiths and Jenks 2012, pp. 25–26).

The Indian Government is actively considering banning the entry of ships which are more than 25 years old (Press Information Bureau 2011). Legislation will be passed requiring that vessels over 25 years of age will only be allowed to enter Indian ports if they are classed by a full member of the International Association of Classification Societies (IACS), have adequate insurance coverage, have an Indian ship agent to represent the owner or operator and have notified the relevant port authority at least 48 hours prior to arrival about all details of the ship, including insurance coverage (McCarthy 2011).

4. Dealing with sub-standard ships

Flag State

Under Article 94 of the 1982 UN Convention on the Law of the Sea (UNCLOS), flag States are responsible for ensuring that ships flying their flag comply with generally accepted international standards and are operated safely, including ensuring that vessels are seaworthy and manned by appropriately qualified seafarers. Flag States are thus the first line of defence in eliminating sub-standard ships. While responsibility for security arrangements onboard ships is not mentioned specifically in Article 94, this has become a flag State responsibility under the ISPS Code.

UNCLOS Article 91 requires that there be 'a genuine link' between a state and the ships entitled to fly the flag of that State. However, it is well accepted now that this is not the case with many ships registered with ORs. The UN Convention on Conditions for Registration of Ships, adopted in 1986, would have confirmed the need for a genuine link, but it has not achieved this outcome, since it has never entered into force (Llacer 2003, p. 519). The lack of a genuine link between the ship and its flag is an unequivocal sign of an OR. However, there is nothing inherently unusual in an international ship registry system in which the owner of a ship may be located in a country other than the state whose flag the ship flies, but a balance has to be struck between the commercial advantages of selecting a particular flag and the need to discourage the use of flags that do not meet their international obligations. It remains a key interest of the international community to develop policies to eradicate flags which do not ensure that ships flying that flag do not put at risk both lives and goods at sea, as well as the marine environment (Llacer 2003, p. 522).

Vetting regimes

Enforcement of required levels of safety and security in shipping is attempted through various types of inspection (Knapp, Bijwaard and Heij 2011, p. 1532). These are both mandatory and non-mandatory. Mandatory ones are required to issue and maintain certificates required by the IMO and to ensure that ships comply with minimum international standards. They are performed by 'Recognized Organizations' (ROs), which may be either inspection units established by the ship registry of a flag State or classification societies on behalf of the registry.

Classification societies were originally established to apply technical standards related to the design, construction and survey of ships and other offshore facilities, but they have now taken over all aspects of ship operations (Branch 2007, pp. 132–135). The International Association of Classification Societies (IACS) represents the 10 major classification societies, such as Lloyd's Register and the American Bureau of Shipping and Det Norske Veritas, but there are many other classification societies that are not members of IACS, some of which are of 'dubious provenance' (Mansell 2009, p. 131). As reports from PSC regimes suggest, a sub-standard ship is more likely to be classified by a non-IACS member. For example, the Annual Report on Port State Control in the Asia-Pacific Region for 2010 classifies all IACS members as high performance ROs, while non-IACS members tend to have very low, low or medium performance (Tokyo MOU 2011, Table 12, pp. 43–44).

Non-mandatory inspections are those performed by industry and by PSC. Industry vetting regimes have been established to allow cargo owners and ship charterers to assess whether a ship is suitable for its purpose. For example, RightShip is a vetting regime for dry bulk carriers and oil tankers based out of Australia. Industry inspections are much more extensive than PSC inspections, especially those for oil tankers, and it has been assessed that these inspections can lead to subsequent cost savings for the industry in terms of the avoidance of casualties and pollution incidents (Knapp, Bijwaard and Heij 2011, p. 1537). It is not surprising that general cargo vessels are the worst performing ship type, because these vessels are not subject to inspection by any of the industry vetting inspection regimes (Knapp and Frances 2007b, p. 472).

Port state control

International law, as codified by UNCLOS, grants a coastal or port state full sovereignty over its internal waters, and thus the right to set conditions on ships entering its waters. This is the legal justification for the PSC regime which allows port states, as a condition of entry to their waters, the right to inspect vessels calling at ports under their jurisdiction. PSC is defined as:

> The inspection of foreign ships in national ports to verify that the condition of the ship and its equipment comply with the requirements of international regulations and that the ship is manned and operated in compliance with these rules. (IMO)

PSC inspectors check to ensure that a ship holds all the necessary certificates. Branch (2007, pp. 105–144) provides a list of the certificates and documents that are required to be carried onboard ships. All ships are required to carry about 17 documents and certifications, while particular categories of vessel (for example passenger ships, chemical tankers, gas carriers and high speed craft) are required to carry additional papers applicable to their category. The inspectors may ask for a demonstration of fire drill or abandon ship drill, including the lowering and operating of the ship's lifeboats. This, however, is often a source of corruption, with the PSC inspector expecting a payoff, such as a bottle of whisky from the captain, not to pursue the practical demonstrations (Purves 2005, p. 68). On the other hand, the offer of a bribe may prompt the inspector to take an even stricter approach to assessing the standard of the ship. If serious deficiencies are found in a ship's safety standards or lead to the assessment that the vessel presents an unreasonable threat to the marine environment, then it may be detained in port until the deficiencies are rectified.

PSC inspections in most cases are the only occasions when state authorities have the right to board a ship without consulting the flag State. PSC inspections allow inspection of the ship, including the cargo hold and crew's quarters. They provide a mechanism to control the movement of targeted ships through detention in port and even a ban from all ports under the same cooperative PSC regime (Griffiths and Jenks 2012, p. 48). PSC regimes apply a targeting methodology based on criteria to determine which vessels, vessel owners and operators, classification societies and flag States are most often associated with sub-standard ships. The targeting methodology applied by the US Coast Guard is described in Ozcayir (2001, pp. 2–6).

The Paris Memorandum of Understanding (Paris MOU) for Europe and the North Atlantic, established in 1982, was the first PSC regime put in place. It became a model for subsequent MOUs (Payoyo 1994). There are currently 10 PSC regimes:

(1) Europe and North Atlantic (Paris MOU);
(2) Asia and the Pacific (Tokyo MOU);
(3) Latin America (Acuardo de Vina del Mar);
(4) Caribbean (Caribbean MOU);
(5) West and Central Africa (Abuja MOU);
(6) Black Sea (Black Sea MOU);
(7) Mediterranean (Mediterranean MOU);
(8) Indian Ocean (Indian Ocean MOU);
(9) Arab States of the Gulf (Riyadh MOU); and
(10) United States (US Coast Guard)

The Paris and Tokyo MOUs and the US Coast Guard appear to be the most efficient and effective PSC regimes. However, many countries involved in these regimes are developed states, able to afford the number of skilled inspectors and management structures required to make the regimes effective. An unfortunate consequence of these regimes being effective is that they tend to drive sub-standard ships away to operate in regions of the world where PSC is less effective. Paradoxically, this means that they may be operating in regions where they are more likely to be exposed to pirate or terrorist attack or to be used for illegal purposes.

There are two PSC regimes applicable to the north-west Indian Ocean and adjacent waters, where Somali pirates are active. These are the Indian Ocean MOU and the Riyadh MOU for the Gulf Region. The Indian Ocean MOU on PSC, to which many successfully hijacked ships should be exposed, is less effective than the Paris and Tokyo MOUs. Some important shipping countries in the region (e.g. Pakistan, Madagascar, Myanmar and the Seychelles) are not parties to the MOU, and of the 15 parties, four (Bangladesh, Eritrea, Maldives and Oman) did not report any inspection activity in 2010 (IO MOU Secretariat 2011, p. 9). Under the IO MOU, parties are committed to inspecting at least 10% of foreign ships visiting their ports (IO MOU Secretariat 2001, Art. 1.3), but inspection rates are low, and the situation is not helped by the fact that just over half the total inspections reported by the MOU (2795 out of 5513) are carried out by Australia. The current effectiveness of the other MOU in the north-west Indian Ocean region, the Riyadh MOU, cannot be assessed as there has been no annual report available publically since 2007. In the light of these factors, it must be concluded that PSC is ineffective in the region and the Horn of Africa and East Africa could well be areas where sub-standard ships are prevalent.

Table 4 compares statistics for four major PSC regimes in 2010. The Tokyo MOU achieved the highest number of inspections, with an overall inspection rate for the region of 66%, although most inspections were carried out by just six members of the MOU: Australia, China, Japan, South Korea, the Philippines and Russia. The lower inspection rates for the Paris MOU and the US Coast Guard may have been due to these two regimes using a tight targeting process to identify ships to be inspected. The number of inspections with deficiencies is roughly the same for the three regional MOUs, but much lower for the US Coast Guard, suggesting that only quality ships

Table 4. Comparative statistics for major PSC regimes 2010.

Regime	No. of inspections	Inspection rate	% inspections with deficiencies	% inspections leading to detention
Paris MOU	24058	30.03	55.21	3.28
Tokyo MOU	33212	66.00	49.91	5.48
Indian Ocean MOU	5513	n/a[a]	52.04	8.54
US Coast Guard	9907	12.97	27.95	1.57

Source: Annual 2010 Reports for regimes.
Note: [a]The IO MOU does not report an inspection rate in its annual report.

visit US ports due to ship owners recognising the strict approach of the United States to ship safety and security. The number of ships detained as a percentage of total inspections with the Paris MOU has shown a steady decline over the years from 9.5% in 2000 to the 2010 figure of 3.28%, showing also that sub-standard ships are steering clear of the European and North Atlantic region covered by the Paris MOU. The higher percentage of inspections leading to the detention of a ship for the Tokyo and Indian Ocean MOUs may suggest more sub-standard ships operating in those regions than in the Paris MOU's region.

5. Way ahead

Scope for improvement

The international community could take greater collective action to deal with sub-standard ships that jeopardise safety and security and pose unacceptable risks to the marine environment. These vessels figure disproportionately in incidents of ship hijacking, in cases of illegal activity at sea, including trafficking in military destabilising commodities, and in casualties leading to pollution of the marine environment. Current measures taken by the international community to address the problem of sub-standard ships have not yet succeeded in reducing the number of sub-standard ships to an acceptable level (Churchill 2007, p. 901).

The primary responsibility for ensuring that ships are not sub-standard rests with the flag State, but it 'has been clear for many years that quite a number of flag States are either unable or unwilling to take the necessary action to ensure such compliance' (Churchill 2007, p. 903). PSC has emerged as the main international system to counter sub-standard vessels, but some PSC regimes appear ineffective, including those applicable in the north-western part of the IOR. Even the Tokyo MOU, which is regarded as one of the most effective regimes, includes some members that make little or no contribution to the inspection effort (Mansell 2009, p. 85).

Maritime security in the IOR is degraded by the ineffectiveness of PSC in the region. There is great scope for improvement in PSC regimes, both in terms of improving the effectiveness of the separate regional regimes, particularly the more poorly performing ones, and with enhancing the global collective ability to deal with sub-standard ships. The targeting of vessels which are more likely to be sub-standard could be improved through developing a global dataset, which allows targeting on the basis of a ship's inspection history (Knapp and Franses 2007a, p. 560). Variables, such as ownership, change of ownership, change of classification society and vetting inspections, might be incorporated into the targeting process to ensure that the ships are identified that require more thorough inspection.

Policy implications

PSC works effectively in the developed world but much less so in the developing world, including in and around the north-western Indian Ocean, paradoxically where the incidence of piracy and armed attacks against ships and the risks of maritime terrorism are higher. It is easy to suggest that PSC and the role of port states in the developing world should be strengthened to ensure greater compliance with minimum international standards and to help rid the oceans of sub-standard ships. However, this suggestion overlooks problems with the lack of capacity in many developing countries to establish an effective national maritime administration and provide the necessary highly-skilled PSC inspectors, as well as the lack of resources in the IMO to monitor the effectiveness of PSC regimes. The levels of corruption that can pervade PSC inspections in some developing countries are an additional problem.

The major MOUs and developed countries do conduct training courses for the PSC personnel of developing countries. The US Coast Guard, for example, has overseas units, such as the US Coast Guard Activities Far East, with offices in Tokyo and Singapore, which has duties including PSC inspections of high risk foreign vessels departing for US ports and providing training and advice on PSC for countries in the Western Pacific and Indian Ocean regions. However, these activities may be just propping up ineffective systems rather than addressing the basic problem, which is the lack of resources and limited capacity.

The IMO has very limited resources. It is ironic that the organisation's annual budget of about US$48 million (IMO 2011) is about the cost of an offshore patrol vessel, a small warship or the cost of maintaining the naval counter-piracy flotilla off Somalia for less than two months, based on the daily operating costs of a naval frigate of about US$50,000 per day (Chalk, Smallman and Burger 2009, p. 2). It would seem that the international community has a rather upside-down view of the priorities for maritime safety, security and marine environmental protection. This situation is not helped when, as in March 2010, at least one of the world's largest flag States had deliberately missed the January deadline to pay its IMO annual membership fee and other states were showing either a reluctance to contribute or were seeking to contribute by periodical instalments (Osler 2010).

Developed countries could do much more to ensure that PSC is implemented effectively. In doing so, they might recognise that by having effective PSC in their own ports, they are in fact exporting the problems to the developing world. Sub-standard ships do not stop trading just because they can no longer enter ports in North America, Europe, Australia or Japan. Rather than just being involved in training courses conducted by the more effective MOUs in poorly performing parts of the world, developed countries could provide direct assistance through their international aid programmes to help build the capacity of developing countries to establish and manage an effective PSC system.

Effective regulation of international shipping can be stifled by conflicts of interest. Flag States and ship owners hold much power and influence at the IMO, but are not fully supportive of PSC. Because the IMO is funded by membership fees based on the size of the respective fleets, flag States provide most of the organization's financial support and are able to exercise influence at the technical committees, where the real power of the IMO lies (Langewiesche 2004, p. 87).

The high incidence of sub-standard ships around the Horn of Africa adversely impacts maritime security generally in the IOR. It is an under-appreciated explanation of the phenomenon of piracy and ship hijackings in the region. Irresponsible shipowners who send poorly prepared ships into piracy-prone areas must accept some share of the responsibility both for the incidence of ship hijackings and for the associated ill treatment of seafarers. If ransoms are not paid promptly, and this is more likely with a less than reputable ship owner operating a sub-standard ship, crews are likely to suffer more. Overall the situation would be improved if the PSC regime was enforced more strictly in the region, and there were fewer poor quality vessels sailing in piracy-prone waters.

Nevertheless, reducing the incidence of sub-standard ships would be just a small contribution to countering piracy. Measures such as improved governance onshore, better enforcement by local security forces, international support for capacity building, enhanced cooperation between foreign navies, more successful prosecutions of pirates and greater vigilance by merchant ships are all necessary parts of a comprehensive counter-piracy regime. Improved governance onshore is the essential requirement, but is also the most difficult to achieve.

References

Bateman, S. (2009), 'Maritime security implications of the international shipping recession', *The Australian Journal of Maritime and Ocean Affairs*, Vol. 1, no. 4, pp. 109–117.

Bateman, S., Ho, J. and Mathai, M. (2007), 'Shipping patterns in the Malacca and Singapore straits: an assessment of the risks to different types of vessel', *Contemporary Southeast Asia*, Vol. 29, no. 2, pp. 309–322.

Branch, A.E. (2007), *Elements of Shipping*, 8th ed. Abingdon: Routledge.

Chalk, P., Smallman, L. and Burger, N. (2009), *Countering Piracy in the Modern Era*. Santa Monica, CA: RAND National Defense Research Institute.

Churchill, R. (2007), 'From port state to court state? International litigation as a possible weapon to combat sub-standard ships', in Y.M. Ndiaye and R. Wolfrum, eds., *Liber Amicorum Judge Thomas A. Mensah: Law of the Sea, Protection of the Marine Environment and Settlement of Disputes*. Leiden: Martinus Nijhoff Publisher, pp. 899–916.

Couper, A.D. (1999), *Voyages of Abuse – Seafarers, Human Rights and International Shipping*. London: Pluto Press.

DeSilva-Ranasinghe, S. (2012), *Fact Sheet: The Indian Ocean Region and Australia's National Interests*. Perth, WA: Future Directions International.

European Maritime Safety Agency (EMSA), *Equasis Data Base*. Available at http://www.equasis.org, accessed 5 February 2012.

Goss, R. (2008), 'Social responsibility in shipping', *Marine Policy*, Vol. 32, no. 1, pp. 142–146.

Griffiths, H. and Jenks, M. (2012), 'Maritime transport and destabilizing commodity flows', *SIPRI Policy Paper 32*. Stockholm: Stockholm International Peace Research Institute (SIPRI).

Indian Ocean MOU Secretariat (2001), *Memorandum of Understanding on Port State Control for the Indian Ocean Region*. Available at www.iomou.org (accessed 19 September 2012).

Indian Ocean MOU Secretariat (2011), *Annual Report 2010*. Available at http://www.iomou.org/armain.htm, accessed 19 September 2012.

International Maritime Bureau (IMB) (2011 and 2012), *Annual Piracy Reports for 2010 and 2011*. London: International Chamber of Commerce.

International Maritime Organization (IMO), *Port State Control*. Available at http://www.imo.org/blast/mainframe.asp?topic_id=159, accessed 5 February 2012.

International Maritime Organization (IMO) (2011), 'IMO assembly adopts wide range of resolutions', *IMO Press Briefing 62*. Available at http://www.imo.org/MediaCentre/PressBriefings/Pages/62-A27-ends.aspx, accessed 5 March 2012.

Kaplan, R. (2009), 'Center stage for the twenty-first century', *Foreign Affairs*, Vol. 88, no. 2.

Kaplan, R. (2010), *Monsoon – The Indian Ocean and the Future of American Power*. New York: Random House.

King, J. (2005), 'The security of merchant shipping', *Marine Policy*, Vol. 29, no. 3, pp. 235–245.

Knapp, S. and Franses, P.H. (2007a), 'Econometric analysis on the effect of port state control inspections on the probability of casualty. Can targeting of substandard ships for inspections be improved?', *Marine Policy*, Vol. 31, no. 4, pp. 550–563.

Knapp, S. and Franses, P.H. (2007b), 'A global view on port state control: econometric analysis of the differences across port state control regimes', *Maritime Policy and Management*, Vol. 34, no. 5, pp. 453–483.

Knapp, S., Bijwaard, G. and Heij, C. (2011), 'Estimated incident cost savings in shipping due to inspections', *Accident Analysis and Prevention*, Vol. 43, no. 4, pp. 1532–1539.

Langewiesche, W. (2004), *The Outlaw Sea: A World of Freedom, Chaos and Crime*. New York: North Point Press.

Llacer, F.J.M. (2003), 'Open registers: past, present and future', *Marine Policy*, Vol. 27, no. 6, pp. 513–523.

McCarthy, L. (2011), 'Indian government tightens restrictions on older vessels', *Lloyd's List*, 5 September. Available at www.lloydslist.com/ll/sector/regulation/article379209.ece

McPherson, K. (1995), *The Indian Ocean – A History of People and the Sea*. Oxford: Oxford University Press.

Mansell, J. (2009), 'Port state control in the Asia-Pacific region: issues and challenges', *Australian Journal of Maritime and Ocean Affairs*, Vol. 1, no. 3, pp. 73–87.

Mejia, M.Q. Jr., Cariou, P. and Wolff, F.-C. (2009), 'Is maritime piracy random?', *Applied Economics Letters*, Vol. 16, pp. 891–895.

Osler, D. (2010), 'Major flag state holds back IMO fees', *Lloyd's List*, 15 March. Available at http://www.lloydslist.com/ll/sector/regulation/article5763.ece, accessed 30 April 2010.

Ozcayir, Z.A.O. (2001), 'Port state control in the USA', *Maritime Studies*, Vol. 121, pp. 2–6.

Payoyo, P.B. (1994), 'Implementation of international conventions through port state control: An assessment', *Marine Policy*, Vol. 18, no. 5, pp. 379–392.

Press Information Bureau, Government of India, Ministry of Shipping (2011), 'Transportation of hazardous chemicals by sea vessels', press release, 15 December. Available at http://pib.nic.in/newsite/PrintRelease.aspx?relid=78728, accessed January 2012.

Purves, B. (2005), *A Sea of Green – A Voyage Around the World of Ocean Shipping*. Hong Kong: Chameleon Press.

Stopford, S. (2009), *Maritime Economics*, 3rd ed. Abingdon: Routledge.

Tokyo MOU Secretariat (2011), *Annual Report on Port State Control in the Asia-Pacific Region 2010*. Available at http://www.tokyo-mou.org/ANN10.pdf, accessed 5 February 2012.

United Nations Conference on Trade and Development (UNCTAD) (2011), *Review of Maritime Transport 2011*. New York: United Nations and Geneva.

International law and counter-piracy in the Indian Ocean

Douglas Guilfoyle

Faculty of Law, University College London, United Kingdom

International discussion of Somali piracy is now largely conducted in the language of law enforcement, not war or terrorism. The aim of this paper is to explain in a brief and practical way to non-lawyers the relevant legal categories and controversies surrounding Somali piracy and to suggest why the response to piracy has remained in the law enforcement 'box'. It does this by considering piracy through the lens of four legal 'paradigms': the law of armed conflict; the international law of piracy; the law of terrorism (including terrorist financing); and the law applicable to transnational organised crime. The contention will be that the law enforcement paradigm is not only legally justifiable but also highly pragmatic and that the other categories may hold fewer benefits than observers might assume.

1. Introduction

Piracy off Somalia continues to plague international shipping in the Indian Ocean, despite significant international efforts to curb it. If Somali piracy represents an exceptional emergency, we might expect the invocation of exceptional legal powers to counter it. Gross and Ní Aoláin posit four legal regimes that can be deployed in response to emergencies generally: 'business as usual', a human rights and law-enforcement paradigm; 'emergency powers', where all legally-permissible derogations from human rights will be made; 'armed conflict', governed by international humanitarian law; and 'an Extra-Legal Measures context', involving unlawful acts by state actors (Gross and Ní Aoláin 2006). Of these, and despite the use of Security Council Resolutions, piracy has largely been addressed by the international community with a 'business as usual' law-enforcement response (Guilfoyle 2010a). The most recent of 12 Security Council Resolutions on point is meticulously legalistic. It refers, in plain law-enforcement language, to 'the need to investigate and prosecute not only suspects captured at sea, but also anyone who incites or intentionally facilitates piracy operations, including key figures of criminal networks involved in piracy' (UNSCR 2020 2011, preamble). It reaffirms 'that international law, as reflected in the United Nations Convention on the Law of the Sea of 10 December 1982 [...] sets out the legal framework applicable to combating piracy', and notes

MARITIME TERRORISM AND PIRACY IN THE INDIAN OCEAN REGION

that the continuing limited capacity and domestic legislation to facilitate the custody and prosecution of suspected pirates after their capture has hindered more robust international action against the pirates off the coast of Somalia, and [...] led to pirates being released without facing justice. (UNSCR 2020 2011, preamble)

The Security Council goes on to commend the efforts of Kenya and the Seychelles to prosecute pirates captured by international forces, and calls on states to enact appropriate national criminal laws (UNSCR 2020 2011, preamble).

This may appear odd, and one might expect more 'robust' legal paradigms to have been considered. After all, the ancient idea that pirates are *hostes humani generis*, 'enemies of all mankind' (Harvard Research in International Law 1932, p. 774), lead nineteenth-century judges to claim pirates are 'universally subject to the extreme rights of war' (*The LeLouis* 1817). We might therefore expect that modern pirates should – or could more effectively – be dealt with under the law of armed conflict, not the law of peace-time policing. Alternatively, we might expect a widespread push to assimilate counter-piracy to the 'war on terror' (Kontorovich 2010), in order to claim the advantages of being able to act outside a criminal justice paradigm and target enemies with lethal force on sight and without warning (Bolton 2011). Instead, however, the response to Somali piracy since 2008 has been particularly resistant to 'securitisation'. By securitisation, I refer to attempts to respond to perceived crises by derogating from ordinary legal paradigms and human rights restraints to give state actors greater freedom to use violence (Bueger and Stockbruegger 2011). Why should this be the case?

The aim of this paper is to explain, in a brief and practical way, the relevant legal categories and controversies surrounding Somali piracy and to suggest why the response to piracy has remained firmly in the law enforcement 'box'. This is done by considering piracy through the lens of four 'paradigms' (legal categories with associated consequences): the law of armed conflict; the international law of piracy; the law of terrorism; and the law applicable to transnational organised crime. In particular, the article challenges the view that the categories of 'terrorist' and 'pirate' are mutually exclusive. Open many international law texts or articles on piracy and one will find a statement that because piracy must be 'for private ends' then a pirate can never be a politically-motivated terrorist. Conversely, it is often presumed that the so-called 'terrorism suppression conventions' apply only to politically-motivated acts. This is not the case. Under the right conditions, one could charge a 'pirate' with offences covered by the terrorism suppression conventions or one could charge certain acts of 'terrorism' as piracy. This follows from the fact that there is no universally-agreed legal definition of terrorism, only agreement on criminalising a series of acts which cannot be justified on any basis. Further, the requirement that piracy be for private ends is widely misunderstood. Finally, piracy will be considered as a transnational organised crime. The suggestion will be that this is the legal model used in practice. First, however, given historical concerns, it is useful to consider the laws of war paradigm.

2. The first legal paradigm: the laws of war or international humanitarian law (IHL)

Commander Dow [Royal Navy]: [...] [EU counter-piracy operation Atalanta] is clearly a law enforcement operation rather than a war against pirate[s] or an armed conflict [...]

MARITIME TERRORISM AND PIRACY IN THE INDIAN OCEAN REGION

> Lord Hamilton of Epsom: You say that it is not a war; it looks quite like one to many of us serving on the side [...] (House of Lords European Union Committee 2010)

To the non-lawyer it may seem peculiar that engagements between warships and pirates are not governed by the laws of war. However, this is the view of most militaries themselves. The EU's public position is that its counter-piracy operation Atalanta is a maritime policing operation and it may use only that degree of force consistent with law enforcement operations (European Union Council Secretariat 2009). The US Navy's *Commander's Handbook* (2007, para. 3.5.3.1) also describes naval counter-piracy operations as an adjunct to law enforcement:

> A pirate vessel or aircraft encountered in [...] international waters may be seized and detained by any U.S. vessel [...] or aircraft [...] The pirate vessel [...] and all persons on board, should be taken [...] to the nearest U.S. port or airfield and delivered to U.S. law enforcement authorities [...] Alternatively, higher authority may arrange with another nation to accept and try the pirates.

Similarly, the view was put without challenge in the NATO Parliamentary Assembly that 'warships engaged in counter-piracy operations are treated as police or law enforcement forces. This also means that captured pirates are not considered prisoners of war, and should [...] be prosecuted in the regular court systems' (Jopling 2009). This reflects the general view that the counter-piracy powers granted by international law are law enforcement powers. In old-fashioned terms, the power to suppress piracy is part of the laws of peace, not the laws of war (François 1950).

However, if it was once said that the pirate has 'declar[ed] war against all mankind, [and therefore] all mankind must declare war against him' (Blackstone 1770), how has the law changed so radically? Would there be advantages to returning to this older paradigm? The first point is that such statements were never very accurate. Talk of the pirate being *hostis humani generis* was always largely 'rhetorical invective' (Harvard Research in International Law 1932, p. 796). Further, public international law has progressively developed to separate out certain types of state violence or enforcement action as categories 'distinct from that of war' (Harvard Research in International Law 1932, p. 826). Under the modern law, there is an increasingly clear conceptual division between actions in war governed principally by international humanitarian law (IHL) and other enforcement action governed by human rights law. Although one should note that human rights continue to apply in war (Milanović 2009), the era of summary execution of pirates on the foredeck has long passed (Harvard Research in International Law 1932, p. 853).

In any event, historically the majority of IHL applied only to international armed conflicts (IACs) between states and states generally resisted the legal regulation of conflicts with non-state actors (non-international armed conflicts or NIACs). This was in part because NIACs were usually civil wars and considered an internal matter (Cryer *et al.* 2010, p. 276). Despite a progressive 'convergence' between the IHL applicable to the two types of conflict, treaty law continues to uphold the IAC/NIAC distinction, and NIACs are subject to different (less detailed) rules of international law. Further, non-state actors in NIACs do not enjoy combatant status under IHL. It thus remains relevant to ask whether any apparent conflict is an IAC, a NIAC, or not an armed conflict in a legal sense.

The existence of an armed conflict is a question of fact. As stated by the ICTY Appeals Chamber in the *Tadić Case* (*Tadić* 1995): '[A]n armed conflict exists whenever there is a resort to armed force between States or protracted armed violence between governmental authorities and organized armed groups or between such groups within a State'. On this basis, an international armed conflict occurs whenever there is either: recourse to violence between states (Cryer *et al.* 2010, p. 279) or a NIAC involving 'organized armed groups' and 'protracted armed violence'.

As Somali pirates do not represent state agents, the only possibility to consider is whether they are an 'armed group' involved in a NIAC (for extended discussion, see Guilfoyle 2010b; Neumann and Salomon 2011). Somali pirates do not satisfy any of the relevant definitions of an 'armed group': they are not organised under responsible military command; they control no territory; they conduct no hostilities within Somalia (Article 1(1), Second Additional Protocol 1977); and their attacks are directed principally against private merchant vessels, not other armed groups or government forces (*Tadić* 1995; Rome Statute 1998). They also are not parties to a conflict in any ordinary sense. To the extent pirates may be peripherally involved in conflict within Somalia, they are the type of economically motivated actor more 'interested in prevent[ing] a re-emergence of effective state control' than in assuming governmental control themselves (Geiss 2009, p. 135). Pirates' sporadic attacks on private craft do not rise to the level of continuous and relatively intense 'protracted armed violence', nor do their occasional and limited exchanges of fire with naval vessels. Pirate activity thus seems closest to 'situations [...] such as riots, [and] isolated and sporadic acts of violence' (Article 1(1), Second Additional Protocol 1977; Rome Statute 1998), falling below the threshold of armed conflict. Nor could a sustained campaign of violent piracy over many years eventually rise to the level of 'protracted armed violence'. The violence must be relatively *continuous* and against some other *party* to a conflict. The random groups of attacked civilians aboard merchant vessels are not (and cannot be) parties to a conflict. If this seems counter-intuitive, one only has to reflect that extremely violent and highly organised criminal groups may exist within states without being 'at war' with the government (Geiss 2009, p. 136).

We must also consider, however, whether UN Security Council authorisation of counter-piracy action under Chapter VII of the UN Charter implicates IHL. UN Security Council Resolutions 1816, 1848 and 1851 (and the subsequent Resolutions re-enacting them, most recently UNSCR 2020 (2011)) authorise states to take 'necessary measures' or use 'necessary means' to suppress piracy. This might be thought to authorise military force under IHL. Several points should be considered. First, Resolutions 1816 (2008, para 7(b)) and 1848 (2008, para 10(b)) authorise the use 'within the territorial waters of Somalia, in a manner consistent with such action *permitted on the high seas with respect to piracy under relevant international law*, all necessary means to repress' piracy (emphasis added). The preamble to both Resolutions affirms that the applicable international law regarding 'action permitted on the high seas' is set out in the UN Convention on the Law of the Sea (UNCLOS). This authorisation, with its reference to 'necessary means', repeated in later Resolutions, therefore, goes no further than UNCLOS (discussed below). Second, Resolution 1851 (2008, para. 6) authorised certain states and regional organisations cooperating with Somalia to:

undertake all necessary measures that are appropriate in Somalia, for the purpose of suppressing acts of piracy and armed robbery at sea, pursuant to the request of the TFG, provided, however, that any measures [...] shall be undertaken consistent with applicable international humanitarian and human rights law.

I note that the reference to IHL applies only *within* Somalia (and has no relevance therefore to maritime operations) and refers to 'applicable' law. IHL is not 'applicable' outside an armed conflict, the existence of which, as discussed, is an objective fact. The reference to IHL in UNSCR 1851 does not, therefore, necessarily imply any determination that IHL presently applies to counter-piracy operations (as to when IHL might become applicable, see Geiss 2009, pp. 139–140; Guilfoyle 2010b, p. 147).

However, if the decision were taken that IHL was applicable in counter-piracy, this would bring with it the fundamental IHL principles of distinction and proportionality (e.g. Turns 2010). Distinction allows persons to be targeted based on their status as a combatant or a direct participant in hostilities. As above, Somali pirates are not participants in hostilities in any IHL sense. They would therefore remain protected civilians. It would be hard to conclude that Somali pirates were targetable as direct participants in hostilities, as there is no relevant NIAC between pirates and each individually-affected flag state. Under IHL, however, force may be used by combatants against civilians consistent with a law-enforcement paradigm in certain cases: e.g. during an IAC occupation, forces may use force against rioting civilians to fulfil their duty to maintain order in occupied territory (Dinstein 2009). However, if this analogy were correct, applying IHL would not grant any greater powers than those ordinarily applying in law-enforcement operations. Even if the above analysis is incorrect, the use of military force would also be governed by the principle of proportionality. This holds that

[l]aunching an attack which may be expected to cause incidental loss of civilian life, injury to civilians, damage to civilian objects, or a combination thereof, which would be excessive in relation to the concrete and direct military advantage anticipated, is prohibited. (Henckaerts and Doswald-Beck 2005)

I note in this context that pirates increasingly hold hostages aboard their mother-ships and in their bases, which would have to be taken into account in planning lawful attacks. Even on the basis of this brief survey it is difficult to see what advantage there would be in considering ourselves 'at war' with pirates.

3. The second legal paradigm: high-seas policing and the law of piracy

As discussed, the general view of counter-piracy operations is that they involve law enforcement authority, using international law high-seas policing powers. To this end, the High Seas Convention 1958 (HSC) and UNCLOS define piracy in almost identical terms. Reference here shall principally be to UNCLOS. The provisions of these treaties, in particular UNCLOS Articles 100 to 107, lay out the legal framework for the repression of piracy.[1] In Article 101, UNCLOS defines piracy as:

any illegal acts of violence or detention, or [...] depredation, committed for private ends by the crew or the passengers of a private ship or a private aircraft, and directed: (i) on

the high seas, against another ship or aircraft, or against persons or property on board
[...]; (ii) against a ship, aircraft, persons or property in a place outside the jurisdiction of
any State. (for more information, see International Law Commission 1956)

The definition includes acts 'of voluntary participation in the operation of a [pirate] ship or of an aircraft', including cases where no piratical attack has yet been attempted (Article 103, UNCLOS), and 'any act of inciting or of intentionally facilitating' piracy (Article 101(c), UNCLOS). The principal legal issues arising under the treaty provisions are therefore:

- the geographic scope of the offence;
- limitations inherent in the definition (including the 'two vessels' and 'private ends' requirements);
- the relationship between the treaty definition and customary international law;
- the extent of powers granted to suppress piracy; and
- whether there are any rules of priority in exercising jurisdiction over pirates.

These are addressed below.

It is also worth noting briefly that Article 100 of UNCLOS provides that: 'All States shall cooperate to the fullest possible extent in the repression of piracy'. The International Law Commission (1956) explained that:

Any State having an opportunity of taking measures against piracy, and neglecting to do so, would be failing in a duty laid upon it by international law. Obviously, the State must be allowed a certain latitude as to the measures it should take to this end in any individual case.

Thus, states may take a range of repressive measures against piracy short of prosecution, including simply disrupting pirate attacks. Historically this duty does not even appear to have required that states criminalise piracy in national law (Harvard Research in International Law 1932, pp. 755–756, 760; Lucchini and Voelckel, 1996, pp. 158–159). While Article 100 may suggest that all states should have such a law, many still do not (UNSCR 2020 2011, preamble).

Returning to the geographic scope of the offence, piracy may be committed anywhere seaward of the territorial sea of a state. Equally, the powers granted to states to suppress piracy apply in all seas outside any state's territorial waters. In Somalia's case, the Security Council has authorised action in Somalia's territorial waters and land territory by states acting in cooperation with the Transitional Federal Government (UNSCR 1816 2008, para. 7 (as renewed)). The reference to piracy occurring on the 'high seas' may be slightly misleading. UNCLOS prima facie excludes the Exclusive Economic Zone (EEZ) from being part of the high seas (Art 86, UNCLOS). However, other provisions make it plain that certain rules applicable to the high seas – including the law of piracy – apply in the EEZ (Art 58(2), UNCLOS; Lucchini and Voelckel 1996, p. 165). No state has been particularly concerned in practice by Somalia's (invalid) declaration of a 200 nm territorial sea (Treves 2009, p. 408).

Taking the 'two vessels' and 'private ends' requirements, the obvious consequence of the first of these is that piracy does not cover the internal seizure of a vessel (International Law Commission 1956). Hijackings such as the *Achille Lauro* incident would therefore not be piracy. Further, the requirement is that the attack is committed from a *private* vessel against *another* vessel. Thus a private craft attacking a warship or government vessel remains piracy. UNCLOS makes it quite clear that government vessels themselves cannot commit piracy, unless the crew mutinies and then commits violence against other ships (Article 102). Absent mutiny and unlawful acts of violence by government vessels are a matter of State responsibility, not piracy.

Much more controversy has been caused by the words 'for private ends'. As noted, it has often been held that the requirement that piracy be for 'private ends' means that an act committed for 'political' motives, i.e. terrorism, cannot be piracy. An alternative view holds that the relevant distinction is not 'private/political' but 'private/public' (Guilfoyle 2009, pp. 36–40; Geiss and Petrig 2011, pp. 61–62). That is, any act of violence on the high seas not attributable to or sanctioned by a state (a public act) is piracy (a private act; on historic debates, see O'Connell 1984, pp. 975–976). This accords with the principle that a public vessel cannot commit piracy, and with some modern case-law indicating that politically-motivated acts of protest can constitute piracy (*Castle John v. NV Mabeco* 1986). In the Somali context, seizing private vessels in order to demand large ransoms from private companies – without any government sanction – can only be an act 'for private ends'.

There is now widespread acceptance that UNCLOS states the relevant customary international law, which thus applies to all states, even those not party to UNCLOS or the HSC (Guilfoyle 2009, pp. 31–32; Geiss and Petrig 2011, p. 41). The powers granted to suppress piracy are broad. A warship or military aircraft, or other ship or aircraft clearly marked and identifiable as being on government service (Article 107, UNCLOS) on the high seas has the power:

- to visit any vessel that it has a reasonable ground for suspecting of piracy and, if suspicions are not resolved by an inspection of its papers, proceed to search it (Article 110, UNCLOS); and
- to seize any pirate vessel and arrest any suspected pirates (Article 105, UNCLOS),
- subject to a duty to compensate a vessel for any loss or injury suffered as a consequence of unjustified inspection/arrest (Articles 106 and 110(3), UNCLOS).

By definition, these powers are granted on the high seas (or in the EEZ) and thus do not extend to pursuing pirates into foreign territorial waters without the coastal state's consent. Without such consent, the exercise of law-enforcement powers by a pursuing warship over a fleeing pirate vessel within foreign territorial waters would prima facie be unlawful (O'Connell 1984, p. 978; Lucchini and Voelckel 1996, p. 165).[2]

A number of possible problems arise from the fact that UNCLOS Article 105 refers only to the power of *the seizing state* and its courts to: first, try a seized pirate (Kontorovich 2010, pp. 270–271); and, second, judge disposition of property (raising awkward questions about the practice of summary disposal of suspect pirates' weapons; Guilfoyle 2010a, p. 141). On the first point, as a matter of customary international law, every state has jurisdiction to prosecute a pirate, irrespective of any connection between the pirate, their victims or the vessel attacked and the prosecuting state ('universal jurisdiction'; Lucchini and Voelckel 1996, p. 182; Guilfoyle 2009, pp. 40–41; Geiss and Petrig 2011, p. 143). On the second point,

UNSCR 1851 (para. 2) plugged any gap by authorising the disposal of equipment suspected of being used or intended for use in piracy.

In addition to the existence of universal jurisdiction, states may also have jurisdiction over suspected pirates on other bases as a matter of national law; for example, where the crime is committed against or aboard a vessel of their flag, or where the victims are their nationals. An act of piracy, like numerous other crimes, may provide several states with equally valid claims to exercise jurisdiction over an offence. In such cases, international law provides no rule of priority between competing jurisdictions (Cryer *et al.* 2010, p. 43). It is sometimes suggested that before exercising universal jurisdiction, a prosecuting state should, for example, offer the suspect for prosecution to a state with stronger 'links' to the offence (Macedo 2001, p. 32). Such suggestions might represent sound policy, but are not legally binding.

Notably, international law places no obligation upon a capturing state to prosecute piracy suspects. UNCLOS simply provides that the seizing state 'may' arrest pirates and its courts 'may' impose penalties (Article 105). This is a discretionary power (Lucchini and Voelckel 1996, p. 176). Nonetheless, a state always has a duty to 'cooperate to the fullest possible extent' in repressing piracy (UNCLOS, Article 100), which may require serious consideration be given to prosecution wherever practicable. However, in the absence of an 'extradite or prosecute' obligation (discussed below), international law does not demand more.

4. The third legal paradigm: the law of terrorism

No naval mission deployed off Somalia has publicly categorised pirates as terrorists. Nor has any state, even the US, attempted to connect counter-piracy with the 'war on terror'. This might be thought of as odd. US arguments that it may be lawful to detain (or directly target with lethal force) armed non-state actors outside the civilian criminal justice system might be thought useful in counter-piracy operations (Bolton 2011). However, such claims are not widely accepted. Few states support the US interpretation of the law of self-defence or armed conflict regarding the targeted killing or detention of enemies abroad (compare Koh 2010; Gray 2008, pp. 227–253), and invoking such doctrines against Somali pirates could endanger the consensus maintaining present efforts (Kontorovich 2010, pp. 246–247). A point of legal theory may also make such a categorisation unthinkable for many. This is the idea that piracy and terrorism are mutually exclusive categories, an idea involving a considerable oversimplification.

There are certainly factual questions about the degree of connection between pirates and terrorists. While scholars have speculated that piracy could be used to fund terrorism, this does not appear to have eventuated in Somalia (House of Commons Foreign Affairs Committee 2012, para. 16). That said, Somali insurgent groups such as al-Shabaab – which have been designated as terrorist entities – appear sometimes able to 'tax' piracy revenues to some degree (Kolb, Salomon and Udich 2011, pp. 113–115). Nonetheless, international actors have generally not alleged significant links between Somali pirates and designated terrorist groups. Nor has the Security Council's legal response to piracy mirrored that of terrorism: there has been no attempt to replicate the 'legislative' use of its Chapter VII powers to create legally binding obligations on all states regarding terrorism (Talmon 2005). Instead,

Security Council resolutions on Somalia have tended to emphasise international cooperation and pre-existing legal mechanisms.

This is not to say that terrorism, as constructed in international law, is irrelevant to Somali piracy. The historic international failure to agree on a single definition of terrorism leaves a fragmentary legal framework (Cryer *et al.* 2010, pp. 334–337), parts of which could apply to piracy. Piratical hostage-taking and hijacking already fall within the acts covered by the Hostages and the Suppression of Unlawful Acts Against the Safety of Maritime Navigation Conventions (discussed below). However, this raises questions about whether invoking these conventions could limit the options of both commercial players (in paying ransoms) and state actors (by requiring a no-exception prosecute or extradite policy).

As explained below, pirates could be prosecuted under a number of 'terrorism' conventions (or, more accurately, 'suppression conventions'). The two suppression conventions considered here are the Convention for the Suppression of Unlawful Acts Against the Safety of Maritime Navigation (hereafter SUA Convention) and the International Convention Against the Taking of Hostages (hereafter Hostage Taking Convention). A terrorist motive does not form any express element of the crimes set out in either treaty. This follows the general historical pattern of the suppression conventions, which was to proceed by criminalising certain acts associated with terrorism, given that no consensus on a universal definition of terrorism could be reached (Cryer *et al.* 2010, pp. 336–340). After discussing these Conventions, a few observations will be offered regarding the implications of international law on terrorist financing.

4.1. The SUA Convention

The SUA Convention was famously inspired by the *Achille Lauro* incident, in which a vessel was internally hijacked and a hostage aboard killed. The sponsoring governments who first introduced the draft Convention at the International Maritime Organization (Austria, Egypt and Italy) cited as part of their reason for doing so the inherent limitations of piracy as an offence: that it necessarily involved an act for private ends, and – crucially – the two vessel requirement excluded the internal seizure of a vessel (International Maritime Organization 1987). Another relevant inspiration for the Convention was General Assembly Resolution 40/61, calling upon the IMO to 'study the problem of terrorism aboard or against ships' (notably, there already existed treaties dealing with hijacking and sabotaging airplanes).[3] The SUA Convention is thus commonly called a 'terrorism suppression' convention. It is important to note, however, that the word 'terrorism' appears *only in its preamble*. As suggested above, a terrorist motive does not form any express element of the treaty offences.

Article 3 of the SUA Convention defines several crimes. Relevantly, Article 3(1)(a) states that '[a]ny person commits an offence if that person unlawfully and intentionally [...] seizes or exercises control over a ship by force or threat thereof'. There is no requirement that the seizure be internal or politically motivated. Thus any pirate seizure of a vessel off Somalia clearly falls within this definition. Attempting, abetting and threatening such an offence are equally SUA Convention crimes (Article 3(2)). The only case in which the Convention would not apply is where the offence was committed solely within a single state's territorial sea *and* the vessel was not scheduled to navigate beyond that sea *and* the suspected offender was subsequently found within that state's territory (Article 4). As pirate attacks off Somalia are generally committed far outside territorial waters, this poses no difficulties. Of course not all piracy will necessarily fall within the SUA Convention. Acts of theft ('depredation') not endangering the safety of a vessel and committed by one vessel against another would be piracy, but would not be a SUA Convention offence. The crime of piracy and SUA Convention offences are thus distinct but may overlap on some facts.

If there is potential overlap, the question becomes whether the SUA Convention offers any advantages over the general law of piracy. It does, in three respects. First, unlike the law of piracy, the SUA Convention creates an express obligation upon parties to enact national laws. Under Article 6, state parties *must* make the offences in Article 3 a crime under national law when committed: against or on board their flag vessels; within their territory or territorial sea; or by one of their nations. In addition, state parties *may* establish criminal jurisdiction on certain other bases.

Second, the SUA Convention contains an obligation to either extradite a suspect or submit the case for potential prosecution (commonly called an 'extradite or prosecute' obligation). Where a state finds a suspect or offender within its territory (the territorial state) and another state party or parties have jurisdiction over the offence, then the territorial state 'shall [...] if it does not extradite him, be obliged [...] to submit the case without delay to its competent authorities for the purpose of prosecution', in accordance with national law (Article 10(1), SUA Convention). To this end, each party *must* enact a law allowing it to prosecute 'in cases where the alleged offender is present in its territory and it does not extradite him' to any states' party having jurisdiction. Put simply, if a state party has a suspect in their territory, and another state party has jurisdiction over the offence, then the first state party must either prosecute that suspect or extradite them to a state which will. This may be described as a limited form of universal jurisdiction, as it allows the prosecution of individuals lacking relevant 'links' to the prosecuting state.

Third, Article 7 provides that a state finding a suspect on its territory is *required* to commence a preliminary investigation and, if necessary, take the suspect into custody pending a decision about extradition or prosecution. That investigating state is also required to communicate with states having jurisdiction. Article 7(5) provides that an investigating state party 'shall promptly report its findings to [those] States and [...] indicate *whether it intends to exercise jurisdiction*' (emphasis added). Thus a state has a free choice whether to extradite or prosecute and need not defer to another state's jurisdiction.

States may be reluctant, however, to invoke the Convention precisely because of this Article 7 extradite or prosecute obligation. It would certainly be awkward if it was found to apply to pirates aboard warships. While a warship is *not* 'territory' in the sense of being a 'floating island' (O'Connell 1984, pp. 736–737), it is an object with a special status in international law. On the high seas *all* vessels are subject to the jurisdiction of their flag state, a status which may be 'assimilated to' territorial jurisdiction (*Lotus Case* 1927). Human rights bodies and courts which have found vessels flagged to, or under the effective control of, a state may fall within its 'jurisdiction' under human rights treaties (*PK et al v Spain* 2008; *Medvedyev v France* 2010; *Hirsi v Italy* 2012). A state's sovereign control over a warship is much stronger than in the case of other vessels (Article 95, UNCLOS). It should therefore be uncontroversial that – on the high seas – a warship may form part of the flag state's 'jurisdiction' on a basis similar to 'territory'. Two different conclusions could be reached. First, because the SUA Convention refers to 'territory' and not 'jurisdiction', it has no application to ships at sea and Article 7 does not apply aboard warships. Alternatively, as the SUA Convention's fundamental purpose is to ensure no suspect goes unprosecuted, and as one should not adopt interpretations which defeat the object and purpose of a treaty, Article 7 should be applied to warships (Geiss and Petrig 2011, pp. 163–164). The point remains untested.

Overall, it is clear that the SUA Convention does not cover piracy *in toto*, but as noted above some acts constituting piracy under UNCLOS may also be SUA Convention offences. While the law of piracy contains a duty to cooperate in the suppression of piracy, but only a discretion to prosecute suspects, the SUA Convention places express obligations upon state parties to both have adequate national laws and to either extradite or prosecute suspects found within their territory. However, only the law of piracy provides an exception to the exclusive jurisdiction of the flag state that can justify the stopping, searching, arrest or seizure of suspect pirate vessels and persons aboard on the high seas. The SUA Convention does not provide any such automatic right of high seas interdiction (although a 2005 Protocol contains a mechanism for seeking the flag state's permission for such a boarding). While piracy is a crime of universal jurisdiction, the SUA Convention creates a more limited form of 'quasi-universal' jurisdiction between parties to the treaty.

4.2. The Hostage Taking Convention

Somali pirates clearly commit offences covered by the Hostage Taking Convention. Article 1 of the Convention states:

> Any person who seizes or detains and threatens to kill, to injure or to continue to detain another person [...] in order to compel a third party [... including] a natural or juridical person [...] to do or abstain from doing any act as an explicit or implicit condition for release of the hostage [commits the offence of hostage-taking].

This definition is clearly met where a hostage is detained and a condition of his or her release is that a private person/company pays a ransom. The Somali model of piracy, involving holding crews for ransom, clearly falls within the Convention.

One might question whether the Convention was intended to encompass maritime crimes potentially covered by the SUA Convention. The Hostage Taking Convention contains no express territorial limitations, a point made clear by Article 5, under which each party must establish jurisdiction over Convention offences committed:

> (a) In its territory *or on board a ship or aircraft registered in that State*; (b) By any of its nationals [...]; [or] (d) *With respect to a hostage who is a national of that State*, if that State considers it appropriate. (emphasis added)

The Convention is thus capable of applying to events at sea.

The Convention includes a substantially similar 'extradite or prosecute' obligation to that in the SUA Convention. Article 13 provides that the Convention has no application: 'where the offence is committed within a single State, the hostage and the alleged offender are nationals of that State and the alleged offender is found in the territory of that State.' These conditions are cumulative and unlikely to be satisfied in any hostage-taking by Somali pirates.

4.3. The question of terrorist financing

One might suspect that these suppression conventions are not invoked because labelling pirates as terrorists could make paying ransoms a breach of terrorist financing laws. This result may follow at national law. Under US law anyone who 'provides material support or resources [...] knowing or intending that they are to be used' in prohibited terrorist acts, defined to include hostage-taking and SUA Convention offences, commits an offence.[4] As a result, arguably, any insurer making 'a ransom payment to pirates [...] is providing material support to terrorists and violating U.S. law' (Lennox-Gentle 2010). At international law, however, such a result is less likely to follow under the Terrorism Financing Convention (International Convention for the Suppression of the Financing of Terrorism 1999).

The Convention sets out something close to a comprehensive definition of 'terrorism', but only for the purpose of prohibiting its intentional financing. Under Article 2(1):

> Any person commits an offence [...] if that person by any means, directly or indirectly, unlawfully and wilfully, provides or collects funds with the intention that they should be used or in the knowledge that they are to be used [...] to carry out:
>
> (a) An act which constitutes an offence within the scope of and as defined in one of the treaties listed in the annex; or
>
> (b) Any other act intended to cause death or serious bodily injury to a civilian [...] when the purpose of such act, by its nature or context, is to intimidate a population, or to compel a government or an international organization to do or to abstain from doing any act.

Relevantly, Article 2(1)(a) covers SUA and Hostage Taking Convention offences. Surely this makes it illegal to finance those who commit such crimes by paying them ransom? Not necessarily. The Convention only criminalises giving money to individuals both 'unlawfully and wilfully' and with either the 'intention' or 'knowledge' that the money will be used for prohibited purposes. A commercial actor paying a ransom to secure the release of a crew and vessel may certainly know that such funds will likely finance future attacks. However, someone who provides money under duress does not do so *wilfully* (*contra* Kolb, Salomon, Udich 2011, p. 127). Arguably, then, the Convention does not criminalise paying Somali pirates ransoms. (For a different approach with a similar conclusion see Kolb, Salomon, Udich 2011, pp. 134–138). On this analysis, the same result follows even where there is evidence that some money paid to Somali pirates finds its way to designated terrorist organisations such as al-Shabaab (Kolb, Salomon, Udich 2011, pp. 113–115).

4.4. Conclusions

Nothing in theory prevents prosecuting pirates under national laws implementing the SUA or Hostages Conventions. Indeed, their obligations to prosecute or extradite might be thought superior to merely permissive universal jurisdiction over piracy. They have not, however, been widely invoked – though national implementing laws have occasionally been used as 'back up' charges in piracy cases.[5] Reluctance to rely on these 'terrorism' conventions may simply reflect the fact that states have used these powers little in practice and in many cases have not implemented them in national law.

5. The fourth legal paradigm: transnational organised crime

As noted above, the response to Somali piracy has fallen within a law-enforcement paradigm. As the 2000 United Nations Convention against Transnational Organized Crime (UNTOC) is in force for many states active in counter-piracy off Somalia, it is worth brief consideration. UNTOC applies to 'serious crimes', which are 'transnational in nature' *and* committed by an 'organized criminal group' (Article 3(1)). Serious crimes are those punishable by at least four years' imprisonment. Most acts of piracy off Somalia involving violent attacks and hostage-taking will therefore involve a 'serious crime'.

Under UNTOC a crime is 'transnational in nature' when it is, inter alia, 'committed in more than one State' or 'committed in one State but a substantial part of its preparation, planning, direction or control takes place in another State' (Article 3(2)). Can this extend to crimes committed on the high seas? Under Article 15(b) states must criminalise conduct prohibited by UNTOC 'committed on board a vessel that is flying the flag of that State Party'. The idea of 'committed in [...] [a] State' thus likely includes events occurring aboard a flag vessel. If so, offences planned or prepared in one state and committed aboard another state's flagged vessel will be 'transnational in nature'.

The requirement of an 'organized criminal group' is met where 'three or more persons' act in concert to commit 'one or more serious crimes [...] in order to obtain, directly or indirectly [...] financial [...] benefit' (Article 2(a)). Again, pirate gangs clearly satisfy this requirement. Thus a pirate raid planned in Somalia and carried out aboard a foreign-flagged vessel could involve one or more 'serious crimes' prepared in one state, committed in another, and carried out by an organised criminal group. It is no obstacle that Somalia is not a party to UNTOC.

UNTOC contains an extradite or prosecute obligation in Article 16(10). Unlike the 'terrorism' treaties discussed above, the obligation to submit the case to prosecuting authorities only follows where another party has made an extradition request and it has been declined. Under UNTOC, extradition can be requested for a 'serious crime' that 'involves an organized criminal group' if 'the person who is the subject of the request for extradition is located in the territory of the requested State Party, provided that the offence for which extradition is sought is punishable under the domestic law of both' states (Article 16(1)). On this reading, the Convention applies a different (and lower) test for 'transnationality' in extradition cases, as the only necessary transnational element is that the person sought for extradition is in another state's territory (UN Office on Drugs and Crime 2004).

Possibly of more consequence are the provisions of Article 18 regarding mutual legal assistance ('MLA'). State parties are required to 'afford one another the widest measure of mutual legal assistance in investigations, prosecutions and judicial proceedings' related to UNTOC covered offences (Article 18(1)). While the extensive provisions of Article 18 cannot be summarised here, one may note that such co-operation extends to '[t]aking evidence or statements from persons', 'providing information, evidentiary items and expert evaluations' and '[f]acilitating the voluntary appearance of persons in the requesting State Party', such as witness. These provisions are sufficiently detailed that they may act as a so-called 'mini-MLA treaty'. That is, they set out a complete MLA regime that parties can apply between themselves if other arrangements are absent. For the purposes of requesting MLA, the requesting state need only have, under Article 18(1), 'reasonable grounds to suspect' that the relevant offence 'is transnational in nature [...] and that the offence involves an organized criminal group'.

UNTOC may thus provide a common framework for facilitating MLA in relation to prosecuting pirates, although MLA activities have clearly already been happening, including under more specific instruments such as those concluded between patrolling naval states and Kenya and the Seychelles (Guilfoyle 2010a; UNSCR 2020 2011, preamble). Indeed, the process involved in states which have captured pirates transferring them (and associated evidence) to another state for prosecution is a classic form of MLA. That process is about to gain a further level of complexity with the conclusion of agreements between states such as the Seychelles for repatriation of convicted prisoners to Somalia, once there are prisons safe enough to which to return them (UN Secretary General 2011).

6. Conclusions

The aim of this paper has been to give a concise overview of the legal paradigms potentially applicable to Somali piracy. In doctrinal terms, the laws-of-war paradigm is both a poor fit and not particularly useful. A narrow, legalistic understanding of terrorism certainly covers some acts committed by Somali pirates but has generally not been invoked. It is possible that states do not wish to fetter themselves with a 'prosecute or extradite' obligation when they are not always willing to prosecute piracy suspects. However, it is legally uncertain whether such obligations would, irrespective, bind states in respect of activities aboard warships. It is more likely the case that poor domestic implementation of these treaties has rendered them of limited utility. The path the international community pursued down looks most like mutual legal assistance under the UNTOC, but relies in practice far more on tailored bilateral agreements. These, ultimately, have as their underpinning the general international law of piracy. Despite its difficulties, this historical curiosity of international law appears to have provided states with all the authority they need to pursue the current programme of counter-piracy off Somalia. The language of counter-piracy as law enforcement is now embedded in the international discussion of Somali piracy. The choice would appear not only entirely legally justifiable but also highly pragmatic.

Notes

1. The preambles to UNSCR 1848 and 1851 (2008) first reaffirmed 'that international law, as reflected in [UNCLOS], sets out the legal framework applicable to combating piracy'. All later Resolutions reiterate the point.

2. However, UNSCR 1816 (para. 7), 1846 (para. 10) and 1851 (para. 6) provide a mechanism for 'co-operating States' to enter the territorial waters and land territory of Somalia. This has been renewed in subsequent resolutions.
3. Convention for the Suppression of Unlawful Seizure of Aircraft, The Hague, 16 December 1970, 860 UNTS 105; Convention for the Suppression of Unlawful Acts against the Safety of Civil Aviation, Montreal, 23 September 1971, 974 UNTS 177.
4. 18 USC 2339A(a) (Supp. III 2009).
5. E.g. Somali piracy suspect Abduwali Abdukhadir Muse was charged in the US both with piracy and offences under 18 USC 2280, implementing the SUA Convention. The charging document is available at http://graphics8.nytimes.com/packages/pdf/nyregion/22pirate_Complaint.pdf.

References

Blackstone, W. (1770), *Commentaries on the Laws of England*, 4th ed., Vol. 4. Oxford: Clarendon Press.

Bolton, J.R. (2011), 'Treat Somali pirates like terrorists', *The Washington Times*, 14 October. Available at http://www.washingtontimes.com/news/2011/oct/14/treat-somali-pirates-like-terrorists/, accessed 24 July 2011.

Bueger, C. and Stockbruegger, J. (2011), 'Security communities, alliances, and macrosecuritization: the practices of counter-piracy governance', in M.J. Struett, J.D. Carlson and M.T. Nance, eds., *Maritime Piracy and the Construction of Global Governance*. London: Routledge.

Castle John v. NV Mabeco (Belgium, Court of Cassation, 1986) 77 *International Law Reports* 537.

Convention for the Suppression of Unlawful Acts against the Safety of Civil Aviation, Montreal, 23 September 1971, 974 UNTS 177.

Convention for the Suppression of Unlawful Acts Against the Safety of Maritime Navigation, Rome, 10 March 1988, 1678 UNTS 221.

Convention for the Suppression of Unlawful Seizure of Aircraft, The Hague, 16 December 1970, 860 UNTS 105.

Cryer, R., Friman, H., Robinson, D. and Wilmshurst, E. (2010), *An Introduction to International Criminal Law and Procedure*, 2nd ed. Cambridge: Cambridge University Press.

Dinstein, Y. (2009), *The International Law of Belligerent Occupation*. Cambridge: Cambridge University Press.

European Union Council Secretariat (2009), 'EU naval operation against piracy (EU NAVFOR Somalia – Operation ATALANTA)', Fact Sheet EU NAVFOR/04, March. Available at http://www.consilium.europa.eu/uedocs/cmsUpload/090507%20Factsheet%20EU%20NAVFOR%20Somalia%20-%20version%207_EN.pdf, accessed 24 July 2011.

François, J.P.A. (1950), 'Regime of the high seas' in *Yearbook of the International Law Commission*, Vol. 2. New York: United Nations, pp. 36–113.

Geiss, R. (2009), 'Armed violence in fragile states: low-intensity conflicts, spillover conflicts, and sporadic law enforcement operations by third parties', *International Review of the Red Cross*, Vol. 91, pp. 127–142.

Geiss, R. and Petrig, A. (2011), *The Legal Framework for Counter-Piracy Operations in Somalia and the Gulf of Aden*. Oxford: Oxford University Press.

Gray, C. (2008), *International Law and the Use of Force*, 3rd ed. Oxford: Oxford University Press.

Gross, O. and Ní Aoláin, F. (2006), *Law in Times of Crisis: Emergency Powers in Theory and Practice*. Cambridge: Cambridge University Press.

Guilfoyle, D. (2009), *Shipping Interdiction and the Law of the Sea*. Cambridge: Cambridge University Press.

Guilfoyle, D. (2010a), 'Counter-piracy law enforcement and human rights', *International and Comparative Law Quarterly*, Vol. 51, no. 1, pp. 141–169.

Guilfoyle, D. (2010b), 'The laws of war and the fight against Somali piracy: combatants or criminals', *Melbourne Journal of International Law*, Vol. 11, no. 1, pp. 141–153.

Harvard Research in International Law (1932), 'Draft convention on piracy', *American Journal of International Law Supplement*, Vol. 26, pp. 739–886.

Henckaerts, J.-M. and Doswald-Beck, L. (2005), *Customary International Humanitarian Law, Vol I: Rules*. Cambridge: International Committee of the Red Cross.

High Seas Convention (HSC), 29 April 1958, 450 UNTS 11.

Hirsi v Italy, European Court of Human Rights (Application No. 27765/09), Judgment of the Grand Chamber, 23 February 2012.

House of Commons Foreign Affairs Committee (United Kingdom) (2012), 'Piracy off the coast of Somalia' (HC 2010-12, 1318), 5 January. London: The Stationery Office.

House of Lords European Union Committee (United Kingdom) (2010), 'Combating Somali piracy: the EU's naval operation Atalanta' (HL 2009–10, 103), 14 April. London: The Stationery Office. Evidence Annexe, p. 29.

International Convention Against the Taking of Hostages, New York, 17 December 1979, 1316 UNTS 205.

International Convention for the Suppression of the Financing of Terrorism, New York, 9 December 1999, 2178 UNTS 197.

International Law Commission (1956), *Yearbook of the International Law Commission*, Vol. 2. New York: United Nations.

International Maritime Organization (1987), IMO Doc. PCUA 1/3, 3 February, Annexe.

Jopling, M. (2009), 'The growing threat of piracy to regional and global security', *NATO Parliamentary Assembly Document 169 CDS 09 E rev 1*. Available at http://www.nato-pa.int/default.asp?SHORTCUT=1770, accessed 24 July 2011.

Koh, H. (2010), 'The Obama administration and international law', *Annual Meeting of the American Society of International Law, Washington, DC, 25 March*. Available at http://www.state.gov/s/l/releases/remarks/139119.htm, accessed 24 July 2011.

Kolb, A., Salomon, T.R. and Udich, J. (2011), 'Paying danegeld to pirates: humanitarian necessity or financing jihadists?', *Max Planck Yearbook of United Nations Law*, Vol. 15, pp. 105–164.

Kontorovich, E. (2010), '"A Guantanamo on the sea": the difficulties of prosecuting pirates and terrorists', *California Law Review*, Vol. 98, no. 1, pp. 234–276.

Lennox-Gentle, T. (2010), 'Piracy, sea robbery, and terrorism: enforcing laws to deter ransom payments and hijacking', *Transportation Law Journal*, Vol. 37, no. 3, pp. 199–218.

Lotus Case, [1927] PCIJ Ser. A No. 10, 25.

Lucchini, L. and Voelckel, M. (1996), *Droit de la Mer*. Paris: Pedone. Tome 2, Vol. 2.

Macedo, S. ed., (2001), *The Princeton Principles on Universal Jurisdiction*. Princeton, NJ: Princeton University Press.

Medvedyev v France, European Court of Human Rights (Application No. 3394/03), Judgment of the Grand Chamber, 29 March 2010.

Milanović, M. (2009), 'A norm conflict perspective on the relationship between international humanitarian law and human rights law', *Journal of Conflict and Security Law*, Vol. 14, no. 3, pp. 459–483.

Neumann, T. and Salomon, T.R. (2011), 'Kein Krieg vor Somalia', *Journal of International Law of Peace and Armed Conflict*, Vol. 24, no. 3, pp. 165–172.

O'Connell, D.P. (1984), *The International Law of the Sea*. Oxford: Clarendon. Vol. 2.

PK et al v Spain, Committee Against Torture, Decision, 21 November 2008, UN Doc. CAT/C/41/D/323/2007, para. 8.2.

Second Additional Protocol to the Geneva Conventions of 12 August 1949, and relating to the Protection of Victims of Non-International Armed Conflicts, 8 June 1977, 1125 UNTS 609.

Rome Statute of the International Criminal Court, 17 July 1998, 2187 UNTS 90. Article 8(2)(d) and (f).

Tadić (1995), Decision on the Defence Motion for Interlocutory Appeal on Jurisdiction. International Criminal Tribunal for the Former Yugoslavia. Appeals Chamber. Case No IT-94-1-AR72. 2 October. Paragraph 70.

Talmon, S. (2005), 'The security council as world legislature', *American Journal of International Law*, Vol. 99, no. 1, pp. 175–193.

The LeLouis (1817) 2 Dodson 210, 244.

Treves, T. (2009), 'Piracy, law of the sea, and use of force: developments off the coast of Somalia', *European Journal of International Law*, Vol. 20, no. 2, pp. 399–414.

Turns, D. (2010), 'The law of armed conflict (international humanitarian law)', in D. Evans, ed., *International Law*, 3rd ed. Oxford: Oxford University Press, pp. 830–832.

UN Convention on the Law of the Sea (UNCLOS), 10 December 1982, 1833 UNTS 3.

UN Convention against Transnational Organized Crime (UNTOC), 15 November 2000, 2237 UNTS 319.

UN Office on Drugs and Crime (2004), *Legislative Guide for the Implementation of the United Nations Convention against Transnational Organized Crime.* New York: United Nations. Paragraph 416(b).

UN Secretary General (2011), 'Report of the Secretary-General on the modalities for the establishment of specialized Somali anti-piracy courts', UN Doc S/2011/360.

UN Security Council Resolution 1816 (2008), UN Doc. S/RES/1816. 2 June.

UN Security Council Resolution 1846 (2008), UN Doc. S/RES/1846. 2 December.

UN Security Council Resolution 1848 (2008), UN Doc. S/RES/1848. 12 December.

UN Security Council Resolution 1851 (2008), UN Doc. S/RES/1851. 16 December.

UN Security Council Resolution 2020 (2011), UN Doc. S/RES/2020. 22 November.

US Navy (2007), 'Commander's handbook on the law of naval operations'. Available at http://www.usnwc.edu/getattachment/a9b8e92d-2c8d-4779-9925-0defea93325c/1-14M_(Jul_2007)_(NWP), accessed 24 July 2011.

BOOK REVIEW

India as an Asia Pacific power, by David Brewster, London, Routledge, 2012, xi + 219 pp., £85 (hardback), ISBN 978-0-415-61761-1

That India might be considered a power of consequence in the Asia Pacific will come as a surprise to many. The world has tended to see India through the prism of the troubled subcontinent and only occasionally has referred to its broader strategic interests in the Indian Ocean Region. Few have had reason to associate India with the East Asian security discourse. Yet, the prospect of India contributing to the balance of power in the Asia Pacific has attracted some academic and much policy attention in the United States and East Asia. This is rooted in the rapid expansion of India's economy in the recent decades, its growing material capabilities and the widespread perception that India is emerging as a great power. David Brewster's volume is the first full-length study on the subject and could well become the benchmark with which to evaluate India's changing role in the rapidly-evolving security dynamic in East Asia.

India's Look East Policy (LEP), announced by Delhi in the early 1990s, has been a subject of interest for those studying India's external relations and their changing orientation since the end of the Cold War. The initial emphasis of the LEP was indeed on India's integration with the booming East Asian economies and the Association of South East Asian Nations (ASEAN)-led regional institutions. The defence and security dimensions of the LEP, however, began to draw greater attention in the second decade of its implementation.

Despite much skepticism in the region about India's relevance, ASEAN decided to invite India into the East Asian Summit process that was launched in 2005. India has also become a part of the ASEAN Defence Ministers Meeting (ADMM Plus) forum, which was initiated in 2010. The unstated assumption in the region was that having India would help generate a better balance of power in East Asia. A similar premise was inherent in the American strategic outreach to India in the second term of the Bush Administration (2005–2009), which saw the United States invest much political capital in building a strategic partnership with India. Washington was betting that India, with its accelerating economic growth, was bound to emerge as a great power, and assisting in India's rise was in the US interest. Delhi's own engagement with the region on security affairs rose steadily through the 2000s, collectively with ASEAN as well as individually with key countries.

Brewster examines the pull factors in East Asia and the push factors in India that have made questions on Delhi's security role in the Asia Pacific relevant. Brewster begins with a review of India's rise and the recent evolution of its strategic thinking about the Asia-Pacific region. He then moves on to assess India's traditional security competition with China, its expanding strategic engagement with the United States, and its growing partnership with Japan. While many others have covered this ground, Brewster's survey of India's relations with the great powers of the region acquires a special salience thanks to its conscious focus on the Asia-Pacific theatre.

The chapters that follow paint a picture of India's deepening political engagement with Vietnam in Indo-China, Singapore, Malaysia and Indonesia in archipelagic South East Asia, and Australia in the Oceanic region. The exploration of India's security ties with regional actors provides the basis for the two penultimate chapters, which take a broader view of India's maritime security ambitions in the western Pacific and examine the internal drivers shaping India's engagement with the region. The concluding chapter raises the prospect for India's emergence as a power in the Asia-Pacific.

Brewster's skeptical eye provides a necessary antidote to the hype on India's rise and the kind of role Delhi could play in the Asia-Pacific region. Brewster's cautious approach is more in line with those in East Asia who argue that the gap between promise and performance of an Indian strategic role in the region is real and is unlikely to be bridged any time soon. Brewster points to the enduring limitations on Delhi arising from its traditional 'defensive strategic thinking'. He insists that India's accelerated economic growth does not automatically give it a strategic role in the Asia-Pacific. To become a credible power in the region, Brewster concludes, India needs to 'go beyond its rhetoric and demonstrate a significant commitment to provide security to the region' (p. 164).

Those familiar with India's past isolation from Asia and its profound commitment to non-alignment recognise the sea change in Delhi's attitudes towards East Asian security politics. Yet the pace of change is clearly not enough to overturn the pessimism about India's possible contributions to stabilising the balance of power in the Asia-Pacific. In fact, India's economic slowdown in the early 2010s, its inability to cope with the growing demands in the region to provide security, and the disappointments in Washington about the pace of movement in the strategic partnership with Delhi would seem to justify Brewster's skepticism.

Yet, India looms even larger over the East Asian horizon amidst the rapid transformation of the regional balance of power. While India continues to move at its unhurried pace, the expansion of Chinese military capabilities, Beijing's growing assertiveness towards its Asian maritime neighbours, and the US 'pivot' to Asia have all made Delhi even more relevant to the balance of power. While Brewster's assessment of India's limitations remains a valid one, the regional context has evolved considerably since the book was written. The US needs to deal with the consequences China's rise has made to collaboration with Delhi critical for Washington's Asian military calculus.

Unsurprisingly then, the US Defence Secretary Leon Panetta, during a visit to Delhi in June 2012, called India the 'lynchpin' of US military strategy in Asia. The trend lines that Brewster identifies in India's security engagement with the Asia-Pacific acquire a new intensity amidst the growing distrust between Washington and Beijing and the increasingly rivalrous nature of their bilateral relationship. Brewster's assessment of the convergence between the Indian and

Pacific Oceans into a single theatre – the Indo-Pacific – amidst the rise of India and China has gained much currency. Besides being an important contribution to the study of India's foreign and security policies, Brewster's volume is a definitive starting point for any scholar interested in India's future role in Asia and the Pacific.

C. Raja Mohan
Observer Research Foundation, New Delhi
© 2012, C. Raja Mohan

BOOK REVIEW

The kingdom and the quarry – China, Australia, fear and greed, by David Uren, Melbourne, Black Inc., 2012, vi + 260 pp., AU$29.95 (paperback), ISBN 978-1-86395-566-9

'China is neither the source of endless super-profits, nor the wolf at the door': this is the conclusion (p. 238) of a fascinating new description and analysis of Australia-China relations – *The Kingdom and the Quarry – China, Australia, Fear and Greed* – which deals with the evolving contours of the relationship primarily from an economic and geostrategic perspective.

Australia's current geopolitical environment is the result of a diverse amalgam of historical, economic and geopolitical forces, but, in essence, represents the product of three compelling, yet sometimes divergent, developmental phases over the past 200 years or so.

(1) Australia is presently in its 'regional' phase of international trade relations. That is, since Federation in 1901, when Australia was trade-dependent upon Britain, its strongest linkages are currently with north-east Asia. China became Australia's largest trading partner in 2007.

(2) Australia is now in its third wave of superpower investment. That is, the trade-dependence on Britain was associated with considerable foreign investment, which still remains important. The second, still very significant, investment wave came with the United States and Japan, and the emergence of the current third Chinese wave is mainly in primary commodities, most notably energy, iron ore and increasingly in agriculture. The second wave was the subject of critical analysis from the left; the third wave is currently the subject of critical analysis from the right.

(3) Of much lesser significance is that Australia is now in its fifth phase of Indian Ocean 'new regionalism' – that is, following the pre-colonial, colonial, Cold War and post-Cold War phases – and thus there is renewed interest in reviving the idea of an Indian Ocean community.

These developmental stages are directly associated with Australia's trilateral geopolitical tension – *culturally*, Australia is close to Europe and especially Britain; *politically and strategically*, Australia is close to the United States; *economically*, Australia is close to Asia. Resultant cross-pressures can invariably complicate the making of difficult and contested evaluations on perceptions of threat that impinge directly upon the making of Australia's security (broadly-defined) policy in the twenty-first century. As an economics correspondent, the author, David Uren, deals in considerable detail with the changing fortunes of the economic relationship and its personal (most notably, the creation of billionaires in peripheral resource-rich Australian states), regional, national and international impacts. However, while the book dwells on a multitude of detail of 'insider' economic perspectives in the course of the evolution of the relationship, inevitably such a discussion impinges upon significant dimensions of the geopolitical relationship.

From a Chinese perspective, the development of the Australian economic relationship has been driven by a growing concern over 'resource security' (Chapter 12). The rapid and immense scale of Chinese economic development has necessitated an increasing reliance on essential imported raw materials, especially energy and iron ore, over the past 15 years. More recently, Africa became a natural resources target in a more focussed 'going out' strategy as part of a 'new geopolitics of energy'.

Uren skillfully discusses the emerging tensions between Asia-Pacific regional economic and security linkages. It was especially during the conservative Howard Government years in Australia that the tensions between regional security and regional trade became particularly evident. On the one hand, in 2000, Australia viewed the United States as 'the bedrock of Australia's security strategy' (p. 114). Indeed, in 1999, a media portrayal emerged of Australia acting as the 'deputy sheriff' to the US in Asia. On the other hand, Australia was keen to develop a 'strategic economic relationship' with China. The diplomatic and analytical ambiguities and contradictions associated with managing this complex duality began to emerge and were often based around misperceptions and careless comments. For example, a view expressed by the then Australian Foreign Minister, Alexander Downer, of ANZUS as being 'symbolic' naturally resulted in a strong negative US response. However, perhaps even more damaging was the misperception that Australia's economic relationship with China might result in a more general 'strategic realignment' away from the United States (p. 117).

It is generally the case in Australia that there is bipartisan support for the maintenance of continuity in Australia's foreign policy, irrespective of which political party is in government. The election of Kevin Rudd as an Australian Labor Prime Minister in 2007 was an important event from various perspectives, not the least of which was that he was both fluent in Mandarin and was also a foreign affairs expert. This elicited various responses, expectations and apprehensions, both domestically and overseas. For example, there were those who took the view that since Australia now had a PM who could uniquely speak an Asian language, this would ensure that Australian ties to China would gain immediate and ongoing strength. This prospect was viewed both negatively and positively by commentators, diplomats and others; for example, some, including some well-respected analysts and politicians, now inexplicably described Kevin Rudd as the 'Manchurian candidate' (p. 41).

However, Rudd's 'brutal realism' over the possibility of a 'Chinese threat' to Australia was seemingly reflected in the 2009 Defence White Paper. As Uren expertly teases out, the preparation of this document was associated with a 'split between the intelligence community and the defence white paper team' (p. 125). From a geopolitical point of view, the most interesting 'revelation', which is contained in Chapter 7 of the book – 'Wrestling a Giant' – is the notion that in the Australian 2009 Defence White Paper there was a 'top-secret chapter' that was excluded from the final Report, which outlined a scenario for waging a war against China. This secret chapter purportedly 'focused on Australia's ability to fight an air-sea battle alongside the United States against China' (p. 128).

While the author is unable to provide concrete public proof of the existence of the top-secret chapter, he does draw attention to some secondary sources and to some interesting supporting evidence from *Wikileaks*. Given the nature of national defence documents in Australia, it is much more likely, however, that there was no secret defence White Paper chapter, but rather that there was one scenario among many that was discussed in its preparation that outlined the *possibility* of war with China. While such scenario-building might be seen to be a valuable exercise, to many Australian commentators, the very idea of going to war with one's largest trading partner defies any realistic permutation of security logic and simply beggars belief. In any event, there have been subsequent muted denials from both the Australian bureaucracy and government leaders on even the *discussion* of such a scenario.

Nevertheless, in Uren's view, Obama's 'pivot' to Asia could initiate a 'new cold war', and, if China's neo-Mahanians are in the ascendancy, then the South China Sea will likely become an arena for regional conflict. As the author points out, such uncertainties inevitably raise the contentious question of whether Australia can indeed satisfy the security demands of *both* the United States *and* China (pp. 224–225). However, little detailed geopolitical analysis is provided as to how this key question might be satisfactorily addressed. The book is far more evidentially convincing in its detailed and insightful *economic* analysis of the behaviour of Chinese state enterprises and their employees and the reactions of Australian mining magnates and various multinational mining corporations to the Chinese resource security strategy. Competition is fierce, greed is ever-present and fear and mistrust are commonplace.

While *The Kingdom and the Quarry – China, Australia, Fear and Greed* does not chart a clear path for future Australia-China relations, some suggestions are made in terms of the need to build mutual trust and confidence-building and of placing a greater degree of emphasis on stronger economic and security cooperation, which will collectively go a long way to removing even the thought of inter-state conflict.

Dennis Rumley
The University of Western Australia
© 2012, Dennis Rumley

Index

Note: Page numbers in **bold** type refer to figures
Page numbers in *italic* type refer to tables
Page numbers followed by 'n' refer to notes

Abdulkadir, Mohamed (John) 13, 18n
Abdullah Azzam Brigades 39
Abdullah, Mohammed 61
Achille Lauro hijacking (1985) 101–2
actors: German 44–9, **48**; Spain 23–7
Afghanistan 27, 39, 67, 70; -Pakistan border 74
Ahmed, Sheikh Sherif 15
aircraft: pilotless aircraft 79
Al Shabaab 1, 36, 72
Al-Hiraak 59–60, 65
Al-Qaeda 1, 39, 59, 65, 67, 72–3, 78; *Limburg* tanker attack (2002) 1, 60, 73, 83; *M Star* attack (2010) 39, 73; 9/11 attacks (2001) 72–3; rise in Yemen 59–60; USS *Cole* attack (2000) 1, 60, 72, 83; USS *The Sullivans* attack (2000) 60, 72
Alakrana hijacking (2009) 21, 26, 29–31
Alpers, E. 4
American Bureau of Shipping 89
Ansar Al-Sharia 59–61
anti-access/area denial capabilities (A^2/AD) 69
Arab Spring 60–1
armaments transportation 27
armed conflicts: international (IACs) 98–100
Australia 91, 116–18
Authorised Economic Operator (AEO) 49
Automatic Identification Systems (AIS) 83
awareness campaigns 16–17

Badey, General Ali 13
Bahadur, J. 13
Bangladesh 67, 71
Baoom, General Hassan Ahmed 60
Bari, Mohamed 62
Bateman, S. 2, 8, 17n, 82–95; Ho, J. and Mathai, M. 87
best management practice (BMP) 87
Black Hawk Down (Bowden) 71

Bowden, M. 71
Branch, A. 90
Brewster, D. 113–15
bulk cargo: non-oil 68, 82, 85–7
Bürgin, A. 2, 21–35

Canadian-Somali Coast Guards 12–13
cargo: non-oil bulk 68, 82, 85–7
Central Intelligence Agency (CIA) 59
China 68–70, 74, 78, 85, 116–18; ship flags 85
coastguards: private companies 15–16; Somali-Canadian 12–13; US 90–3
Coffen-Smout, S. 5
Commander's Handbook (USN) 98
communications: seal-lines of (SLOCs) 69
Confederation of European Shipmasters' Association (CESMA) 50
conflict: Yemeni *4.5* 59–65
Contact Group on Piracy off the Coast of Somalia (CGPCS) 49
Container Security Initiative (CSI) 49
Convention for the Suppression of Unlawful Acts Against the Safety of Maritime Navigation (IMO 1988) 104–7
Cooperative Strategy for 21st Century Seapower (USN) 70
corporate terrorism 2; illegal fishing 4–18; waste dumping 4–18
corruption 63, 84; political 67; in Port State Control 90; Yemen 63
counter-piracy 96–110
crime: transnational organised 108–9
Customs-Trade Partnership Against Terrorism (C-TPAT) 1, 49

damage: environmental 8–10, 22
deliberate restraint 50–3
democratic control of armed forces (DCAF) 30–1

INDEX

Denmark 53; and Maersk maritime strategy 53
Det Norske Veritas 89
Downer, A. 117
drugs 22

Enrica Lexie incident (2012) 43
environmental damage 22; Somalia 8–10
Eritrea 62, 65; and Yemeni fishing clash (1996) 63
Ethiopia 62, 65, 67
EULEN 27
European Parliament (EP) 23; constructive
    abstention clause 23–4
European Union (EU) 1, 49, 53, 76; Common
    Information Sharing Environment (CISE) 45;
    Common Security and Defence Policy (CSDP)
    23–5, 50; Internationally Recommended
    Transit Group Corridor (IRTC) 25; Maritime
    Security Centre-Horn of Africa (MSC-HOA)
    25; NAVCO 23; NAVFOR Atalanta 1–2,
    21–3, 26, 30, 38–9, 45, 53; Western 25
EUROPOL 50
Exclusive Economic Zone (EEZ) 16, 47, 101
extradition 106–8

Al Fadhil, Tareq 60
finance 107
fish stock depletion 11–14
fishing: illegal *see* illegal, unreported and
    unregulated (IUU) fishing; Somali private
    structure 10–14, **11**; tuna 27–9; Yemen
    importance 63
flag states 2, *85*, 89, 94; certification 41;
    German 41–3
fleet vessel types 86, *86*

Galtung, J. 6, 17
German Insurance Association (GDV) 50
Germany 2, 85; actors involved 44–9, **48**; Armed
    Forces 49, 55n; *Bundeskriminalamt* (BKA)
    39; Constitution 55n; deliberate restraint
    factors 50–3; economic relevance of maritime
    trade 37–9, 52; Federal Criminal Police Office
    45–7, 50; Federal Crisis Response Task Force
    (KRZ) 41, 47; Federal *Länder* structure 44–7,
    52; Federal Maritime and Hydrographic
    Agency (BSH) 46; Federal Office of
    Economics and Export Control (BAFA) 46;
    Federal Police (BPOL) 40, 44–7, 53, 54–5n;
    flag state 41–3; Foreign Office (AA) 47–9;
    Inter-Ministerial Working Group for Maritime
    Security (AK MarSi) 46; Joint Emergency and
    Reporting Assessment Centre 45; key player
    involvement **48**, 49–50, **51**; Maritime Safety
    and Security Centre 45; maritime security
    relevance and governance 2, 36–55; Ministry
    of Defence 45; Ministry of Economics and
    Technology (BMWi) 46–7; Ministry of

Food, Agriculture and Consumer Protection
    (BMLEV) 46; Ministry of Interior (BMI) 46,
    49, 55n; Ministry of Transport, Building and
    Urban Development (BMVBS) 46, 49; Naval
    Control of Shipping (MSLtSt) Cooperation
    Points (SCP) 50; Navy 45; Parliamentary
    Participation Act (2005) 24; piracy incidents
    41, *42*; priority competition 52–3; and PSCs
    41–9; raw energy import 37–8; security
    structure categories 47; Ship-Owners
    Association (VDR) 41, 47, 50; shipping and
    private security companies (PSCs) 41–9
global financial crisis (GFC) 86
governance *see* maritime security governance
Greenpeace-Italy 8
Gross, O.: and Ni Ailáin, F. 96
Grygriel, J.: and Mitchell, W. 77
Guilfoyle, D. 1–3, 96–112
Gulf Cooperation Council (GCC) 60
Gupta, M. 53–4

Hansen, S. 1–2, 5–6, 59–66
Harper, M. 15
Hart Group 12–13
Hartkorn, S. 60
Hersi, Abdiwahid Mohamed 12
Hersi, Asha Abdulkarim 11
High Seas Convention (HSC) 100–2
High Seas Task Force 7
hijacking: *Alakrana* (2009) 21, 26, 29–31;
    shipping 83–8, *88*, 94; statistics *88*
Ho, J.: Mathai, M. and Bateman, S. 87
Ho, K. 7
Hostage Taking Convention (UN 1979) 106–7;
    Article 1 and definition 106; and extradition
    106–8
Houthi rebellion (2004) 63–4; Zayidi Shiism 64
human rights 7, 105; violations 7
humanitarian law: international (IHL) 97–100

Ibbi, Abdirahman 14
illegal, unreported and unregulated (IUU)
    fishing 2, 63–4, 68; definition 17–18n;
    poaching vessels 5; in Somalia 4–18
immigration 22; illegal 22
India 67–71, 74–8, 113–15; Look East Policy
    (LEP) 113; Mumbai bombings (2008) 72,
    74, 79
India as an Asia Pacific Power (Brewster)
    113–15
Indonesia 67, 75–6
insurance companies 38
international armed conflicts (IACs) 98–100;
    non- (NIACs) 98–100
International Association of Classification
    Societies (IACS) 88–9
International Chamber of Commerce (ICC) 50

INDEX

International Chamber of Shipping (ICS) 50
International Convention Against the Taking
of Hostages (UN 1979) *see* Hostage Taking
Convention (UN 1979)
International Convention for the Suppression of
the Financing of Terrorism (UN 1988) 107
International Convention for the Safety of Life
at Sea (IMO 1974) 46, 83
International Federation of Shipmasters'
Associations (IFSMA) 50
international humanitarian law (IHL) 97–100
international law *see* law, international
International Law Commission (ILC) 101
International Maritime Bureau (IMB) 26,
32n, 39–40; perpetrator attacks *40*; Piracy
Reporting Centre 50
International Maritime Organisation (IMO)
41–3, 49, 83, 87, 93, 104; Convention for
the Suppression of Unlawful Acts Against
the Safety of Maritime Navigation (1988)
104–7; International Convention for the
Safety of Life at Sea (1974) 46, 83; Marine
Environment Protection Committee (MEPC)
17n; vetting regime 89–90
International Ship and Port Facility Security
(ISPS) 1, 49; Code 83
International Studies Association (ISA) 1; San
Diego Convention (2012) 1
International Union of Marine Insurance
(IUMI) 50
INTERPOL 7, 50
Iran 69–70, 76–8; and Saudi cooperation 64–5
Iraq 24, 27; US-led intervention 24

Japan 68, 85, 91–3

kidnappings: officer 63–5
Kingdom and the Quarry (Uren) 116–18
König, D.: and Salomon, T. 43, 55n
Korea 68

Lashkar-e-Taiba (LeT) 1, 67, 72–5; Mumbai
bombings (2008) 72, 74, 79
Law on Foreign Trade of Defense Materials
and Dual Use Goods (2007) 27
law, international 3, 96–110; and counter-piracy
96–110; financing 107; high-seas policing
100–3; Hostage Taking Convention (UN
1979) 106–8; humanitarian (IHL) 97–100;
piracy definition (UNCLOS) 100–1; SUA
Convention (1988) 104–7; and terrorism 96,
103–8; transnational organised crime 108–9
legal responses 2, 16–17; and international rule
of law 3; and restrictions 77; and rights at
sea 75–6
Liberation Tigers of Tamil Eelam (LTTE) 1, 67,
72–4, 78; and SLN battles 73–4

Limburg tanker attack (2002) 1, 60, 73, 83
Line Shipping Connectivity Index (UNCTAD
LSCI) 38
Lisbon Treaty (2009) 23
Lloyds Register 89
lobster exports *12*
Long Range Maritime Patrol and
Reconnaissance Aircraft (LR-MPRA) 53

M Star bomb detonation (2010) 39, 73
Madrid terrorist attacks (2004) 24
Maersk shipping line 53–4
Malaysia 69–70
Malaysia/Singapore/Indonesia (MALSINDO)
49
Manaa, Fares Mohamed Hassan 62
maritime security governance 2; framework for
analysis 21–2; Germany 2; Spain 2, 21–32
maritime trade: German economic relevance
37–9, 52
Mathai, M.: Bateman, S. and Ho, J. 87
Memorandum of Understanding (MOU) 91–3;
comparative statistics *92*; Indian Ocean 91;
members 91; Paris 91; Riyadh 91; Tokyo 91–3
MEND politico-criminal group 78
Menkhaus, K. 4, 17n
Mesøy, A. 60
mineral deposits 67–8
mines: sea 13
Mitchell, W.: and Grygriel, J. 77
Mohamed, Khalid Sheik 72
Mohan, C. 113–15
munitions: precision-guided (PGMs) 79
Murphy, M. 1–5, 67–81

National Maritime Conference 46
naval activity pattern 69–70; risk factors 70
NAVFOR (EU) 1–2, 21; Common Security
and Defence Policy (CSDP) 50; Operation
Atalanta 2, 23, 26, 30, 38–9, 45, 50, 53;
Spanish contribution 23–6
Naxalite insurgency 69
Ni Ailáin, F.: and Gross, O. 96
Nigeria 76; oil companies 77
non-oil bulk cargo 68, 82, 85–7
non-state violence, maritime 67–80; Al-Qaeda
67, 72–3, 78; economic emphasis 75–8;
economic promise 68–70; implications
75–9; Lashkar-e-Taiba 67, 74–5; LTTE 67,
73–4, 78; pirate opportunity 70–1; political
authority 70–2, 76; political uncertainty
68–70; and terrorism nexus 71–5
North Atlantic Treaty Organisation (NATO) 39,
49–50, 53; *Naval Cooperation and Guidance
for Shipping* 50; Operation Active Endeavour
(OAE) 39; Parliamentary Assembly 98
Norway 85

INDEX

officer kidnappings: ransom payments 63–5
oil reserves: Somalia 68
oil transportation 60, 77–8, 82, 85; Yemeni 61
open registry (OR) 85, 89
Operation Enduring Freedom (OEF) 1, 39
opium 68
Organisation of German Shipmasters and Ship
    Officers (VDKS) 50
organised crime: transnational 108–9
Otto, H-J. 46
Ould Abdallah, Ahmedou 9
over-the-horizon (OTH) surveillance 79
Ozcayir, Z. 90

Pakistan 67, 70, 78; -Afghan border 74;
    Inter-services Intelligence (ISI) 74, 79;
    and Islamist group LeT 67, 74–5; Mumbai
    atrocity 74, 79, 83; railway bombing (2006)
    74; *Rak* sinking 84; Special Operations
    Forces (SOF) 79
Panetta, L. 114
Paris: Memorandum of Understanding (MOU)
    91
Philippines 75; Joint Special Operations Task
    Force (JSOTF-P) 78; Moro groups 78
pilotless aircraft (UAVs) 79
piracy: definition (UNCLOS) 100–1
Piracy Prevention Centre (BPOL/Germany)
    40–1, 45–7
PiraT data bank 54n
poaching vessels 5
policing: high-seas 100–3
political corruption 67
pollution 2, 88; toxic waste dumping 4–18
Port Security Initiative (PSI) 49
Port State Control 2, 82–94; Annual Report
    (2010) 89; four major regimes 91–3; maritime
    security 83–4; mechanisms 8; ship ownership
    and registration 84–6, *see also* shipping
poverty 6
precision-guided munitions (PGMs) 79
private security companies (PSCs) 26–8,
    38, 41, 77; approval process 46; Best
    Management Practice (BMP4) Handbook
    41–3; certification 41–3, 46–7; and German
    shipping 41–9; Law (1992) 31; regulation
    43–4; in Spain 26–8; training 28
Puntland State of Somalia 9–15

Qatan, Brigadier Salim Ali 61
Qayad, Mahdi Gedi 4–5, 8

Rak sinki (2011) ng 84
ransom payments 6, 14–16, 18n, 21, 36, 40,
    107; officer kidnappings 63–5
restraint: deliberate 50–3
Rice, C. 59

rights: human 7, 105
rights at sea 75–6
Riyadh: Memorandum of Understanding
    (MOU) 91
Rudd, K. 117
Rumley, D. 116–18
Russia 76

Saadah rebellion 60, 65
safety: shipping 88
Safety of Life at Sea (SOLAS) Convention
    (IMO 1974) 46, 83
Saleh al-Ahmar, Mohammed 61
Saleh, Ali Abdellah 60, 61
Salomon, T.: and König, D. 43
Samatar, A.: *et al* 5
Saudi-Iran cooperation 64–5
Schneider, P. 1–3, 36–58
Scorpeneclass submarines (SSKs) 69
sea lines of communications (SLOCs) 69
sea mines 13
securitisation 97
security: maritime shipping 83–4, *see also*
    private security companies (PSCs); maritime
    security governance
Segur Ibérica 27
Sen, Amartya 7
shahat (beggar) 16, 18n
shipping 82–94; building programmes 69;
    classifications 89; downturn 86–7; German
    and private security companies (PSCs)
    41–9; hijacking and statistics 83–8, *88*, 94;
    improvement scope 92–3; inspections 89–94;
    international 84–7; largest flags and states
    85, 89, 94; maritime security 83–4; nature
    84; ownership and registration 84–94; policy
    implications 93–4; and Port State Control
    90–2; safety and pollution 88; sub-standard
    87–92; vessel age 87–8; vetting regimes
    87–90; vulnerability 87; world fleet vessel
    types 86, *86*
smuggling 22, 62; weapons 68
Somali High Seas Fishing Company 10;
    demersal fish export 10
Somali National Movement (SNM) 5–6
Somali-Canadian Coast Guards 12–13
Somalia 2, 68, 71, 75–6, 83, 87, 96–9; current
    piracy dynamics 14–16; defensive piracy
    evolution 14; environmental effects 8–10;
    fish stock depletion 11–14; Fisheries
    Ministry 12–14; government collapse 10,
    15; illegal fishing and waste dumping 4–18;
    lobster exports *12*; local responses 12–14; oil
    reserves 68; private fishing structure 10–14,
    11; Puntland State of 9–15; *shahat* (beggar)
    16, 18n; ship hijacking 83–8, *88*; structural
    violence and corporate terrorism 6–7;

INDEX

territorial sea declaration 101–2; Transitional Federal Government (TFG) 15

Spain 2; actors involved 23–7; *Alakrana* hijacking (2009) 21, 26, 29–31; *Armada Española* (Navy) 23; Constitution 24, 27; contribution to Atalanta 23-6; driving forces 25, 28–9; effectiveness 25–6, 29; *Ejército del Aire* (Air Force) 23; *Guardia Civil* 26; identified threats 22; *Instituto Tecnológico 'La Marañosa'* (armed forces facility) 26; Madrid terrorist attacks (2004) 24; maritime security governance 2, 21–32; Ministry of Agriculture (MARM) 27; Ministry of Defence (MDE) 23, 26; Ministry of Interior (MoI) 26–7; national legal issues and decision-making 24, 27–8; National Police 26; *Operación Centinela Indico* 23; *Partido Populare* (PP) 24; *Partido Socialista Obrero Español* (PSOE) 24; private security companies (PSCs) 26–9; reform reasons 29–31; *Security Strategy* (2011) 22–9; tuna-fishing industry 27–9

Sri Lanka 73; Navy (SLN) 73–4

SSDF 12

state instability 69

states and flags *85*, 89, 94

submarines: Scorpene-class (SSKs) 69

suicide attack: Yemen (2012) 61

Suppression of Unlawful Acts (SUA) Convention (1988) 1, 83, 104–7; Article 3 and acts of theft 104–5; Article 7 and investigation requirements 105; Safety of Maritime Navigation Protocol 83; warship control 105–6

surveillance: over-the-horizon (OTH) 79

Tadić case (1995) 99

Tamil Eelam *see* Liberation Tigers of Tamil Eelam (LTTE)

terrorism: corporate 2, 4–18

terrorism, definition 6–7; and financing 107; and law 96, 103–8; suppression conventions 97, 104–7

Terrorism Financing Convention (1999) 107

Tokyo: Memorandum of Understanding (MOU) 91–3

Tolba, M. 8

toxic waste dumping 2; and contamination 8–10; in Somalia 4–18; truth 17n

trade: maritime 37–9, 52

trafficking 22; human 62; weapons 22

transnational organised crime 108–9

tribal issues 60

tsunami (2004) 9, 12

tuna-fishing industry 27–9

United Nations Conference on Trade and Development (UNCTAD) 37–8, 86; Line Shipping Connectivity Index (LSCI) 38

United Nations (UN) 4–5, 11, 49; Convention Against Transnational Organised Crime (UNTOC) 108–9; Convention on Conditions for Registration of Ships 89; Convention on the Law of the Sea (UNCLOS) 89–90, 99–106; Environmental Programme (UNEP) 8–9; Interim Force in Lebanon-Operation (UNIFIL) 39; International Convention Against the Taking of Hostages (1979) 106–8; International Convention for the Suppression of the Financing of Terrorism (1988) 107; Resident/Humanitarian Coordinator 9; Security Council (SC) 9, 23, 50, 96–103, 109–10n; Somalia Monitoring Group 5, 9–10

United States of America (USA) 69; Coast Guard 90-3; Navy (USN) 69–70, 77, 98; USS *Cole* attack (2000) 1, 60, 72, 83; USS *The Sullivans* attack (2000) 60, 72

Uren, D. 116–18

vessel types: world fleet 86, *86*

violence: structural 6–7, *see also* non-state violence, maritime

Waldo, Mohamed Abshir 5–6

warship control 105–6

waste dumping *see* toxic waste dumping

water-borne improvised explosive devices (WBIEDs) 73

weapons 68; trafficking 22

weapons of mass destruction (WMDs) 22, 82–4

Weldemichael, A.T. 1–3, 4–20

Winner, A.C. 1–3

world fleet vessel types 86, *86*

World Food Programme (WFP) 25, 39

Wyler, L. 59

Yemen 2, 83; and 4.5 conflicts 59–65; Al-Hiraak 59–60, 65; Al-Qaeda 59–60, 65; Arab Spring aftermath 60–1; corruption 63; Council of the Peaceful Southern Revolution (2009) 60; fishing clash (1996) and Eritrea 63; fishing importance 63; government transition 60; Houthi rebels 63–4; maritime highways 62–4; Military Retirees Co-ordination Council 60; oil transportation 61; regional two great games 64–5; Saadah rebellion (2004) 60, 65; security analyses 59–61; strategic importance 62; suicide attack (2012) 61; terrorist attacks 61; threats 59; tribal issues 60

Yusuf, Abdullahi 12, 15

Zu Guttenberg, K-T. 39